# None other name

# None other name

## Daily devotional readings
## from 19th century Scottish ministers

Compiled by Leen J. van Valen

REFORMATION PRESS
2020

**British Library Cataloguing-in-Publication Data**
A catalogue record for this book is available from
the British Library

**PAPERBACK EDITION**
**ISBN 978-1-872556-45-1**

© **Reformation Press 2020**

Published by
Reformation Press, 11 Churchill Drive, Stornoway
Isle of Lewis, Scotland HS1 2NP

www.reformationpress.co.uk

Cover photo: 'Loch Tummel Queen's View' by Andy Hawkins is licensed
under CC BY-SA 2.0

Printed by www.lulu.com

Also available as a Kindle e-book
ISBN 978-1-872556-46-8

All rights reserved. No part of this publication may be reproduced,
stored in a retrieval system, or transmitted, in any form or by any means,
without the prior permission in writing of Reformation Press, or as
expressly permitted by law, by licence, or under terms agreed with the
appropriate reprographic rights organisation.

There is none other name under heaven given among men, whereby we must be saved

*Acts 4:1*

# Foreword

THIS book has been compiled by the Dutch church historian and author, Leen van Valen. As well as being a biographer of Robert Murray McCheyne, he has written extensively in both Dutch and English about the religious history and literature of Britain and North America. He has drawn on his wide knowledge of Scottish devotional literature to provide daily portions from an era when evangelical religion flourished throughout the country.

These daily readings have been taken from the published works of twelve ministers, each of whom had his personal style of preaching and writing. In assembling this volume, editorial changes have been confined to updating punctuation to present-day conventions and to using uniform spelling. Explanations of unfamiliar words have been supplied in brackets. Where necessary, lengthy sentences and paragraphs have been divided to allow for easier reading. As the daily portions have been extracted from longer works, occasional minor rewording has been necessary to give the reader context.

The book lists the original sources of the readings. The majority of the nineteenth-century originals are available online at www.archive.org. Modern editions of many of these books are in print, available from publishers such as Free Presbyterian Publications and The Banner of Truth Trust. The publisher hopes that readers will derive spiritual benefit from the daily portions in this book, and that they will be given an appetite to read further from the works of these men.

Reformation Press, Stornoway

# Preface

THIS book of daily readings consists of excerpts from works by twelve eminent Scottish writers of the nineteenth century, a time when the Lord raised up may eminent preachers of the gospel throughout Scotland.

Robert Murray McCheyne is probably the most famous of the men whose works are featured in this book. He was at the centre of a circle of ministers who contributed vastly to the spiritual life of that time. Among his closest friends I would especially mention the brothers Andrew and Horatius Bonar. Along with McCheyne, these men experienced times of great blessing in their own congregations and were instrumental in promoting vital godliness throughout Scotland and far beyond. It is a testimony to the quality of their work that their writings are among the great spiritual classics of the English-speaking world, and many of them have been continuously in print since they were first issued.

These excerpts give an impression of the practical tone of the sermons and writings of the twelve ministers. It is an outstanding characteristic of this material that these men assigned a preeminent place to the person and the work of Jesus Christ. Each with his own individual way of expression, they sought to put Christ at the centre of their ministry. When we consider the works in this light, the title of this book expresses its rich content: *None other name.*

The daily readings largely consist of related excerpts from the source texts, with a named writer for each month. Biographical information about the writers is given, along with details of the sources from which the excerpts have been taken.

It is hoped that the passages will stimulate interest in these godly ministers, their lives, and their writings. It is my earnest wish that the Lord may bless these daily portions to touch, challenge, and comfort the hearts of all who read them.

L. J. van Valen

# Acknowledgments

REFORMATION PRESS acknowledges the kind permission of the Banner of Truth Trust (banneroftruth.org) to use excerpts from a book by Hugh Martin, *Christ For Us* (Edinburgh, 1998).

The photograph of Hugh Martin has been reproduced by courtesy of the London Mathematical Society.

# January

Robert Murray McCheyne (1813–1843) was born in Edinburgh. He studied at the University of Edinburgh, where he won prizes in all the courses he attended. The death of his elder brother David in July 1831 made a deep impression on his soul. The Holy Spirit convinced him of his ungodliness and the pollution of his own nature. Later he was able to reflect on his spiritual experience and he was brought to a clear understanding of the way of acceptance with God through reading *The Sum of Saving Knowledge* by David Dickson and James Durham. He described his conversion in his famous poem: *Jehovah Tsidkenu*—The Lord, my righteousness.

McCheyne studied theology under Thomas Chalmers and was licensed to preach in July 1835. After being assistant minister for a year in the joint charge of Larbert and Dunipace, he became the settled minister of St Peter's Church in Dundee.

A revival of religion began in Dundee during McCheyne's absence on a trip to Palestine, a trip he undertook as a member of a mission to the Jews. His friend William Burns, who replaced McCheyne during his absence, was closely involved in that work.

The years that followed were a blessing for McCheyne. God richly blessed his labours in that bustling industrial city and in other places he visited. However, he was subject to poor health and he died in 1843 after a short illness. His writings have been continuously in print since then.

## Sources of daily readings

January 1–11: Andrew A. Bonar, *Memoir and Remains of the Rev. Robert Murray M'Cheyne* (Dundee, 1844).

January 12–31: Andrew A. Bonar (ed.), *Additional Remains of the Rev. Robert Murray M'Cheyne* (Edinburgh, 1846).

## Biography

Leen J. van Valen, *Constrained by His Love: A new biography on Robert Murray McCheyne* (Tain, 2002).

# 1 January

*Who being the brightness of his glory, and the express image of his person, and upholding all things by the word of his power, when he had by himself purged our sins, sat down on the right hand of the Majesty on high.*
*Hebrews 1:3*

Question: Where is Jesus now? Answer: 'He is set down at the right hand of the Majesty on high.'

He is upon the throne with God in his glorified body, and his throne is for ever. A sceptre is put into his hand—a sceptre of righteousness—and the oil of gladness is poured over him. All power is given to him in heaven and on earth. Oh, brethren, if you and I could pass this day through these heavens, and see what is now going on in the sanctuary above—if you could see what the child of God now sees who died last night—if you could see the Lamb with the scars of his five deep wounds in the very midst of the throne, surrounded by all the redeemed, every one having harps and golden vials full of odours—if you could see the many angels round about the throne, whose number is ten thousand times ten thousand, and thousands of thousands, all singing, 'Worthy is the Lamb that was slain'—and if one of these angels were to tell you, 'This is he that undertook the cause of lost sinners. He undertook to bear their curse and to do their obedience. He undertook to be the second Adam—the man in their stead, and lo, there he is upon the throne of heaven!'

Consider him—look long and earnestly upon his wounds, upon his glory—and tell me, do you think it would be safe to trust him? Do you think his sufferings and obedience will have been enough? 'Yes, yes!' every soul exclaims. Lord, it is enough! Lord, stay thy hand! Show me no more, for I can bear no more. Oh, rather let me ever stand and gaze upon the almighty, all-worthy, all-divine Saviour, till my soul drink in complete assurance that his work undertaken for sinners is a finished work! Yes, though the sins of all the world were on my one wicked head, still I could not doubt that his work is complete, and that I am quite safe when I believe in him.

## 2 January

> The LORD said unto my Lord, Sit thou at my right hand, until I make thine enemies thy footstool.
> Psalm 110:1

Oh, brethren, if I could lift you away to the eternity that is past—if I could I bring you into the council of the Eternal Three, and as it was once said, 'Let us make man'—if I could let you hear the word, 'Let us save man'—if I could show you how God from all eternity designed his Son to undertake for poor sinners—how it was the very plan and the bottommost [fundamental] desire of the heart of the Father that Jesus should come into the world, and do and die in the stead of sinners, how the Holy Spirit breathed sweetest incense and dropped like holiest oil upon the head of the descending Saviour—if I could show you the intense interest with which the eye of God followed Jesus through his whole course of sorrow and suffering and death—if I could show you the anxious haste with which God rolled away the stone from the sepulchre while it was yet dark, for he would not leave his soul in hell, neither suffer his Holy One to see corruption—if I could show you the ecstasies of love and joy that beat in the bosom of the infinite God when Jesus ascended to his Father and our Father, how he welcomed him with a fulness of kindness and grace which God alone could give and God alone could receive, saying, 'Thou art my Son, this day have I begotten thee. Thou art indeed worthy to be called my Son; never till this day wast thou so worthy to be called mine. Thy throne, O God, is for ever and ever; sit thou on my right hand until I make thine enemies thy footstool.'

# 3 January

> And one of the elders answered, saying unto me, What are these which are arrayed in white robes? and whence came they? And I said unto him, Sir, thou knowest. And he said to me, These are they which came out of great tribulation, and have washed their robes, and made them white in the blood of the Lamb.
> *Revelation 7:13–14*

The saved in heaven had washed their robes. This leads us back to their conversion. Once every one of that company had filthy garments. They were like Joshua—their garment was spotted by the flesh. It was like a garment with the leprosy in it. Some stained with blood—spots of blood upon their garments, some with adultery, some with disobedience to parents, some with pride, falsehood, evil speaking. All—all—were stained!

Everyone was convinced that he could not make himself clean. He could not wash his garments nor throw them off. He was brought to see himself lost and helpless. Jesus was revealed to him, and his precious blood shed for sinners, even the chief, saying to the heavy laden, 'Come to me!' Of all that company, there is not one stands there in any other way. All are washed in blood. It is their only way of standing. Have you been washed in blood? You will find not one in heaven who went there in any other way. You think to go to heaven by your own decency, innocency, attention to duties. Well, you would be the only such one there: all are washed in blood. Come and let us reason together (Isaiah 1:18).

They came out of great tribulation. Everyone that gets to the throne must put their foot upon the thorn. The way to the crown is by the cross. We must taste the gall if we are to taste the glory. When justified by faith, God led them into tribulations also. When God brought Israel through the Red Sea, he led them into the wilderness. So, when God saves a soul, he tries it.

# 4 January

But God forbid that I should glory, save in the cross of our Lord Jesus Christ, by whom the world is crucified unto me, and I unto the world.
*Galatians 6:14*

Dear friends, have you been brought to glory only in the cross of Christ? Have you given over the old way of salvation by the deeds of the law?

Your natural heart is set upon that way. You are always for making yourself better and better, till you can lay God under obligation to pardon you. You are always for looking in for righteousness. You are looking in at your convictions, and sorrow for past sins—your tears and anxious prayers. Or you are looking in at your amendment—forsaking of wicked courses and struggles after a new life. Or you are looking at your own religious exercises—your fervency and enlarged heart in prayer or in the house of God. Or you are looking at the work of the Holy Spirit in you—the graces of the Spirit.

Alas, alas! The bed is shorter than that you can stretch yourself on it, the covering is narrower than that you can wrap yourself in it (Isaiah 28:20). Despair of pardon in that way! Give it up for ever! Your heart is desperately wicked. Every righteousness in which your heart has anything to do is vile and polluted, and cannot appear in his sight. Count it all loss, filthy rags, dung, that you may win Christ!

Betake yourselves to the Lord Jesus Christ! Believe the love of the Lord Jesus Christ! He delighteth in mercy; he is ready to forgive; in him compassions flow; he justifies the ungodly. Have you seen the glory of the cross of Jesus? Has it attracted your heart? Do you feel unspeakably pleased with that way of salvation? Do you see that God is glorified when you are saved?

# 5 January

Being confident of this very thing, that he which hath begun a good work in you will perform it until the day of Jesus Christ
*Philippians 1:6*

Learn how certain it is that you shall one day soon be with Christ. It is the will of the Father, it is the will of the Son. It is the prayer of Christ.

If you have really been brought to Christ, you shall never perish. You may have many enemies opposing you in your way to glory. Satan desires to have you, that he may sift you like wheat. Your worldly friends will do all they can to hinder you. Still you shall be with Christ. We shall see your face at the table of glory. You have a hard heart, an unbelieving heart, a heart deceitful above all things, and desperately wicked. You often think your heart will lead you to betray Christ. Still, you shall be with Christ. If you are in Christ today, you shall be ever with the Lord. You have lived a wicked life. You have dreadful sins to look back upon. Still, if you are come to Jesus, this is his word to thee: 'Thou shall be with me in paradise.'

In truth, Christ cannot want [be without] you. You are his jewels—his crown. Heaven would be no heaven to him, if you were not there. This may give you courage in coming to the Lord's table. Some of you fear to come to this table, because, though you cleave to Christ today, you fear you may betray him tomorrow. But you need not fear. 'He that hath begun a good work in you will perform it till the day of Jesus Christ.' You shall sit at the table above, where Christ himself shall be at the head.

# 6 January

And about the ninth hour Jesus cried with a loud voice, saying, Eli, Eli, lama sabachthani? that is to say, My God, my God, why hast thou forsaken me?
*Matthew 27:45*

On the cross the wounds of Christ were the greatest outlets of his glory that ever were. The divine glory shone more out of his wounds than out of all his life before. The veil was then rent in twain, and the full heart of God allowed to stream through. It was a human body that writhed, pale and racked, upon the accursed tree; they were human hands that were pierced so rudely by the nails; it was human flesh that bore that deadly gash upon the side; it was human blood that streamed from hands and feet and side; the eye that meekly turned to his Father was a human eye; the soul that yearned over his mother was a human soul.

But oh, there was divine glory streaming through all! Every wound was a mouth to speak of the grace and love of God! Divine holiness shone through. What infinite hatred of sin was there when he thus offered himself a sacrifice without spot unto God! Divine wisdom shone through. All created intelligences could not have devised a plan whereby God would have been just, and yet the justifier. Divine love; every drop of blood that fell came as a messenger of love from his heart to tell the love of the fountain. This was the love of God. He that hath seen a crucified Christ hath seen the Father. Oh, look on the broken bread, and you will see this glory still streaming through! Here is the heart of God laid bare—God is manifest in flesh.

# 7 January

> The voice of my beloved! behold, he cometh leaping upon the mountains, skipping upon the hills.
> *Song of Solomon 2:8*

Christ's coming to the desolate believer is often sudden and wonderful. We saw in the parable that it was when the bride was sitting lonely and desolate that she heard suddenly the voice of her lord. Love is quick in hearing, and she cries out, 'The voice of my beloved!' Before, she thought the mountains all but impassable, but now she can compare his swiftness to nothing but that of the gazelle or the young hart. Yea, while she speaks, he is at the wall—at the window—showing himself through the lattice.

Just so is it oftentimes with the believer. While he sits alone and desolate, the mountains of separation appear a vast and impassable barrier to the Saviour, and he fears he may never come again. The mountains of a believer's provocations are often very great. 'That I should have sinned again, who have been washed in the blood of Jesus. It is little that other men should sin against him; they never knew him—never loved him as I have done. Surely I am the chief of sinners, and have sinned away my Saviour. The mountain of my provocations hath grown up to heaven, and he never can come over it any more.'

Thus it is that the believer writes bitter things against himself, and then it is that oftentimes he hears the voice of his beloved. Some text of the Word, or some word from a Christian friend, or some part of a sermon, again reveals Jesus in all his fulness—the Saviour of sinners, even the chief.

# 8 January

And I heard a voice from heaven saying unto me, Write, Blessed are the dead which die in the Lord from henceforth: Yea, saith the Spirit, that they may rest from their labours; and their works do follow them.
*Revelation 14:13*

'Blessed are the dead.' The world says, 'Blessed are the living,' but God says, 'Blessed are the dead.' The world judges of things by sense—as they outwardly appear to men; God judges of things by what they really are in themselves—he looks at things in their real colour and magnitude. The world says, 'Better is a living dog than a dead lion.' The world looks upon some of their families, coming out like a fresh blooming flower in the morning, their cheeks covered with the bloom of health, their step bounding with the elasticity of youth, riches and luxuries at their command, long, bright summer days before them. The world says, 'There is a happy soul.'

God takes us into the darkened room, where some child of God lately dwelt. He points to the pale face where death sits enthroned, the cheek wasted by long disease, the eye glazed in death, the stiff hands clasped over the bosom, the friends standing weeping around, and he whispers in our ears, 'Blessed are the dead.'

Ah, dear friends, think a moment! Whether does God or you know best? Who will be found to be in the right at last? Alas, what a vain show you are walking in! Disquieted in vain. 'Man that is in honour, and understandeth not, is like the beasts that perish.' Even God's children sometimes say, 'Blessed are the living.' It is a happy thing to live in the favour of God—to have peace with God—to frequent the throne of grace—to burn the perpetual incense of praise—to meditate on his Word—to hear the preached gospel—to serve God; even to wrestle, and run, and fight in his service, is sweet. Still God says, 'Blessed are the dead.'

# 9 January

> These shall make war with the Lamb, and the Lamb shall overcome them: for he is Lord of lords, and King of kings: and they that are with him are called, and chosen, and faithful.
> *Revelation 17:14*

Union to the Lord has a beginning. Every one that is blessed in dying has been converted. You may dislike the word, but that is the truth. They were awakened—began to weep—pray—weep as they went to seek the Lord their God. They saw themselves lost, undone, helpless—that they could not be just with a holy God. They became babes. The Lord Jesus drew near, and revealed himself. 'I am the bread of life.' 'Him that cometh to me I will in no wise cast out.' They believed and were happy—rejoiced in the Lord Jesus—counted everything but loss for Christ. They gave themselves to the Lord. This was the beginning of their being in Christ.

Dear friends, have you had this beginning? Have you undergone conversion—the new birth—grafting into Christ? Call it by any name you will, have you the thing? Has this union to Christ taken place in your history? Some say, 'I do not know.' If at any time of your life you had been saved from drowning, if you were actually drowned and brought to life again, you would remember it to your dying hour. Much more if you had been brought to Christ. If you had been blind, and by some remarkable operation your eyes were opened when you were full grown, would you ever forget it? So, if you have been truly brought into Christ, you may easily remember it. If not, you will die in your sins. Whither Christ has gone, thither you cannot come. 'Except ye repent and be converted, ye shall all likewise perish.'

# 10 January

Every branch in me that beareth not fruit he taketh away: and every branch that beareth fruit, he purgeth it, that it may bring forth more fruit.
*John 15:2*

Not all that seem to be branches are branches of the true vine. Many branches fall off the trees when the high winds begin to blow—all that are rotten branches. So in times of temptation or trial or persecution, many false professors drop away. Many that seemed to be believers went back, and walked no more with Jesus. They followed Jesus—they prayed with him—they praised him—but they went back, and walked no more with him.

So is it still. Many among us doubtless seem to be converted; they begin well and promise fair, who will fall off when winter comes. Some have fallen off, I fear, already; some more may be expected to follow. These will not be blessed in dying. Oh, of all deathbeds, may I be kept from beholding the deathbed of the false professor! I have seen it before now, and I trust I may never see it again. They are not blessed after death. The rotten branches will burn more fiercely in the flames.

Oh, think what torment it will be, to think that you spent your life in pretending to be a Christian, and lost your opportunity of becoming one indeed! Your hell will be all the deeper, blacker, hotter, that you knew so much of Christ, and were so near him, and found him not. Happy are they who endure to the end, who are not moved away from the hope of the gospel, who, when others go away, say, 'Lord, to whom can we go?'

# 11 January

> Ephraim shall say, What have I to do any more with idols? I have heard him, and observed him: I am like a green fir tree. From me is thy fruit found.
> *Hosea 14:8*

If you are this day united to Jesus, the Spirit will come like dew upon your soul. The Spirit is given to them that obey Jesus: 'I will pray the Father.' When all nature is at rest, not a leaf moving, then at evening the dew comes down—no eye to see the pearly drops descending, no ear to hear them falling on the verdant grass. So does the Spirit come to you who believe. When the heart is at rest in Jesus—unseen, unheard by the world—the Spirit comes, and softly fills the believing soul, quickening all, renewing all within. 'If I go away, I will send him unto you.'

Dear little ones, whom God hath chosen out of this world, you are like Gideon's fleece—the Lord will fill you with dew when all around is dry. You are his vineyard of red wine—he says, 'I will water it every moment'—silently, unfelt, unseen, but surely. But, ah, that Spirit is a Holy Spirit! 'I the Lord thy God am a jealous God.' He cannot bear an idol in his temple. When the ark of God was carried into the temple of Dagon, the idol fell flat before it. Much more when the Holy Spirit comes into the heart will he cast out the idols. If you have received the Spirit, you will be crying now in your heart. 'Lord, take these things hence! Drive them out of my heart! What have I to do any more with idols?'

# 12 January

The Spirit of the Lord GOD is upon me; because the LORD hath anointed me to preach good tidings unto the meek; he hath sent me to bind up the brokenhearted, to proclaim liberty to the captives, and the opening of the prison to them that are bound.
*Isaiah 61:1*

Christ was anointed not only to bind up the broken-hearted, but also to proclaim liberty to the captives, so that if it be good and wise to direct the poor broken-hearted sinner, who has no way of justifying himself, to Jesus as his righteousness, it must be just as good and wise to direct the poor believer, groaning under the bondage of corruption, having no way to sanctify himself, to look to Jesus as his wisdom, his sanctification, his redemption.

Thou hast once looked unto Jesus as thy covenant head, bearing all wrath, fulfilling all righteousness in thy stead, and that gave thee peace. Well, look again to the same Jesus as thy covenant head, obtaining by his merits gifts for men, even the promise of the Father, to shed down on all his members, and let that also give thee peace. 'Trust in the Lord with all thine heart.'

Thou hast looked to Jesus on the cross, and that gave thee peace of conscience. Look to him now upon the throne, and that will give thee purity of heart. I know of but one way in which a branch can be made a leafy, healthy, fruit-bearing branch, and that is by being grafted into the vine and abiding there. And, just so, I know of but one way in which a believer can be made a holy, happy, fruitful child of God, and that is by believing in Jesus, abiding in him, walking in him, being rooted and built up in him.

# 13 January

For as many as are led by the Spirit of God, they are the sons of God.
*Romans 8:14*

In a mill where the machinery is all driven by water, the working of the whole machinery depends upon the supply of water. Cut off that supply, and the machinery becomes useless. Set on the water, and life and activity is given to all. The whole dependence is placed upon the outward supply of water; still, it is obvious that we do not throw away the machinery through which the power of the water is brought to bear upon the work.

Just so in the believer: the whole man is carried on by the Spirit of Christ, else he is none of his. The working of every day depends upon the daily supply of the living stream from on high. Cut off that supply, and the understanding becomes a dark and useless lump of machinery, for the Bible says that unconverted men have the understanding darkened. Restore the divine Spirit, and life and animation is given to all—the understanding is made a new creature. Now, though the whole leaning or dependence here is upon the supply of the Spirit, still it is obvious that we do not cast away the machinery of the human mind, but rather honour it far more than the world.

Now, however difficult it may be to explain all this to the world, it is most beautiful to see how truly it is acted on by the simplest child of God. If you could overhear some simple cottage believer at his morning devotions, how simply he brings himself in as lost and condemned, and therefore cleaves to Jesus, the divine Saviour.

## 14 January

> But when he saw the multitudes, he was moved with compassion on them, because they fainted, and were scattered abroad, as sheep having no shepherd.
> *Matthew 9:36*

Christ saw the multitudes. He had gone through the crowded cities and villages of populous Galilee, and oh, how many faces he had looked upon! This made him sad.

There is something very saddening to a Christian to look upon a multitude. To stand in the crowded streets of a large metropolis and to see the current of human beings flowing onward to eternity brings an awful sadness over the spirit. Even to stand in the house of God and look upon the dense mass of assembled worshippers fills the bosom of every true Christian with a pitiful [heart-breaking] sadness.

Why is this? Because the most are perishing souls. Ah, it was this that filled the bosom of the Redeemer with compassion! Of all the bustling crowds that hurry through the streets of your town, of all the teeming multitudes that issue forth from your crowded factories, ah, how few will stand on the right hand of Jesus!

Nay, to come nearer still—of the hundreds now before me in this house of God, souls committed to my care and keeping, willing and anxious as you are to hear, yet how few believe our report! How few will be to me a crown of joy and of rejoicing in the day of the Lord Jesus! Just think how dreadful, my friends, if there be one soul here that is to perish—one body and soul with us, in health and strength today, that is to be with devils in a short while, feeling the worm and the flames and the gnashing of teeth. If there were but one in the whole town, I do think it would be enough to sadden the soul. But, ah, does not the Bible say, 'Many are called, but few are chosen'?

# 15 January

Then saith he unto his disciples, The harvest truly is plenteous, but the labourers are few; pray ye therefore the Lord of the harvest, that he will send forth labourers into his harvest.
*Matthew 9:37–38*

Jesus Christ is the same yesterday, today, and for ever. Just as he went through the towns and villages of Galilee beholding the multitudes, so does he now go through the towns and villages of our beloved land. And, oh, if his the heart was moved with compassion over the thousands of Galilee, surely it must be breaking with intensest pity over the tens of thousands of Scotland!

There may be some of you who can look coldly and carelessly on the fifty thousand of Edinburgh that never cross the threshold of the house of God. There may be some of you who can hear unmoved of the eighty thousand of Glasgow who know neither the melody of psalms nor the voice of prayer. There may be some of you who can look upon the haggard and vice-stricken countenances of the mill-population of your own town, thousands of whom show, by their dress and air and open profligacy, that they are utter strangers to the message of a preached Saviour. Some of you may look on them and never shed one tear of pity—never feel one prayer rising to your lips. But there is one above these heavens, whose heart beats in his bosom at the sight of them. And if there could be tears in heaven, that tender Saviour could weep, for he sees the multitudes fainting and scattered, and, oh, worst of all, as sheep that have no shepherd!

## 16 January

> For ye know the grace of our Lord Jesus Christ, that, though he was rich, yet for your sakes he became poor, that ye through his poverty might be rich.
> *2 Corinthians 8:9*

Oh, brethren, this is good news for the most wicked of men! Are there some of you who feel that you are like a beast before God—or all over sin, like a devil? Some of you have lived in the abominations of Corinth. Some of you are like the Romans—without strength, ungodly, sinners, enemies. Yet for your sakes Christ became poor. He left glory for souls as vile as you. He left the songs of angels, the love of his Father, and the glories of heaven, for just such wretches as you and me. He died for the ungodly. Do not be afraid, sinners, to lay hold upon him! It was for your sakes he came. He will not—he cannot—cast you out.

Oh, sinners! You are poor indeed, but he will make you rich. All the riches he left he is ready to raise you to. He will make you rich in the love of God—rich in the peace that passeth all understanding—if you truly lay hold on him. The wrath of God will pass away from you, and he will love you freely. The love wherewith God loves Christ shall be on you. He will make you rich in holiness. He will fill you with all the fulness of God. He will make you rich in eternity. You will behold his glory—you will enter into his joy—you will sit with him on his throne.

## 17 January

> And you, that were sometime alienated and enemies in your mind by wicked works, yet now hath he reconciled.
> *Colossians 1:21*

He hath reconciled us: 'Yet now hath he reconciled.' Sinners, we are not reconciled in the day of our election, nor at the death of Christ, but in the hour of conversion.

Oh, that is a precious 'now': '*Now* hath he reconciled.' It is a happy moment, when the Lord Jesus draws near to the sinful soul, and washes him clean in his precious blood, and clothes him in his white raiment, and so reconciles him to God. A double reconciliation takes place in the hour of believing. God becomes reconciled to the soul. When the soul is found in Christ, the Father says, 'I will heal his backsliding, I will love him freely: for mine anger is turned away from him' (Hosea 14:4). The soul replies to God, 'I will praise thee: though thou wast angry with me, thine anger is turned away, and thou comfortedst me' (Isaiah 12:1). God does not impute to that soul his trespasses; he reckons to him the obedience of the Lord Jesus. God justifies him. 'He will save, he will rejoice over thee with joy; he will rest in his love, he will joy over thee with singing' (Zephaniah 3:17).

The soul is reconciled to God. The Holy Spirit, who bends the soul to submit to Jesus, changes the heart to love him. When the beasts came into the ark, their natures were changed—they did not tear one another to pieces, but lovingly entered two and two into the ark. The lion did not devour the gentle deer, nor did the eagle pursue the dove. So, when sinners come to Christ, their heart is changed from enmity to love.

# 18 January

And in that day thou shalt say, O LORD, I will praise thee: though thou wast angry with me, thine anger is turned away, and thou comfortedst me.
*Isaiah 12:1*

There is abundant provision for the pardon and peace of the sinner, for God's anger is turned away on the head of Christ. The thing which troubles the conscience of awakened souls is the anger of God. It is this which makes them tremble, by night and by day, in public and in secret.

An awakened soul feels that he has broken God's law and is exposed every moment to his wrath. He can find no rest in his bed, no peace at his meals, no joy in his friends. The heavens are black above his head, the earth is ready to open and devour him. If God be a just and holy God, he will pour out his anger. If he be a true God, he will fulfil all his threatenings.

If such a soul would take Christ as his surety, he would find abundant peace. The anger of God has already been turned away on the head of Christ. All the clouds of wrath have been directed, like a waterspout, upon that one head. If you are willing that Christ be your surety, you do not need to fear. The law has had its course, and God does not demand a second punishment.

There is no reason for your standing trembling, when there is such a glorious way of pardon. Christ offers himself as a surety to every one of you, and if you accept of him, your wrath is past—it will never fall on you to all eternity.

## 19 January

> In that day there shall be a fountain opened to the house of David and to the inhabitants of Jerusalem for sin and for uncleanness.
> *Zechariah 13:1*

A fountain is seen in a pierced Christ. The first look to Christ makes the sinner mourn; the second look to Christ makes the sinner rejoice. When the soul looks first to Christ, he sees half the truth—

he sees the wrath of God against sin, that God is holy and must avenge sin, that he can by no means clear the guilty. He sees that God's wrath is infinite. When he looks to Christ again, he sees the other half of the truth—the love of God to the lost, that God has provided a surety free to all. It is this that fills the soul with joy. Oh, it is strange that the same object should break the heart and heal it! A look to Christ wounds; a look to Christ heals.

When the Spirit is teaching, he gives a full look at Christ, a look to him alone for righteousness. What does the sinner see? The wounds of Christ—a fountain for sin and for uncleanness. Oh, trembling sinners, come and get this look at Christ! Come and see a fountain for sin and for uncleanness, opened on Calvary all those years ago. 'I cannot, for my sins are very great.' Are you all sin and uncleanness—nothing but sin, a lump of sin? In your life, in your heart, are you one bundle of lusts? Here is a fountain opened for you. Look to a pierced Christ, and weep; look to a pierced Christ, and be glad.

# 20 January

> For the Son of man is as a man taking a far journey, who left his house, and gave authority to his servants, and to every man his work, and commanded the porter to watch. Watch ye therefore: for ye know not when the master of the house cometh, at even, or at midnight, or at the cockcrowing, or in the morning.
> *Mark 13:34–35*

Christ will come back suddenly. The whole Bible bears witness to this. In one place it is compared to a snare which suddenly entraps the unwary wild beast: 'As a snare shall it come on all them that dwell on the face of the whole earth.' Again, to a thief: 'The day of the Lord so cometh as a thief in the night.' Again, to a bridegroom coming suddenly: 'At midnight there was a cry made, Behold the bridegroom cometh.' Again, to the waters of the flood. Again, to the fiery rain that fell on Sodom and Gomorrah. And here to the sudden coming home of the master of the house: 'Ye know not when the master of the house cometh.'

Now, my dear friends, I am far from discouraging those who, with humble prayerfulness, search into the records of prophecy to find out what God has said as to the second coming of the Son of man. We are not like the first disciples of Jesus, if we do not often put the question, 'What shall be the sign of thy coming, and of the end of the world?' But the truth which I wish to be written on your hearts is this, that the coming shall be sudden—sudden to the world—sudden to the children of God.

'In such an hour as ye think not, the Son of man cometh.' 'Ye know not when the master of the house cometh, at even, or at midnight, or at cockcrowing, or in the morning.' Oh, my friends, your faith is incomplete if you do not live in the daily faith of a coming Saviour.

# 21 January

> Who shall separate us from the love of Christ? shall tribulation, or distress, or persecution, or famine, or nakedness, or peril, or sword?
> *Romans 8:35*

Who was it that loved? It was Jesus, the Son of God, the second person of the blessed Godhead. His name is 'Wonderful, Counsellor, the mighty God, the everlasting Father, the Prince of Peace', 'King of kings and Lord of lords', Immanuel, Jesus the Saviour, the only begotten of his Father. His beauty is perfect: he is the brightness of his Father's glory, and the express image of his person. All the purity, majesty and love of Jehovah dwell fully in him. He is the bright morning Star, he is the Sun of righteousness and the Light of the world. He is the rose of Sharon and the lily of the valleys—fairer than the children of men.

His riches are infinite. He could say, 'All that the Father hath is mine.' He is Lord of all. All the crowns in heaven were cast at his feet, all angels and seraphs were his servants, all worlds his domain.

His doings were infinitely glorious. By him were all things created that are in heaven and that are in earth, visible and invisible. He called the things that are not as though they were—worlds started into being at his word. Yet he loved us. It is much to be loved by one greater in rank than ourselves—to be loved by an angel. But oh, to be loved by the Son of God! This is wonderful—it passeth knowledge.

# 22 January

> Then spake Jesus again unto them, saying, I am the light of the world: he that followeth me shall not walk in darkness, but shall have the light of life.
> *John 8:12*

There is no happier life under the sun than to follow Christ all our days. There is not a more miserable creature on earth than a backslider. Every time we turn aside from following Christ, we are providing misery for ourselves—hidings, desertions and broken bones. The only happy life is to follow with all our heart. We generally think it is happy to have this or that idol, but we are quite mistaken. Your true happiness is in self-surrender, in giving up your heart and all to him.

Any one inconsistency mars your joy, mars communion. Are you not far happier in your times of closest walking with God? Oh that it were so with me always! Decays bring darkness and misery. The only happiness is to suffer the loss of all things. Many Christians are not willing to deny themselves, to suffer for Christ's sake—not willing to bear reproach or persecution. Christ will give a hundredfold more—peace of conscience. It is the thriving Christian that is the useful Christian—the one that follows Christ fully. The blessing to Abraham was, 'I will bless thee, and make thee a blessing.' This was eminently true of Paul. He followed Christ fully, and what a blessing he was! So would you be, if you followed Christ fully. If you bore all the features of Christ about with you, what a blessing you would be to this place and to the world—not a cumberer of the ground. How useful to your children and neighbours!

## 23 January

> Let him kiss me with the kisses of his mouth: for thy love is better than wine.
> *Song of Solomon 1:2*

When a labouring, heavy laden sinner is brought to the feet of Jesus, he finds a joy and peace in believing he never felt before. He gets a discovery of the love of Christ that he never had before—the love of Jesus in coming for the ungodly and dying for them, the freeness of Christ to every creature—to sinners, even the chief—to publicans and sinners coming to him, the wisdom and excellency of this way of salvation, the amazing glory and perfection of the righteousness of God. When the Spirit thus takes the veil from the eyes, he gets a sight of Christ which he never will—and never can—forget. This is the spiritual relish and discerning of the Lord's body.

Every new exhibition of Jesus calls up again this sweet sense of his goodness and beauty. He cannot hear his name but his heart is caught away to him. His name is like ointment.

When ministers preach his Word, the memory rushes back to Jesus, and when the broken bread and wine are set before his eyes, his heart is drawn away to remember Jesus. As when the widows stood by Peter weeping, showing the coats and garments that Dorcas had made, every new piece of handiwork of their departed friend called up fresh love in their bosom and fresh tears to their eyes, so to those that know Jesus, the broken bread and poured-out wine stir up their inmost souls to remember Jesus.

## 24 January

> I have showed you all things, how that so labouring ye ought to support the weak, and to remember the words of the Lord Jesus, how he said, It is more blessed to give than to receive.
> *Acts 20:35*

These words form part of a most touching address, which Paul made to the ministers of Ephesus when he parted with them for the last time. He took them all to witness that he was pure from the blood of all men: 'For I have not shunned to declare unto you all the counsel of God.'

It is deeply interesting to notice that the duty of giving to the poor is marked by him as one part of the counsel of God—so much so, that he makes it his last word to them: 'I have shewed you all things, how that so labouring ye ought to support the weak, and to remember the words of the Lord Jesus, how he said. It is more blessed to give than to receive.' These words, which he quotes from the mouth of the Saviour, are nowhere to be found in the Gospels. It is the only traditional saying of our Lord that has been preserved. It seems to have been one of his household words—a commonplace—uttered by him again and again: 'It is more blessed to give than to receive.'

I am glad of having this opportunity of laying before you this part of the counsel of God—for God knows there is no part of it I wish to keep back from you—that you ought to labour to support the weak. And the only argument I shall use with you is that of our blessed Lord: 'It is more blessed to give than to receive.'

# 25 January

As the hart panteth after the water brooks, so panteth my soul after thee, O God.
*Psalm 42:1*

When a soul comes to close with Christ, he is not made perfectly holy all at once: 'The path of the just is as the shining light, that shineth more and more unto the perfect day.' Just as you have seen the day struggling with the darkness, then with clouds, till the sun bursts forth in meridian splendour, so it is with the holiness of a Christian. Just as in the richest lands, after the deepest ploughing, weeds will still grow up among the corn, so, many roots of bitterness remain in the believer's heart.

Paul thanked God for the grace that was given to the Corinthians—that they came behind in no gift—and yet he says they had strife and envy and divisions, so that he could not call them spiritual, but carnal. So it is with every Christian heart. Weeds grow up in the best cultivated gardens. There is enough in Christ to supply all our need. It is our own fault that we are not holy as God is holy. It is not in Christ, but in ourselves, that we are straitened. The shower of grace is plentiful enough, and more than enough; we do not open our mouth wide. But every soul in Christ hates sin and pants after holiness. Nothing makes him pant more after God than corruption striving within.

# 26 January

I have fought a good fight, I have finished my course, I have kept the faith.
*2 Timothy 4:7*

How blessed it is to stand by the deathbed of God's children! How different from that of the wicked! The wicked sometimes die in anguish. Some have been known to cry out, 'Lost, lost, lost! Oh eternity! Oh for half an hour to pray!' Some die in blasphemy, cursing God for their pains and their sores. The greater number die like a beast, without any thought or care except for the body: 'They have no bands in their death: but their strength is firm.' 'Like sheep they are laid in the grave … and the upright shall have dominion over them in the morning.'

How sweet, compared with these, is the departure of God's children! They fall asleep in Jesus: 'I am ready to be offered, and the time of my departure is at hand.' Paul here compares it to the pouring out of a drink offering: 'Yea, and if I be offered upon the sacrifice and service of your faith, I joy, and rejoice with you all' (Philippians 2:17). He felt so entirely dedicated and given away to God, that his death was like the pouring out of the wine offering, which already belonged to God. He compared it also to the departure of a ship: 'The time of my departure is at hand.' The things of time were like the cables that bound him to this world, but soon his bark [sailing ship] was to be loosed from the shore, to sail forward to the shore of glory, to be moored for evermore.

# 27 January

> For I am not ashamed of the gospel of Christ: for it is the power of God unto salvation to every one that believeth; the Jew first, and also to the Greek.
> *Romans 1:16*

'I am not ashamed of the gospel of Christ.' More is meant in these words than is expressed. He does not mean only that he was not ashamed of the gospel, but that he gloried in it. It is very similar to Galatians 6:14: 'God forbid that I should glory, save in the cross of our Lord Jesus Christ.'

Two things are implied in this.

(1) That he was not ashamed of it before God. He had ventured his own soul on this way of salvation. He could say, like David, 'This is all my salvation—this is all my desire.' The way of salvation by Jehovah our Righteousness was sweet to Paul. His soul rested there with great delight. He came thus to God in secret, thus in public, thus in dying. He hoped to stand before God through all eternity clothed in this divine righteousness.

(2) That he was not ashamed of it before men. Though all the world had been against him, Paul would have gloried in this way of salvation. He had a burning desire to make it known to other men. He felt it so sweet, he saw it to be so glorious, that he could have desired a voice so loud that all men might hear at one moment the way of salvation by Christ.

Men would laugh at the idea of a poor worm like Paul going to subdue mighty Rome with a few words of his lips, but Paul saw such a divine power in the gospel that he was not ashamed of it. He knew it could break the hardest heart, and bind up the most broken.

# 28 January

> For I am not ashamed of the gospel of Christ: for it is the power of God unto salvation to every one that believeth; the Jew first, and also to the Greek.
> *Romans 1:16*

No wonder Paul went so boldly to Rome, when he had such a weapon in his hand. He knew that the hearts of the Romans were hard as adamant, proud as Lucifer, and full of lusts as hell is full of foul spirits. He knew that Satan held that proud city in his arms, yet still here was a power—the simple truth as it is in Jesus—by which God could bring low the proudest and hardest, to sit at the feet of Jesus, clothed and in their right mind.

This is what enables us to continue preaching among you. I have now some experience of the hardness of your hearts, and that it is easier to create a world than to convert one of your souls. But the gospel is 'the power of God', and I do not despair of the conversion of any one of you. God is able to do it through his mighty gospel, 'for with God nothing shall be impossible'.

O brethren, have you felt the power of the gospel? Has the gospel come to you, not in word only, but in power, and in the Holy Ghost, and in much assurance? Has it broken your heart and bound it up? Mighty gospel! It alone can save! Awakened sinner, the gospel is 'the power of God unto salvation to every one that believeth'. Though you may have the sins of the Jew and the Greek, there is enough in Jesus to cover all. Though your heart is hard, God is able, through this mighty gospel, to subdue it.

# 29 January

> Now a certain man was sick, named Lazarus, of Bethany, the town of Mary and her sister Martha.
> *John 11:1*

Bethany is a sweet retired village, about two miles from Jerusalem, in a ravine at the back of the Mount of Olives. It is at this day embosomed in fig trees and almond trees and pomegranates. But it had a greater loveliness still in the eyes of Christ: it was 'the town of Mary and her sister Martha'. Jesus knew it only as the town of Mary and her sister Martha.

Probably they lived in a humble cottage under the shade of a fig tree, but that cottage was dear to Christ. Often, as he came over the Mount of Olives and drew near, the light in that cottage window gladdened his heart. Often he sat beneath their fig tree telling them the things of the kingdom of God. His Father loved that dwelling, for these were justified ones. And angels knew it well, for night and day they ministered there to three heirs of salvation. No wonder he called the place 'the town of Mary and her sister Martha'—that was its name in heaven.

So it is still. When worldly people think of our town, they call it the town of some rich merchant—some leading man in public matters—some great politician, who makes a dash [flourish] as a friend of the people, or the town near which some wealthy nobleman dwelleth. But in heaven our town is known as the town of our Marthas and Marys. Perhaps some poor garret where an eminent child of God dwells gives this town its name and interest in the presence of Jesus.

# 30 January

> I am the good shepherd: the good shepherd giveth his life for the sheep.
> *John 10:11*

The shepherd of the sheep is the Lord Jesus Christ. 'I am the good shepherd, and know my sheep, and am known of mine' (verse 14).

Why does he get this name?
(1) Because he died for the sheep. He is not a thief nor a robber, he is not a stranger nor a hireling, but the shepherd of the sheep: 'All we, like sheep, have gone astray: we have turned every one to his own way; and the LORD hath laid on him the iniquity of us all' (Isaiah 53:6).
(2) Because he finds the sheep. 'What man of you, having an hundred sheep, if he lose one of them, doth not leave the ninety and nine in the wilderness, and go after that which is lost, until he find it?' (Luke 15:4). Every sheep in the fold has been found by Jesus.
(3) Because he carries the sheep. 'And when the hath found it, he layeth it on his shoulders, rejoicing' (Luke 15:5). He gathers the lambs with his arm, and carries them in his bosom.

(4) Because he leads and feed the sheep. They 'go in and out, and find pasture' (verse 9). 'The Lord is my shepherd; I shall not want: he maketh me to lie down in green pastures: he leadeth me beside the still waters' (Psalm 23:1–2). 'For the Lamb which is in the midst of the throne shall feed them, and shall lead them unto living fountains of waters: and God shall wipe away all tears from their eyes' (Revelation 7:17).

# 31 January

> I am the good shepherd: the good shepherd giveth his life for the sheep.
> *John 10:11*

Faithful pastors have a peculiar care for the sheep. How remarkably is this exemplified in the case of Paul!

(1) He prayed for them. 'I would that ye knew what great conflict I have for you' (Colossians 2:1). 'God is my witness, whom I serve with my spirit in the gospel of his Son, that without ceasing I make mention of you always in my prayers' (Romans 1:9). 'We give thanks to God and the Father of our Lord Jesus Christ, praying always for you' (Colossians 1:3).

(2) What labours he underwent for them! 'Ye know, from the first day that I came into Asia, after what manner I have been with you at all seasons' (Acts 20:18). 'Remember, that by the space of three years I ceased not to warn every one night and day with tears' (Acts 20:31). 'And I will very gladly spend and be spent for you; though the more abundantly I love you, the less I be loved' (2 Corinthians 12:15). 'So being affectionately desirous of you, we were willing to have imparted unto you, not the gospel of God only, but also our own souls, because ye were dear unto us. For ye remember, brethren, our labour and travail: for labouring night and day, because we would not be chargeable unto any of you, we preached unto you the gospel of God' (1 Thessalonians 2:8–9).

(3) What tears did he shed for them: 'For, out of much affliction and anguish of heart, I wrote unto you with many tears' (2 Corinthians 2:4). 'I fear lest when I come again, my God will humble me among you, and that I shall bewail many that have sinned already' (2 Corinthians 12:21).

# *February*

A LEXANDER MOODY STUART (1809–1898) was born in Paisley as Alexander Moody. He married Jessie Stuart in 1839 and thereafter added her surname to his own name.

After studying at the universities of Glasgow and Edinburgh he was licensed as a minister in 1831. The following year he was sent as an evangelist to Lindisfarne (Holy Island) off the coast of Northumberland, in the north of England. Early in 1835 he became the assistant minister to Robert Candlish in St George's, Edinburgh. In 1837 he was inducted as the minister of the newly established St Luke's Church in Edinburgh. After the Disruption in 1843 the congregation became Free St Luke's.

His preaching was deeply experiential. For many years he attracted many hearers who appreciated such a pulpit ministry. Moody Stuart was a close friend of 'Rabbi' John Duncan, the pious professor of

Hebrew at New College, the theological college of the Free Church of Scotland, and Duncan became a member in his congregation. Both these men had a rich spiritual life, both in the heights and depths of spiritual warfare.

Moody Stuart played an influential role in the Free Church of Scotland. He wrote extensively on a wide variety of topics, including Christian biography, biblical commentary, devotional works, evangelism, and polemical topics.

## Source of daily readings

Alexander Moody Stuart, *The Three Marys* (Edinburgh, 1862).

## Biographies

Kenneth Moody-Stuart, *Alexander Moody Stuart D.D.: A memoir, partly autobiographical* (London, 1899).

Robin Gray, *Alexander Moody Stuart: His spheres of influence* in *Scottish Reformation Society Historical Journal*, Vol. 10 (2020), pp. 227–237.

# 1 February

> But who may abide the day of his coming? and who shall stand when he appeareth? for he is like a refiner's fire, and like fullers' soap.
> *Malachi 3:2*

Seeking soul, you desire to find the Lord Jesus, and you pray for his gracious appearing. 'The Lord, whom ye seek, shall suddenly come … behold, he shall come, saith the LORD of hosts. But who may abide the day of his coming? … For he is like a refiner's fire, and like fullers' soap' (Malachi 3:1–2).

Consider this image of the fuller's soap and test yourself by it, whether you truly desire his coming and can abide it. The garment is put into the fuller's hands, to be cleansed unsparingly from every spot and stain, and made thoroughly clean and white. If you welcome this cleansing, you can abide his coming, but if you welcome not the cleansing, you cannot abide the coming, nor do you truly desire it.

Mark, however, that the question is not whether you are so clean as to endure the Lord's judgment, which will become the inquiry at his second appearing. The question is not now, if you are white and clean as the fuller's soap can make you, for then his coming would have no resemblance to the soap and the washing of the fuller. But are you willing to be subjected in your mind, soul and conscience to this fuller's soap, or are you not? It matters not how clean you are, how few your stains; you cannot receive him if you desire to retain one of them all. It matters not how defiled you are, how crimson and scarlet your sins, if you are willing to be cleansed from them all. Then you welcome Jesus with his cleansing blood.

## 2 February

> Jesus saith unto her, Mary. She turned herself, and saith unto him, Rabboni; which is to say, Master.
> John 20:16

My Lord is 'the Lord that bought me'. What we purchase is ours: the field we purchase and the yoke of oxen bought are ours. So also we are purchased by Christ, but with this difference, that we have a will of our own that must consent to the transference. The price was paid without our consent. Yet against our will the actual transference of the property is never made, for Christ has no slaves. It is, however, not a transference of bonds, but a ransom from bondage. Nevertheless we are not redeemed to be lords and owners of ourselves, but to be the servants of the Lord Jesus Christ, whose servants are all freemen. We are not our own; we are 'bought with a price'. We love to be claimed by him as our owner, and we love to serve him as our master. We serve him freely and from the heart; yet our service is not a gratuity which we may give or withhold, but we are bound to serve Christ our Lord.

We are loosed from all other masters for this very end, that we may serve our crucified and risen Lord, who has redeemed us with his blood. 'I am thy servant: ... thou hast loosed my bonds' (Psalm 116:16). Servants we are, yet friends of the Lord whom we serve. He calls us friends, yet adds, 'Ye are my friends, if ye do whatsoever I command you' (John 15:14). The believer glories in him to others as his friend: 'This is my beloved, and this is my friend' (Song 5:16). But to himself he never says 'my friend', but always 'my Lord'. 'Ye call me Master and Lord: and ye say well; for so I am' (John 13:13).

## 3 February

> Jesus saith unto her, Touch me not; for I am not yet ascended to my Father: but go to my brethren, and say unto

them, I ascend unto my Father, and your Father; and to my God, and your God.
*John 20:17*

Some professed Christians appear to cultivate fellowship with Christ, and speak much of spiritual joy; yet when testimony is to be borne to Christ they fail. In such a case there is little fellowship. The same world that stops the lips in witness-bearing will grieve the Spirit of grace and supplication, and will close the heart in prayer. To profess a secret communion with Christ and to shun open testimony gives little glory to Jesus, brings little profit to man, and is accompanied with little life in the soul. To every such soul Jesus saith, 'Touch me not … but go'. Speak what you have known, and testify what you have seen. If God has lit your candle, you must let that light shine before men. You may be seeking more oil, when he would have you use what you have, and then to him that hath shall be given, but he will not give you more to hide beneath a bushel. You wonder that you have not more light, but the truth is that now you need no more. The instant you hold forth the lamp of life to others, you will need more light for yourself, and be sure that you shall have it in abundance.

It is true that Christ would have fellowship with you, and that without him you can do nothing, but he will have fellowship with many more besides, and he will not have your fellowship with him hinder the communion he desires with many. Your service in bringing others into his fellowship is more glory and pleasure to him than mere present communion with yourself. And the communion you desire he will bestow, not merely in seeking his face but in doing his will.

# 4 February

Now Jesus loved Martha, and her sister, and Lazarus.
*John 11:5*

In a deeper sense than the saying, 'He loved Martha, and her sister, and Lazarus,' every believer can say, 'He loved me, and gave himself for me.' It is not merely the sacrifice of his life for us, but the depth of his love prompting that sacrifice. As he has not spared his life for us, so he has kept back no thought of his heart from us: 'All things that I have heard of my Father I have made known unto you' (John 15:15). He has withheld from us no inward thought of love, but opened all his mind, and he has concealed no lurking ill that might overtake us, or covert snare into which we might fall.

'In my Father's house are many mansions: if it were not so, I would have told you' (John 14:2). Jesus has kept nothing secret from us, of either good or evil, which it concerns us to know. And opening all his heart to us, he invites and enables us to open all our heart to him in return. The whole church is his Bride, yet each believer is personally betrothed to him, as if there were no other. He knows his sheep every one, loves them every one, names them every one. And each one walks with him in an intimacy and a fellowship which the closest of mere human friendships can never approach. 'I ... know my sheep, and am known of mine. As the Father knoweth me, even so I know the Father' (John 10:14–15).

## 5 February

> And Jesus answered and said unto her, Martha, Martha, thou art careful and troubled about many things: but one thing is needful.
> *Luke 10:41–42*

The one great need of man is God; the one need of lost man is peace with God, and therefore the one need of every man is Christ, who is our peace and is himself Immanuel, God with us.

The one great need of every man is God. For the life that now is, man needs God, for man lives not by bread alone, but by every word that proceeds from the mouth of God. Man lives, moves, and has his being in God, without whom bread cannot feed him, and air can breathe no life into him. If God withdraws his upholding hand, man returns to his dust though all things else remain to him unchanged. If God remains with him, he can draw water from the rock beneath for his thirst, if need so be, and shower manna from heaven above for his hunger.

But still more the soul of man needs God. In his own image he created him, and for communion with himself, and with his own finger wrote it on his inmost being that 'man's chief end is to glorify God and to enjoy him for ever'.[1] The handwriting can neither be altered nor effaced. Man can never sink into one of the beasts that perish. Like them in stupidity he does become, but for ever unlike in the great void that is left in his being when man is without God in the world. Like them he may be in heedlessness of God above him and of eternity before him, but only because he is sunk in death-like torpor. Awakened out of that sleep, man is sore athirst as one perishing for want of water, and he cries, 'My soul thirsteth for God, for the living God. O God, … my soul thirsteth for thee, my flesh longeth for thee in a dry and thirsty land, where no water is' (Psalms 42:2; 63:1).

# 6 February

And Jesus answered and said unto her, Martha, Martha, thou art careful and troubled about many things: but one thing is needful.
*Luke 10:41–42*

---

[1] Westminster Shorter Catechism, answer to question 1: *What is man's chief end?*

Martha was preparing various bread for earthly hunger, but one bread for the soul was indispensable and Jesus had announced regarding it, 'I am that living bread.'

Every soul of man needs this bread, for except we eat the flesh of the Son of man, and drink his blood, we have no life in us (John 6:53). Till it is received by faith, all is death within us, and death before us for ever. Every man needs it daily, for except in eating the flesh of the Son of man we have no life in us; it is the only origin of life, and the only sustenance of life in our souls. And as we need this one thing, so it is the only thing that we need. All things else are lifeless to us, and having this, all things else are needless. Jesus himself certifies to us that it is our one and only need.

One of the few grand eras opens in human life when a man first discovers that one thing only is needed by him. His soul has been befooled till that time—trifled with, teased, allured, distracted. He is now awakened to one thing great, one thing needful, one thing alone for his soul, for himself.

'One need,' Mary said, and leaving all things else, in the midst of the manifold preparations for the feast, she hastened to the feet of Jesus to fill the aching void in her soul. One thing needful, O dying sinner! One thing needful for you—and if not quickly found, there is before you one vast yawning want [lack] for ever.

# 7 February

And Jesus answered and said unto her, Martha, Martha, thou art careful and troubled about many things: but one thing is needful.
Luke 10:41–42

When we must die, we need no more bread, for it will soon remain before us untasted; clothing we need not, it will soon lie beside us useless. But Christ we need in life, in death, in eternity. In the body we need Christ, out of the body we need Christ. Yesterday we needed Christ, today Christ, and tomorrow Christ. One need and one alone—the same to all, the same everywhere, and the same always.

But if life itself is not needed, much less do we need the varied accompaniments and comforts of life. The love of father, mother, husband, wife, brother, sister, you need it not; you need one thing only, the love of God in Christ. The esteem and praise of man, naturally so dear to us all, you need it not, but the praise that comes from God only. The countenance [approval] of friends, patrons, customers, you need it not, but only the light of God's countenance, and the light of the Lamb. The wealth, wisdom, learning, science, taste of this world, you need them not, but only to be wise unto salvation, and rich for the world to come.

In seeking first the kingdom of God and his righteousness, there is the promise that other things will be added. And so far as they are good for us, we shall not lack them, but rather have them a hundredfold in this present life. But it is an immense relief to the spirit to come down to the great root of all realities, to ask what we truly need, and to answer, 'One thing I need, and no more.'

# 8 February

> And Jesus answered and said unto her, Martha, Martha, thou art careful and troubled about many things: but one thing is needful.
> *Luke 10:41–42*

'One thing is needful' is the utterance of Jesus Christ—himself the one thing needed, and close beside the soul which he warns of the need. The bread come down from heaven is freely presented to Martha, and at the same moment she is warned that she dies without it. 'There is bread enough and to spare in my father's house,' presents itself to the thoughts of the famished child of folly, and then, but not before, he dares to own to himself, 'and I perish with hunger!'

Friend, there is one thing needful for you, and you die without it, but of all things it is both the nearest, with no distance to reach it, and the freest, with no price to pay for it. 'Say not in thine heart, Who shall ascend into heaven? (that is, to bring Christ down from above:) or, Who shall descend into the deep? (that is, to bring up Christ again from the dead.) But what saith it? The word is nigh thee, even in thy mouth, and in thy heart: ... that if thou shalt confess with thy mouth the Lord Jesus, and shalt believe in thine heart that God hath raised him from the dead, thou shalt be saved' (Romans 10:6–9).

If one thing were ever so needful and yet by no means within the grasp of the needy, the soul might plead that there is nothing for it but to seek the many things that can profit neither much nor long, but that can at least be found. But the exact reverse is the case. The many things are hard to get, and burdensome to keep, while the one [one thing] is the free and irrevocable gift of God to every one that accepts it, to every one that believes.

# 9 February

> But one thing is needful: and Mary hath chosen that good part, which shall not be taken away from her.
> *Luke 10:42*

Mary saw that she needed Christ—that Christ had come unto their house not for their services but for their salvation, not to receive many things from them but to give all things to them. She needed Christ—he had come into the world for the very purpose of giving himself for her need, and it was in her owning his mission and feeding on his words that he would see of the travail of his soul and be satisfied.

It is far easier and more natural for every one of us to seek to serve Christ than to be willing to be saved by his service and suffering for us. The doctrinal knowledge of the truth often makes no practical difference in this respect, and the soul seeking salvation ever attempts many things to make itself acceptable to Christ. It is an exceeding great joy when we discover that Christ has no need of us and our labours, but that we need him, and that without any works of ours he gives himself freely to us.

Martha represents the legal inquirer, Mary the believer in Jesus Christ. But Martha represents also the legal Christian, working many things that give Christ little honour or pleasure, peradventure none, and Mary sets forth the believing soul alive to its own wants, and honouring Christ by ever hungering for him, and by receiving him as the very bread of its life.

# 10 February

> And she had a sister called Mary, which also sat at Jesus' feet, and heard his word.
> *Luke 10:39*

Working (in the believer) is the blessed fruit of life, but working otherwise is only death. To purge the conscience from dead works is amongst the chief virtues of the blood of Jesus, and the carnal mind, in its busy works, is ever doing that which requires to be covered by the blood of sprinkling.

'To him that worketh not but believeth' lays an awful pause upon the soul. There is a solemn silence within—a deathlike stillness—when the soul first dares to cease talking and stop working, and, beginning to listen to the word of life, hears that it may believe in

Jesus unto salvation. But how glorious the result! How different the false life wrought out from within by our own legal efforts, and the true life coming down from above through Jesus Christ!

What reality and power of life are given to the soul by feeding on Christ, the bread of heaven! What freshness and eternity of life spring up as a well of living water within the heart, by the Holy Ghost given in believing! What fulness and variety of living food are received in the words of life, by every soul that 'hears and lives'! Let us therefore follow Mary, let us take her lowly seat at the feet of Jesus and, in so doing, let us reckon that blessed are our ears, because they hear what many prophets and righteous men have desired to hear, but have not heard.

# 11 February

> He hath holpen his servant Israel, in remembrance of his mercy; as he spake to our fathers, to Abraham, and to his seed for ever.
> *Luke 1:54–55*

In all the preparation of this elect vessel by nurture in the Word, by love to Israel and by the hope of the Messiah, the divine wisdom shines brightly. Mary occupying a place altogether singular in the human family and in the church of God, as the mother of Jesus, is singular also among the saints by the crowning event of her life occurring in early youth. Youthful believers had from the beginning formed a noble cloud of witnesses, as children of the covenant made with their father Abraham. But in Joseph, in Moses, in David, the crowning events of life were not in youth but in manhood, after a long and fiery trial of their faith.

So it was also in the peculiar exercise of faith for the promised Deliverer. To Eve, the 'man from the Lord' was neither through her first-born Cain nor through the righteous Abel, but when both were lost in one day, it was through Seth, given to her in his martyred brother's stead. To Abraham the child of promise came not, till old age had left himself as good as dead. Mary's own cousin Elisabeth is stricken in years before she is honoured to be the mother even of the Messiah's forerunner, John the Baptist. But with Mary herself all this is reversed. It is not nature exhausted and then miraculously revived, but nature anticipated, set aside. It is not faith tried by a succession of disappointments, hope deferred till the heart is sick and it becomes hope against hope, but it is gift unforeseen, blessing of which there had been no forethought, unlooked-for favour and grace.

# 12 February

He hath filled the hungry with good things; and the rich he hath sent empty away.
*Luke 1:53*

In the ministry of the Lord Jesus Christ, these were among the first of all the words he uttered, 'Blessed are they which do hunger and thirst after righteousness: for they shall be filled' (Matthew 5:6). And Mary describes herself as partaking of that hunger and sharing in that blessedness.

How few there are amongst us that hunger and thirst after righteousness! And how few, after having tasted, continue to hunger and to thirst more intensely than before!

How many of you are rich, and increased with goods, and have need of nothing; and know not that ye are wretched, and miserable, and poor, and blind, and naked! How foolish the fancied spiritual wealth, how wise the spiritual poverty! How miserable the fulness—how empty and void, how utterly unsatisfying and vain; in the end, how accursed!

How happy the hunger, how sure of satisfaction! How pleasant in its very exercise, because it is healthy hunger for living bread! How blessed now, because it cannot be disappointed but is sure to be filled! How blessed for ever, because it is God, it is Christ, it is the Spirit that meets the heart's desire! The soul is filled with bread that can never cloy, with living water that is ever fresh, with satisfaction which instantly creates more desire and longing, with hunger which is ever met by soul satisfaction.

Longing believer, to all eternity you will join Mary in her song, 'He hath filled the hungry with good things.' May God in his mercy grant that none of us may have cause for ever to say of ourselves, 'But he hath sent the rich empty away.'

## 13 February

> And Mary said, Behold the handmaid of the Lord; be it unto me according to thy word. And the angel departed from her.
> *Luke 1:38*

Mary believes in the power of God, which, simple as it appears, is rarer far than is thought. David speaks of it as a special revelation to himself, 'Once have I heard, yea twice, that power belongeth unto God' (Psalm 62:11) because it is a truth known and believed by few, when our own strength is gone, that power belongs to him. But he adds, 'Unto God also belongeth mercy,' connecting love with power, for knowledge of mere divine power would bring no hope.

Even so is it with Mary. She believes in the power, she believes also in the goodness of God. Like David, she too declares that 'his mercy is on them that fear him' (Luke 1:50). She believes in his mercy and she accepts his goodness: 'Hail, highly favoured' (Luke 1:28). 'Be it unto me according to thy word.' The gift of God's great goodness she receives in simple faith—that as nothing is too hard for the Lord to do for the weakest, so nothing is too good for him to bestow upon the vilest. It is believing submission to the gracious pleasure of God, believing acceptance of unmerited goodness.

Such is all true faith. It is belief in the free favour of God through Jesus Christ, with nothing in us to call forth that favour, but everything to provoke wrath. It is belief in the forgiveness of sins, under the confessed desert [deservedness] of condemnation. It is not, however, a mere general faith in the forgiving God, but the acceptance of the pardon that is freely given. Mary believes in the Lord's goodness, but she accepts the blessing for which she believes: 'Behold the handmaid of the Lord; be it unto me according to thy word.'

# 14 February

> And Mary said, Behold the handmaid of the Lord; be it unto me according to thy word. And the angel departed from her.
> *Luke 1:38*

Mary, believing God's power and goodness, confides also in his *truth*. 'Be it according to thy promise' is the expression of her faith. The whole transaction is strange and unexpected to her, but she is not a stranger to God and his Word, and the inquiries she makes are not in unbelief but in holy simplicity and faith.

The angel's appearance is new and marvellous in her experience, and she is troubled at first by an event so wholly unexpected. His glorious tidings are also strange and unlooked for, and the manner of their fulfilment incomprehensible. But she never doubts the truth of God's Word.

Does not the like trial constantly find many of us wanting? We believe the truth of God's words to others, but are slow to believe them for ourselves. We believe that Jesus Christ came into the world to save sinners—sinners in general, other sinners, any other except ourselves. We believe the saying to be faithful and worthy of acceptation by all, yet we oft distrust it, as if not worthy of our acceptance. This did not Mary: she believed that the word of God, true to Abraham, was true also to her, and blessed she was in believing. The like faith in us will receive the same blessing. Let us not put it from ourselves by unbelief, but let us take God at his word, let us trust his truth, let us accept his promise. In believing we shall be blessed now, and we shall not be put to shame, world without end, for there shall for ever be 'the performance of the things spoken unto us by the Lord'.

## 15 February

> For he hath regarded the low estate of his handmaiden: for, behold, from henceforth all generations shall call me blessed. For he that is mighty hath done to me great things; and holy is his name.
> Luke 1:48–49

Mary's noble outburst of joy is not in Nazareth, but in the house of Zacharias; not in Galilee, but in the hill-country of Judea. Like the birth in Bethlehem, this seems not to be accidental, but divinely ordered. As the birth of Jesus is to be in the land of Judah, so is also this song of praise for the incarnation—Christ being of the tribe of Judah, and Judah signifying praise. There is joy in Mary for the favour shown her, but with no mingling of pride.

And with this joy there mingles no pride: 'He hath regarded the low estate of his handmaiden. ... He hath exalted them of low degree.' The signal favour is received with the deepest humility under the consciousness of her own unworthiness and unmeetness. Goodness so great as to remove all plea of desert does not uplift but humbles. If the favour is less or the merit more, so that the disparity between the two is not so marked, pride finds occasion to enter.

But when the distance is extreme between the gift and the recipient, the effect is to humble the soul under a sense of unworthiness.

So it is with Mary in receiving Christ, and so also with every soul that receives the forgiveness of sins through his name. The distinction above others in Mary's case was greater, but the joy in itself could not be more than when a condemned sinner is forgiven through Christ's blood and has the full sense of the pardon of sin.

## 16 February

> For he hath regarded the low estate of his handmaiden: for, behold, from henceforth all generations shall call me blessed. For he that is mighty hath done to me great things; and holy is his name.
> *Luke 1:48–49*

Nothing can exceed the change from being a child of wrath into becoming a child of the most high God, from a fearful looking for of judgment to be begotten again to an inheritance eternal in the heavens, from being condemned and accursed of God to being justified, accepted, beloved.

A change greater than this, if fully realised, cannot take place upon the soul of any son of man, nor can stronger reasons for joy be stated or conceived. Christ himself declares that Mary's own happiness was not so great: 'Blessed is the womb that bare thee, and the paps which thou hast sucked. ... Yea rather, blessed are they that hear the word of God, and keep it' (Luke 11:27–28).

Be assured of this, that there is not a more groundless imagination than that by which you refuse the free favour of God lest its reception should fill you with pride. The pardon of your sins and the knowledge that all your sins are pardoned, adoption into the family of God and assurance of your adoption, the heirship of heaven and the full persuasion of your inheritance, will not lift you up with pride but most certainly humble you in the dust. Our natural hope of partial blessing may elate us because we trust to meet half-way the favour shown us. But God's own grace is so great to us [who are] so vile, that the firmer our assurance of it and the closer home it comes to us, we are only the more ashamed of ourselves. 'That thou mayest remember, and be confounded, and never open thy mouth any more because of thy shame, when I am pacified toward thee for all that thou hast done, saith the Lord GOD' (Ezekiel 16:63).

# 17 February

*He hath shewed strength with his arm; he hath scattered the proud in the imagination of their hearts.*
*Luke 1:51*

There is the seal of the Spirit to Mary's faith, and this gives her great joy in the Lord.

These words of the apostle Paul are full of instruction: 'In whom also, after ye believed, ye were sealed with that holy Spirit of promise' (Ephesians 1:13). At first it will often be true, in the language of Luther, that 'faith is a certain dark confidence'. It is trust in that which we see not, and for that which we do not feel. It is confidence in the bare word of God. Fruitless hitherto in the soul that word may have been, yet it is received as true. The soul rests upon it as God's truth, not because the word is working love in the heart or filling the mind with light, but simply because it is God's truth. Hundreds of inquiring souls believe not, because they feel not—looking for the fruit and the seal of faith in order to believing, instead of simply believing the word itself and leaving the rest to follow according to the will of God.

'After we believe, we are sealed with the Holy Spirit.' It is the Spirit that works faith in us, but the conscious gift and seal of the Spirit follow, for we 'receive the Spirit by the hearing of faith'. There is certainty in the Spirit's seal to faith in Christ Jesus, because 'him hath God the Father sealed'. He hath sealed Christ in his own wondrous person and in his glorious work, and he seals Christ wherever he is, and in every soul that receives him.

## 18 February

> And it came to pass, that, when Elisabeth heard the salutation of Mary, the babe leaped in her womb; and Elisabeth was filled with the Holy Ghost: and she spake out with a loud voice, and said, Blessed art thou among women, and blessed is the fruit of thy womb.
> *Luke 1:41–42*

There is sovereignty both in the time and the manner of the seal. With Mary, there is manifest sovereignty in the *time* of the Spirit's seal. It is not immediately on the angel's departure, but after the lapse of days or weeks. Calm and childlike confidence would seem to have been the state of Mary's mind in Nazareth, without any outburst of holy joy. There was simple and unwavering faith, but the Spirit's full seal to that faith seems not to have been given till Elisabeth had saluted her, 'Blessed is she that believed: for there shall be a performance of those things that were told her from the Lord' (verse 45).

The *manner* of the seal was also sovereign, for it was not in the solitude of Mary's chamber, as we should have expected, but in holy fellowship with a sister saint. The two meet together in the name of the coming Messiah. Elisabeth calls the unborn child 'my Lord', which she must surely have done only because she owned him as Immanuel, God with us. She is filled with the Holy Ghost for herself. Full of the Spirit, she addresses Mary, and Mary is filled with the Holy Ghost and breaks out into her glorious song. So in substance it is to every believer in Christ Jesus. The faith is sealed to each according to the measure of the gift of God, and according to his holy sovereignty in time and manner, but always the simpler and stronger the faith, the more full will be the seal of the Spirit, because the simplest faith most owns and honours Christ, whom alone the Father seals.

# 19 February

> And Mary said, My soul doth magnify the Lord, and my spirit hath rejoiced in God my Saviour.
> *Luke 1:46–47*

Mary enjoying the Lord's goodness, rejoicing in the Lord himself, gives praise and thanks unto his name. The Lord had exalted her, and she uses her exaltation only to exalt the Lord. The Mighty One had done great things for her, and she extols him alone as mighty: 'My soul doth magnify the Lord.' All else are forgotten, for he only is great, and greatly to be praised. It is not Mary that is great through the great things done for her, but the Lord that does them is great. Mary does not magnify herself in receiving great things, does not magnify her people Israel on whose account she receives them, does not magnify her father David through whom they come to her, but Mary magnifies the Lord.

We have noted this last, but it is greatest, and with her it is first. With her the favour shown to herself is last, her own joy in the Lord precedes it, and the Lord's own greatness is first of all. 'My soul doth magnify the Lord' is the first outburst of her song, and it is an outburst of praise and blessing unto God most high. The mighty One, the only mighty One, he that is mighty—the holy One, the only holy One, holy is his name—the merciful One, with his mercy on them that fear him, and the faithful One, as he spake to Abraham and his seed.

# 20 February

> Now the birth of Jesus Christ was on this wise: When as his mother Mary was espoused to Joseph, before they came together, she was found with child of the Holy Ghost. Then Joseph her husband, being a just man, and not willing to make her a public example, was minded to put her away privily.
> *Matthew 1:18–19*

The echoes of the Virgin's songs have scarcely died away among the hills of Judah, when a dark cloud overshadows all her life, and her bright morning of joy is turned into a night of bitter weeping. Through the Lord's singular goodness to her, and through her childlike faith in him, she is like to become an outcast in the eyes of men, as one that has forsaken the guide of her youth and broken the covenant of her God. A darker cloud never rested upon a child of God on earth, purely for the sake of Christ; a sorer trial could not fall to the lot of any child of man. There is much, indeed, to support the youthful sufferer, yet the crisis is dark in the extreme.

There is *strong consolation* to Mary's soul in her sorrow. First of all, there is the answer of a *good conscience* toward God, for hers is no buffeting for sin, but doing well and suffering for it. Christians often suffer, not for Christ's sake but for their own sins, and when they suffer for the Lord's sake, the mingling of the will of man with the work of God often aggravates their sorrow and furnishes their foes with an excuse for evil-entreating them. There is nothing of this with Mary; her faith and obedience are the only cause of her reproach. The sting is thus taken out of suffering. When there is no secret rankling of conscience, but all is clear toward God, there is much to lighten the heaviest load of grief.

## 21 February

Now the birth of Jesus Christ was on this wise: When as his mother Mary was espoused to Joseph, before they came together, she was found with child of the Holy Ghost. Then Joseph her husband, being a just man, and not willing to make her a public example, was minded to put her away privily.
*Matthew 1:18–19*

The case of most believers is substantially the same as Mary's—blessed in believing, and rejoicing greatly in the Lord, but when Christ is formed in us the hope of glory, soon exposed to reproach for his name. We must all take up the cross if we are to follow Christ, and through tribulation we must enter into the kingdom, suffering with him before we reign with him.

Next, there is the *favour* of God, which is ample compensation for the loss of human esteem—the favour of God previous to the reproach and producing it, and the favour of God consequent on the suffering for his sake and healing it. If we be reproached for the name of Christ, happy are we, for the Spirit of glory and of God resteth upon us (1 Peter 4:14). Christ's cross borne by us ever draws down Christ's Spirit, and prayer itself is not more effectual for this end. The joy of the Lord is then most of all our strength when other joy is taken away, for Christ has promised not to leave us comfortless, but to come unto us, when without him all comfort would be gone. When others cast us out for his sake, Jesus himself ever seeks and finds us, nor will he leave us while our need remains.

## 22 February

Now the birth of Jesus Christ was on this wise: When as his mother Mary was espoused to Joseph, before they came together, she was found with child of the Holy Ghost. Then

> Joseph her husband, being a just man, and not willing to make her a public example, was minded to put her away privily.
>
> *Matthew 1:18–19*

Foul crime, base hypocrisy, and horrible blasphemy are about to be laid to Mary's charge in Nazareth, in Galilee, in Israel. What a weight of sorrow, what a load of shame! How unequal to such a burden would most maidens in Israel have been! Of her conduct in this fiery trial we know this only, that she appears to have said nothing and done nothing to vindicate herself, but there is enough in this simple fact. The record indeed does not declare so much, and is only silent, but the fact of God's express interposition warrants the conclusion that Mary did not interfere in her own behalf. Doubtless, when demanded, she would state the truth for God's glory and her own justification, but otherwise she abides in silence and in meekness. She believed at first, and was blessed; she believes now, and does not make haste. She does not strive nor cry, nor make her voice to be heard in the streets. She complains not to man of wrong and appeals not to man for pity, but in patience possesses her soul.

Yet they know little of the human heart, who conceive that under this outward calm all is quiet within. And they know little of the mind of God, who think that in such a case he spares his own from present tribulation because he is soon to send them deliverance. But a soul that can praise as Mary did, and as so few others could, can also pray as few besides. The lips that can so well adduce the ancient promises in a song of thanksgiving can likewise plead those promises in earnest supplication.

## 23 February

And we know that all things work together for good to them that love God, to them who are the called according to his purpose.
*Romans 8:28*

Let us remember that the nearer we are to Christ, the nearer are we to his cross. The glorious revelation of Christ to Paul is accompanied with the intimation: 'I will show him how great things he must suffer for my name's sake' (Acts 9:16). But if we suffer with him, we shall also reign with him; if we bear his cross, we shall also wear his crown.

Mary's joy would seem to many all too little to compensate her sorrow. But the joy is not simply good and the grief simply evil, but if from the Lord both are good and both are among the 'all things' that work together for good to them that love him. The sorrow indeed is usually more fruitful than the joy, and therefore 'whom the Lord loveth he chasteneth, and scourgeth every son whom he receiveth' (Hebrews 12:6).

The believer, rejoicing in the hope of the glory of God, has received therewith a golden secret which turns all darkness into light, and all the bitter into sweet. For not only do we rejoice in the hope of glory, 'but we glory in tribulations also: knowing that tribulation worketh patience; and patience, experience; and experience, hope; and hope maketh not ashamed; because the love of God is shed abroad in our hearts by the Holy Ghost which is given unto us' (Romans 5:3–5).

Are you a stranger to the reproach of Christ? If so, you have reason to fear that Christ has never been formed in you the hope of glory. Has that reproach, once tasted, become again a strange thing to you? Then you have reason to inquire if the cross of Christ has not lost its power within you. Christ and his cross are never far apart, and the absence of the cross may be warning you to seek an absent Christ.

# 24 February

> Then Joseph being raised from sleep did as the angel of the Lord had bidden him, and took unto him his wife: and knew her not till she had brought forth her firstborn son: and he called his name JESUS.
> *Matthew 1:24–25*

After Joseph's dream and Mary's entrance into his house, there is an interval of silence in the gospel narrative till the enrolment, ordered by the Roman emperor, summons them both to Bethlehem. It must have been to Mary an interval of blessed peace, of gratitude, of joy, of hope, of prayer. To Joseph and Mary together it was doubtless a season of much quiet waiting on the Lord, of humble inquiry into his mind and will, of supplication for grace and wisdom in the nurturing of the child who was to redeem the Israel of God. The mother of Jesus is a Nazarene, but Jesus himself is to be born in Bethlehem, the city of his father David. Bethlehem is the 'house of bread', fit birthplace for him who is 'the bread of God', that 'cometh down from heaven, and giveth life unto the world' (John 6:33).

But Jesus is also the fountain of living water for the sons of men, bearing this inscription, 'If any man thirst, let him come unto me, and drink' (John 7:37). Nor is the type of this living water lacking in Bethlehem. It was the place of David's birth and boyhood, and in his manhood of hardship and war he longed to drink of the well from which in earlier years he had so often quenched his thirst. He is in the cave of Adullam with his hardy comrades in arms, long shut out from the house of the Lord, and sighing, 'As the hart panteth after the water brooks, so panteth my soul after thee, O God. … When shall I come and appear before God?' (Psalm 42:1–2).

## 25 February

But Mary kept all these things, and pondered them in her heart.
*Luke 2:19*

Mary keeps the Lord's *words*—his words spoken by his messengers concerning herself or her holy child and Saviour, and afterwards, the child's own words.

First of all, she has such words to keep, for Christ says, 'He that hath my commandments, and keepeth them.' The first great point with her and with us is to possess the words of life. Many, in the multitude of holy words around them and even within their memories, never possess one of them for themselves, and 'from him that hath not shall be taken away even that which he hath'. The words of life shall be taken from them for ever, because they have them not. They both have, and have not—they have them in their lips and in their hands, yet they are never truly theirs in the heart, and from them they are taken to all eternity.

But blessed is he that hath even one saying of the Lord, that hath it for himself and not for another, that hath it from the Lord and given to his own soul. He is blessed because it shall never be taken away, and blessed because to him that hath shall be given, and he shall have more; word shall be added to word, promise to promise, warning to warning, till he is rich toward God by having the words of everlasting life dwelling in him richly.

## 26 February

But Mary kept all these things, and pondered them in her heart.
*Luke 2:19*

Meanwhile the scene of most dazzling magnificence that has ever been enacted on earth is witnessed on the high plains of Bethlehem. A few months ago in that same country, and possibly in that neighbourhood, Mary's full heart had burst into the heavenly song, 'My soul doth magnify the Lord.' And now the heavens are opened to respond to that noble hymn from earth.

There are shepherds watching their flocks by night, who are doubtless men of God that wait for the consolation of Israel, as those that watch for the morning. They are thrown into sore alarm, not by the dreaded lion or leopard bounding in upon their sleeping flocks, but by the glory of the Lord suddenly breaking forth around them, and an angel announces, 'Behold, I bring you good tidings of great joy, which shall be to all people. For unto you is born this day in the city of David a Saviour, which is Christ the Lord' (Luke 2:9–10). Instantly, from angel and archangel, from cherubim and seraphim, there bursts a loud song of rapturous joy—there appears a multitude of the heavenly host, praising God and saying, 'Glory to God in the highest, and on earth peace, goodwill toward men' (Luke 2:14). The shepherds, filled with wonder, hasten to tell the vision and report the words in Bethlehem, and in the mean abode of Mary. Heaven opened, to announce the birth of Jesus, is in strange contrast to the meanness of that birth, and the lowly manger in which he is laid is the very sign by which the angels intimate that the great King is to be recognized. All that hear wonder at the tidings told them by the shepherds: Mary alone marvels not, but thoughtfully ponders all in her heart.

# 27 February

Now when Jesus was born in Bethlehem of Judaea in the days of Herod the king, behold, there came wise men from the east to Jerusalem.
*Matthew 2:1*

And again, there come wise men from the distant east to the city of David. In their own land they have seen the star of the Messiah, which guides them to Palestine; at Jerusalem they are instructed to proceed to Bethlehem, and there they behold the heavenly lamp shining over Mary's humble home.

They enter and tell the thoughtful mother of their journey from afar, and of their guide by night in the heavens. They see the child, and fall down before him with offerings of gold and frankincense and myrrh. Mary's heart overflows with gratitude and joy: with gratitude for the Lord's goodness in so seasonable a supply for their poverty; with joy at so honourable a recognition of the infant Lord and King.

The wise men take leave of the holy family, and depart for their own country. Night comes on, and Joseph and Mary with the child resign themselves to thankful repose. At midnight she is suddenly awakened by her husband. He tells her that the angel of the Lord, who had before enjoined him in a dream to own her without fear, has again appeared in like manner, warning him to flee with her for the child's life from the sword of Herod. And in haste in that same hour they make ready for their flight. In the dark night the tender mother and child go forth out of Bethlehem, to leave their native country and the holy land and go down into Egypt, the land of heathen idols and of Israel's ancient bondage. So unexpectedly lifted up and so suddenly cast down, Mary has enough thrown into the balance now, when she ponders these things in her heart.

# 28 February

> Ponder the path of thy feet, and let all thy ways be established.
> Proverbs 4:26

'Ponder the path of thy feet, and let all thy ways be established' (Proverbs 4:26) is the counsel of Wisdom to every son of man. Next to prayer and reading the Word of God, there is nothing better for men, for young and old, than pondering the path of the feet. Without it, no man can understand his own way, and all his goings will be uncertain and crooked.

A man's goings are indeed of the Lord, and 'it is not in man that walketh to direct his steps'. But if the Lord has a way for every man, he is willing to teach him its waymarks, and it is the wisdom of the prudent 'to understand his way' (Proverbs 14:8). It is only by pondering the path of the feet, in considering the dealings of the Lord with us and his guiding hitherto, that we are enabled to discern the path in which he would have us to go, and to walk in 'footsteps ordered by the Lord'. And there is nothing either more interesting or more profitable for a man than often to weigh the Lord's various dealings with him, alike in providence and in grace.

Nor let any man say that it was interesting to Mary to ponder her path, for there were great events, and of world-wide interest, continually occurring in her course, but that his own life is insignificant and mean. The difference is far less than you conceive. If you are a follower of Christ, your life will be full of greatness and of interest.

# 29 February

But the path of the just is as the shining light, that shineth more and more unto the perfect day.
*Proverbs 4:18*

If you are a follower of Christ, your life will be full of greatness and of interest. The wrath to come is great—you are delivered from it. Look down with joy and trembling over the brink of the deep pit from which you have been drawn. Sin is great—Christ has given and is giving you the victory over it, and it is still a great conflict and great victory continually. Satan is the strong one among all the sons of strength, and yet he is bruised under your feet by your stronger Redeemer. Grace is great, and it abounds toward you; heaven is great, and it is your own sure inheritance. Great sorrow, great joy, great fear, great hope in your own heart, with great works of the Lord wrought on your behalf, all belong to your course on earth, and yours therefore is no mean or common life, but a grand and eventful life.

Yet much depends on your pondering the ways of the Lord with you, for the old saying holds true that 'to those who are given to observation, things happen that are worth observing'. Much of Mary's life would have been thrown away on another less thoughtful than she, but the Lord, who gave so much to think upon, raised up his handmaid with a heart to ponder it all. And if you will ponder well the little that seems to have been allotted to you, you will first of all find that it is your own blindness alone that makes it little instead of great, and dull instead of replete with interest. And next, the Lord will show you greater things, when once your heart is directed to observe and improve [profit from] what he has already wrought for you.

# March

HORATIUS BONAR (1808–1889) was born in Edinburgh. He attended the High School and University in this city. As a student, he and his brother Andrew became friends with Robert Murray McCheyne. The bonds of Christian fellowship between these three men endured and they became the centre of evangelical activity within the Church of Scotland and, after the Disruption, in the Free Church of Scotland.

In 1837 Horatius Bonar became the minister of the North Church in Kelso and he joined the Free Church of Scotland in 1843. He remained in Kelso until 1866, when he was translated to the newly formed Chalmers Memorial Free Church in the Grange district of Edinburgh.

Bonar was an influential figure on both sides of the Atlantic. He was a distinguished poet, known for composing spiritual songs and he was also the author a large number of books, many of which remain in print.

## Sources of daily readings

March 1–3: Horatius Bonar, *The Blood of the Cross* (Kelso, 1857).

March 4–6: Horatius Bonar, *Follow the Lamb; or Counsels to Converts* (London, 1861).

March 7–8: Horatius Bonar, *God's Way of Peace: A book for the anxious* (London, 1869).

March 9–10 and 27–31: Horatius Bonar, *The Night of Weeping: or Words for the Suffering Family of God* (London, 1845).

March 11–16 and 25–26: Horatius Bonar, *Christ, the Healer* (London, 1867).

March 17–24: Horatius Bonar, *Kelso Tracts* (Kelso, 1846).

## Biography

*Horatius Bonar, D.D.: A memorial* (London, 1889).

# 1 March

*But into the second went the high priest alone once every year, not without blood, which he offered for himself, and for the errors of the people.*
*Hebrews 9:7*

One of God's chief controversies with this world is respecting this blood. He has many other such controversies, but this is one of the chief. For here his estimate and man's are at utter variance with each other, in respect both of the value and efficacy of this blood, no less than regarding the guilt of shedding it. On many points they differ in their estimates. As to the value of the soul, of earth, of time, of eternity, they differ. But here they differ most of all, and on this difference the sinner's eternity hinges. For it is according to what he thinks of this blood that he is saved or lost. This is the turning point of his salvation. He may count it strange or hard that his everlasting welfare should be thus determined. Yet God declares that it must be so. He will not consent to treat that blood so lightly as the sinner. Nor will he consent to deal favourably with the sinner that slights or scorns that blood. Here he is inexorable. For the honour of his own Son is involved in it, and that honour must be maintained inviolable.

And why should it be thought an incredible thing that it should be so? Grant but that this blood is what it is, the blood of God's beloved Son, and it is not difficult to see why he should, on such a point, be so awfully inflexible. Nay, shall we not say, 'How can it be otherwise?' And wonder only how he can bear so much as one single slight offered to blood so precious in his eyes.

# 2 March

*How much more shall the blood of Christ, who through the eternal Spirit offered himself without spot to God, purge your conscience from dead works to serve the living God?*
*Hebrews 9:14*

What think you, then, of the blood of Christ? Is that which is so precious in God's eyes as precious in yours? Has the controversy between him and you upon this point been solidly adjusted? And are you at one with him in his estimate of the blood of his dear Son? If so, it is well. For this is faith, and it is by this faith that you are saved. It was unbelief that led you to form so low an estimate of that blood, and it is faith which has led you to throw aside your own estimate and adopt that of God. Thus it is that we believe.

The Holy Spirit shows us the real nature of that blood we have been slighting. He shows us whose blood it is—what wonders it is intended to effect—what power it has to cleanse—what efficacy to give peace. He tells us what God has written concerning this blood. He tells us God's opinion of its value. And making known these things to us he leads us to immediate peace. The new estimate which he enables us to form of this at once infuses peace. If that estimate which God had given of it be true, then all that is needful for our peace has been accomplished. That infinitely precious blood sheds peace and sunshine into our souls. We see that blood as God sees it, and our consciences are unburdened, our souls are set at rest.

# 3 March

And Aaron shall lay both his hands upon the head of the live goat, and confess over him all the iniquities of the children of Israel, and all their transgressions in all their sins, putting them upon the head of the goat, and shall send him away by the hand of a fit man into the wilderness.
*Leviticus 16:21*

It is the blood whose shedding has provided a propitiation for sin, and whosoever will consent to take this as his propitiation becomes a partaker of the blessings which it contains. It was the high priest's laying of his hand upon the goat that established the connection between it and the people, so that Israel's sins passed over to the substitute; and so it is our believing that connects us with the divine Substitute, and brings to us all the benefits of the divine bloodshedding.

It is our unbelief that intercepts the communication; it is faith that establishes it. Faith may seem a slight thing to some, and they may wonder how salvation can flow from believing. Hence they try to magnify it, to adore it, to add to it, in order that it may appear some great thing, something worthy of having salvation as its reward. In so doing, they are actually transforming faith into a work, and introducing salvation by works under the name of faith. They show that they understand neither the nature nor the office of faith. It saves, simply by handing us over to the Saviour. It saves, not on account of the good works which flow from it, not on account of the love which it kindles, not on account of the repentance which it produces, but solely because it connects us with the saving One. Its saving efficacy does not lie in connection with righteousness and holiness, but entirely in its connection with the righteous and holy One. Thus it is that unbelief ruins, because it cuts off all communication with the source of life, and thus faith blesses because it establishes that communication.

## 4 March

Therefore, my beloved brethren, be ye stedfast, unmoveable, always abounding in the work of the Lord, forasmuch as ye know that your labour is not in vain in the Lord.
*1 Corinthians 15:58*

You were neither born nor reborn for yourselves alone. You may not be able to do much, but do something: work while it is day. You may not be able to give much, but give something—according to your ability, remembering that the Lord loveth a cheerful giver. Take heed, and beware of covetousness, for the love of money is the root of all evil. Whenever worldliness comes in, in any shape, whether it be love of money or love of pleasure, you cease to be faithful to Christ, and are trying to serve both God and mammon.

Do something, then, for God, while time lasts. It may not be long, for the day goeth away, and the shadows of evening are stretched out. Do something every day. Work, and throw your heart into the work. Work joyfully and with a right good will, as men who love both their work and their master. Be not weary in well-doing. Work, and work in faith. Work in love and patience and hope. Don't shrink from hard labour or disagreeable duties, or a post trying to flesh and blood. 'Endure hardness, as a good soldier of Jesus Christ' (2 Timothy 2:3). 'Be steadfast, unmoveable, always abounding in the work of the Lord' (1 Corinthians 15:58). Don't fold your hands, or lay aside your staff, or sheathe your sword. Don't give way to slothfulness and flesh-pleasing, saying to yourselves, 'I can get to heaven without working.'

# 5 March

> Whosoever believeth that Jesus is the Christ is born of God: and every one that loveth him that begat loveth him also that is begotten of him.
> *1 John 5:1*

'I am the Lord your God' was God's greeting of love to Israel (Leviticus 11:44). It is no less now his salutation of grace to every one who has believed on the name of his Son, Christ Jesus. God becomes our God the moment that we receive his testimony of his beloved Son. This new relationship between God and us, in virtue of which he calls us *his,* and we call him *ours,* is the simple result of a believed gospel.

If anyone reading these lines is led to ask, 'How may I become a son?' we answer in the words of truth, 'He that believeth that Jesus is the Christ is born of God.' Nothing less than believing can bring about this sonship, and nothing more is needed. The joy and the peace and the love and the warmth, these are the *effects* of faith, but they are not faith. They are the fruits of a conscious sonship which has been formed by the belief of the divine testimony to Jesus as the Son of God and the Saviour of the lost. 'As many as received him, to them gave he the right to become the sons of God, even to them that believe on his name' (John 1:12, marginal reading).

God's simple message of grace contains peace for the sinner. And the sinner extracts the peace therein contained, not by effort or feeling, but by the simple belief of the true sayings of God. Good news makes glad by being believed, and they refuse to yield up their precious treasure to anything but to simple faith. Believe the tidings of peace from God, and the peace is all your own.

## 6 March

But to him that worketh not, but believeth on him that justifieth the ungodly, his faith is counted for righteousness.
Romans 4:5

It is not to him that worketh, or feeleth, or loveth, but to him that believeth that God says, 'I am the Lord your God.' And when God used the word 'believing', he just meant what he said, and intended nothing else than what man means by that word. Had he meant anything else, he would have told us, and not suffered us to be misled or deceived by our misunderstanding of a word of which the Bible is full. Had he meant working, or feeling, or loving, he would have said so, and not allowed us to suppose that believing was really all. What a book of deception and mystery the Bible would be, if 'believing' does not mean 'believing', but something less or something more! To make it something less would be to take from God's Word as truly as if we had struck out a book from the Bible. To make it something more would be to add to God's Word, as truly and as sinfully as if we had forged another gospel or another Epistle, or accepted the Apocrypha as part of the inspired record.

We make God a liar when we refuse to take him at his word, or give him credit for speaking that simple truth, in believing which we are saved. But let us remember the other side of his statement, namely, our being found liars by reason of our adding to his word. 'Every word of God is pure' (Proverbs 30:5). Can we make it purer, or more transparent, or more simple? We add to it, lest it should be too simple, too childlike, too blessed; we put something of our own into it to make it more *substantial* and complete; and that 'something' (call it feeling, or realizing, or loving) destroys the divine simplicity and transparency of faith.

# 7 March

> When he shall come to be glorified in his saints, and to be admired in all them that believe (because our testimony among you was believed) in that day.
> *2 Thessalonians 1:10*

It is the Holy Spirit alone that can draw us to the cross and fasten us to the Saviour. He who thinks he can do without the Spirit has yet to learn his own sinfulness and helplessness. The gospel would be no good news to the dead in sin if it did not tell of the love and power of the divine Spirit as explicitly as it announces the love and power of the divine Substitute.

But, while keeping this in mind, we may try to learn from Scripture what is written concerning the bond which connects us individually with the cross of Christ, making us thereby partakers of the pardon and the life which that cross reveals. Thus then it is written, 'By grace are ye saved, through faith; and that not of yourselves: it is the gift of God.'

Faith then is the link, the one link, between the sinner and the sin-bearer. It is not faith, as a work or exercise of our minds, which must be properly performed in order to qualify or fit us for pardon. It is not faith, as a religious duty, which must be gone through according to certain rules, in order to induce Christ to give us the benefits of his work. It is faith, simply as a receiver of the divine record concerning the Son of God. It is not faith considered as the source of holiness, as containing in itself the seed of all spiritual excellence and good works. It is faith alone, recognizing simply the completeness of the great sacrifice for sin and the trueness of the Father's testimony to that completeness—as Paul writes to the Thessalonians, 'Our testimony among you was believed.'

# 8 March

God is not a man, that he should lie; neither the son of man, that he should repent: hath he said, and shall he not do it? or hath he spoken, and shall he not make it good?
*Numbers 23:19*

God is not a man that he should lie. He means what he says when he speaks in pity, as truly as when he speaks in wrath. His words are not mere random expressions, such as man often uses when uttering vague sentiment, or trying to produce an impression by exaggerated representations of his feelings. God's words are all true and real. You cannot exaggerate the genuine feeling which they contain, and to understand them as figures is not only to convert them into unrealities, but to treat them as falsehoods.

Let sinners take God's words as they are: the genuine expressions of the mind of that infinitely truthful being, who never uses but the words of truth and soberness. He is sovereign, but that sovereignty is not at war with grace, nor does it lead to insincerity of speech, as some seem to think it does. Whether we can reconcile the sovereignty with the pity, it matters not. Let us believe them both, because both are revealed in the Bible.

Nor let us ever resort to an explanation of the words [as being] of pity, which would imply that they were not sincerely spoken, and that if a sinner took them too literally and too simply he would be sorely disappointed, finding them at last mere exaggerations, if not empty air.

Oh, let us learn to treat God as not merely the wisest, and the highest, and the holiest, but as the most truthful of all beings. Let the heedless sinner hear his truthful warnings and tremble, for they shall all be fulfilled. Let the anxious sinner listen to his truthful words of grace, and be at peace.

# 9 March

Was then that which is good made death unto me? God forbid. But sin, that it might appear sin, working death in me by that which is good; that sin by the commandment might become exceeding sinful.
*Romans 7:13*

We are not at all persuaded that there is so very much evil in us. We do not know ourselves. Our convictions of sin have been but shallow, and we are beginning to imagine that the conflict between the flesh and the spirit is not so very fierce and deadly as we had conceived it to be. We think we have rid ourselves of many of our sins entirely, and are in a fair way speedily getting rid of all the rest. The depths of sin in us we have never sounded; the number of our abominations we have never thought of marking. We have been sailing smoothly to the kingdom, and perhaps at times were wondering how our lot should be so different from the saints of old.

We thought, too, that we had overcome many of our corruptions. The old man was crucified. It seemed dead, or at least feigned itself to be so in order to deceive us. Our lusts had abated. Our tempers had improved. Our souls were calm and equable. Our mountain stood strong, and we were saying, 'We shall never be moved.' The victory over self and sin seemed, in some measure, won.

Alas, we were blind! We were profoundly ignorant of our hearts. Well, the trial came. It swept over us like a cloud of the night, or rather through us like an icy blast, piercing and chilling us to the vitals. Then the old man within us awoke and, as if in response to the uproar without, a fiercer tempest broke loose within.

# 10 March

And thou shalt remember all the way which the LORD thy God led thee these forty years in the wilderness, to humble thee, and to prove thee, to know what was in thine heart, whether thou wouldest keep his commandments, or no.
*Deuteronomy 8:2*

'The Lord thy God led thee these forty years in the wilderness, to humble thee, and to prove thee, to know what was in thine heart.' Their desert trials put them to the proof. And when thus proved, what iniquity was found in them! What sin came out which had lain hidden and unknown before! The trial did not create the evil: it merely brought out what was there already, unnoticed and unfelt, like a torpid adder. Then the heart's deep fountains were broken up, and streams of pollution came rushing out, black as hell. Rebellion, unbelief, fretfulness, atheism, idolatry, self-will, self-confidence, self-pleasing—all burst out when the blast of the desert met them in the face and called Egypt to remembrance with its luxurious plenty. Thus they were proved.

Even so it is with the saints still. God chastens them, that he may draw forth the evil that is lying concealed and unsuspected within. The rod smites us on the tenderest part, and we start up in a moment as if in arms against God. The flesh, the old man, is cut to the quick, and forthwith arouses itself, displaying all of a sudden much of its former strength. When it was asleep we did not know its power, but now that it has been awakened, its remains of strength appal us. It is not till the sea is troubled that its waters cast up mire and dirt. When all was calm, there seemed naught but purity pervading it, and ripple folded over ripple in the still brightness of its transparent green. But the winds break loose, the tempest stirs its lowest depths, and then all is changed.

# 11 March

> And he came to Nazareth, where he had been brought up: and, as his custom was, he went into the synagogue on the sabbath day, and stood up for to read.
> *Luke 4:16*

It is as a preacher of the gospel that the Lord here announces himself. He was sent of the Father, that he might 'testify the gospel of the grace of God'. Both in that which he *spoke* and in that which he *did*, he shewed himself the revealer of the free love of God.

Not to *create* that love, nor to *call it forth*, but to *reveal* it; not to *buy* it, but to *make a way* for its reaching us, did the Son of God take flesh, and live, and die. It was as the messenger of peace between God and man that he came from the Father and dwelt among us. It was as the bringer of good news that he was born at Bethlehem and died on Golgotha. And it is as such that he stands up to read in the synagogue of Nazareth.

This Nazareth, to which he brought his first message of grace, had no claim for such favour and honour. It was not one of the holy or famous cities of the Old Testament. It was neither a city of refuge nor a Levitical city. It had no name in Israel in former days, and, when the Lord made it his dwelling, it was noted for its evil, not for its good.

But where sin abounded, there grace did much more abound, and it was this abounding grace that now visited this home of abounding sin. The Son of man came to seek and to save that which was lost, and on these hills of Zebulon we find the good Shepherd pursuing his stray sheep, bent upon their recovery, as if they had been the choicest of his flock.

## 12 March

The Spirit of the Lord is upon me, because he hath anointed me to preach the gospel to the poor; he hath sent me to heal the brokenhearted, to preach deliverance to the captives, and recovering of sight to the blind, to set at liberty them that are bruised, to preach the acceptable year of the Lord.
*Luke 4:18–19*

Jehovah's acceptable year is the season during which he is revealing himself as the 'Lord God, merciful and gracious, long-suffering, and abundant in goodness and truth, keeping mercy for thousands, forgiving iniquity, and transgression, and sin'. It is the season during which he is shewing himself able to save to the uttermost, and to quicken the dead in sin with an everlasting life. It is the season during which he is giving bread to the hungry and water to the thirsty, and health to the sick, and clothing to the naked, and riches to the poor, and abundance to the needy; during which he is forgiving sin, cleansing guilt, loosing chains, opening prisons, finding lost ones, welcoming prodigals, receiving sinners, stretching out his hand all the day to a disobedient and gainsaying people.

The gracious character of this era continues to the very last. It began in love and it ends in love—and not the less so because it is to be succeeded by vengeance and wrath. There is no diminution of the blessing, no drying up of the blessed stream, no narrowing of the heart out of which the gracious wonders come. Nay, as rivers grow fuller and deeper in passing downward, and as they are widest at their entrance on the great ocean, so does this acceptable year preserve its character to the last, and the free love which marks it seems to increase and enlarge as the time of the end draws nigh. The last messages of grace which the Bible contains, and which are specially meant for the last days, are the fullest and the largest of all: 'Whosoever will, let him take of the water of life freely.'

# 13 March

> For the life was manifested, and we have seen it, and bear witness, and shew unto you that eternal life, which was with the Father, and was manifested unto us.
> *1 John 1:2*

The life has been manifested! This is our gospel. It is not 'the life *is*', but the life has come forth from its eternal mystery: the life has been *manifested*, so as to be seen and heard and handled. In the Word was life; nay, the Word was *the* life. 'In him was life, and the life was the light of men' (John 1:4). The 'light of the world' is the Word made flesh, the manifested life of God. The life was manifested, and we beheld his glory—the glory as of the only begotten of the Father, full of grace and truth. In the light we have the life, and in the life we have the light.

The life has been manifested! But what has drawn it out? What has given it opportunity to come forth? Death! It is not life that has attracted life, nor light that has given occasion for the outshining of light. No, but death and darkness—utter death, absolute darkness. Thus God, the God of all grace, has spoken out, and revealed the breadth and length of his infinite love. Thus we learn the true meaning and discover the essence of that grace which has been proclaimed to us by the lips, and embodied in the person of the incarnate Son.

It was the manifestation of *death* on earth that called forth this manifestation of *life* from heaven. Man's utter death has drawn out the fulness of the life of God. The entrance of death was the signal for the entrance of life.

# 14 March

For whether is greater, he that sitteth at meat, or he that serveth? is not he that sitteth at meat? but I am among you as he that serveth.
*Luke 22:27*

'I am among you as he that serveth.' Thus he speaks to us now, coming into the midst of us, and offering his gracious services. I am come, not to receive, but to give; not to be filled, but to fill; not to be healed, but to heal; not to be gladdened, but to gladden; not to be ministered unto, but to minister! Oh, who is there that can listen coldly to such an announcement, or refuse such a proffer of service? Shall condescending love like this be trifled with or set at nought? Is there some one here, like Peter, ready to say, 'Surely this is too much! Lord, thou shalt never wash my feet! I cannot bear the thought that thou shouldst perform an act so menial for such as I am.' Then hear the answer: 'If I wash thee not, thou hast no part in me. If thou wilt not allow me thus to minister, then thou canst not be mine!'

Strange, yet blessed thought! We cannot be saved, we cannot have any part in him, unless we allow him thus to perform for us his service of lowly love. It is as the servant that he is the Saviour! In saving, he serves, and in serving, he saves!

Do we not often lose sight of this? And, in losing sight of it how much do we miss! We should be holier as well as more blessed men if we did but allow the Master to serve us as he desires.

# 15 March

For she said, If I may touch but his clothes, I shall be whole.
*Mark 5:28*

Here, we may say, we have the record of one who had learned to do justice to the love of God—to the grace of the Lord Jesus Christ. Not of many can this be said, in a world of unbelief like ours, but here is one. We do not know her name; no other part of her history is told us. She is brought before us simply as one who trusted in the Son of God, who had tasted that the Lord was gracious. Like a sudden star, she shines out and then disappears. But her simple faith remains as our example. It is not the great multitude thronging Christ that here draws our eye. It is the woman and the Lord, the sick one and her healer, the sinner and the Saviour. From every one else our eye is turned, and fixed on these.

As with the woman, so with us. We need Christ! And what an amount of need is implied in this! A man that needs a hundred pounds is needy, but the man who needs ten thousand is far more so. That we need *Christ*—nothing less than Christ, yet nothing more—is the most appalling, yet also the most comforting announcement of a sinner's state that could be made. Nothing could be said more fitted to awaken, to alarm, to humble, than this: you need *Christ*. Such is the nature and the extent of your need, that less than the incarnate Son and his fulness cannot avail you. We need *Christ*! This is the reason for our coming to him, and for his receiving us.

## 16 March

For she said, If I may touch but his clothes, I shall be whole.
*Mark 5:28*

Does it sound strange to say that Christ needed the woman? It is true, and as blessed as it is true. The speaker needs his audience as truly as the audience needs the speaker. The physician needs the sick man as truly as the sick man the physician. The sun needs the earth as truly as the earth needs the sun. You may say, 'What would the earth be without the sun?' Yes, but what would the sun be without an earth to shine upon? What would become of its radiance? All wasted. It would shine in vain. So Christ needed objects for the exercise of his skill and love and power. His fulness needed emptiness like ours to draw it out, otherwise it would have been pent up and unemployed.

He is glorified, not simply in the possession of fulness, but in the *using* of it. If it remain within himself, he is unglorified, and the Father is unglorified. He needed opportunities for drawing out his treasures. He needed the publican as truly (though not in the same sense and way) as the publican needed him. He needed Mary Magdalene and the woman of Sychar, and Simon the leper and Lazarus of Bethany, as truly as they needed him. How cheering! The Lord hath need of us! He needs guilty ones to pardon, he needs empty ones to fill, he needs poor ones to enrich. How precious and how ample is the gospel contained in this blessed truth!

# 17 March

> Which of you convinceth me of sin? And if I say the truth, why do ye not believe me?
> *John 8:46*

In these simple words, our Lord appeals to the *truth* of what he was saying as the ground upon which he expected to be *believed*. By this he shows us that the truth of a thing is the real ground of faith. Our reason for believing a thing is that we think it to be true, and our reason for not believing a thing is that we do *not* think it true. If we see it to be really true, we cannot help believing it. And if what is thus seen to be true be also good, we cannot help being made glad by it (Proverbs 12:25; Acts 12:48).

Faith, then, is the receiving as true what God declares to be so, and unbelief is not receiving as true what he declares to be so. Saving faith is the believing that as true which God has made known for our salvation. Christ and his work are the things which God has revealed for salvation, and therefore saving faith is believing that to be true which God has told us regarding Christ and his work (John 20:31).

In order, then, to faith in God's Word, the only question that arises is, 'Is this word perfectly *true*?' In order to faith in Christ, the question is, 'Is all that God has told us about Christ perfectly *true*?' (John 5:31–32; 3 John 12). Is Christ really altogether worthy of our trust? If we are satisfied of this, then straightway we believe; nay, we cannot but believe. If we do not believe, it must just be because we are not satisfied that what is told us is really true, or that Christ is so worthy of our confidence as God represents him to be.

# 18 March

Which of you convinceth me of sin? And if I say the truth, why do ye not believe me?
*John 8:46*

Remember that the very first act of a sinner's return to God is that by which—believing all that God has declared about his love in Christ and his willingness to welcome every sinner who will return—he puts his trust in him and says, 'Abba, Father!' Here is no mystery and no mistake. God says, 'Return!' (Isaiah 44:22; Jeremiah 31:12, 21), and that one word is sufficient for you, for it shows you the posture in which God is standing towards you, and that his feelings towards you are those of unutterable compassion and benignity.

What more could you have to give you confidence in God? With such evidence of his character, how can you help trusting him? Or how could any amount of feeling in you give you greater ground of confidence than you will at this moment possess? Whether you will believe it or not, you have already most ample ground of confidence towards God—ground which remains the same whatever the state of your feelings may be. All you have to do is to avail yourself of this, by going to him in confidence as one who no longer doubts what he has told you about himself and his Son. Believing that testimony, go to him as your Father. Speak to him as your Father. Ask of him what you will, and it shall be done unto you. When, then, at any time, you lose your peace or hope, it is because you are forgetting the ground of your confidence, and letting go your hold of the testimony.

## 19 March

> And sent his servant at supper time to say to them that were bidden, Come; for all things are now ready.
> Luke 14:17

Weary sinners, here are glad tidings for you! There is but a step between you and life! This very moment you may enter into peace! This very moment you may come and say, 'Abba, Father!' All things are ready and *you* are welcome! Your Father seeks you. He has no pleasure in your death. He is in real earnest when he asks you to turn and live. His interest in your welfare is sincere and deep. Oh, then, return and be at rest! Believe what he has told you about the finished work of his Son, and arise and go to him—enter again your forgotten home, take your place at the table, and rejoice with them that rejoice over you. 'This our brother was dead, and is alive again; he was lost, and is found.'

Ho, ye that are afar off, wandering in misery through the waste howling wilderness, return, return! The storm is rising—the last fatal storm—and where will you find shelter? Here is the refuge from the storm and the covert from the tempest—in the finished and accepted work of Immanuel (Isaiah 25:4; 26:20; 32:2; Matthew 23:37). Place yourselves beneath this precious covert! Here is the paternal wing stretched out. Oh flee, flee to its shadow, that you may be sheltered there! Oh, ere that wing be folded up, and all who have taken refuge beneath its ample stretch be gathered up along with it—ere the covert be withdrawn and you left unsheltered amid the approaching storm—ere grace be gone and wrath begun—oh, flee, flee to the everlasting shelter of the all-protecting wing! 'He shall cover thee with his feathers, and under his wings shalt thou trust.'

# 20 March

Therefore hath he mercy on whom he will have mercy, and whom he will he hardeneth.
*Romans 9:18*

Why was Abel saved? It was not because he chose God any more than his brother Cain, but because God chose him. Therefore it is written, 'He hath mercy on whom he will have mercy, and whom he will he hardeneth' (Romans 9:18).

What is true of Abel is true of all that ever have been, or ever shall be saved. It is God's electing love that saves them. It is God's choice, not their own, that makes them to differ from those who are consigned to wrath. What shall we say then? Is there unrighteousness with God? God forbid! (Romans 9:14). God cannot be unrighteous in saving whom he pleases, or in passing by whom he pleases. Hath not the potter power over the clay, of the same lump to make one vessel unto honour, and another unto dishonour? (Romans 9:21). Shall worms of the dust say, 'What doest thou?' His decreeing to save *man,* did not make it unjust or cruel to pass by the *angels.* It could not be so unless they had *deserved* to be saved, which they did not. He decreed to save *none* of the angels, but he decreed to save *some* from among men. He needed not have saved any. He might have left them all to perish, just as he left the angels. But he determined to save *some.* He did not determine to save all, else all would have been saved, just as all the angels were kept from falling whom he decreed to keep. It would have been infinite love to have saved one single soul, but it was far greater love to save so many.

## 21 March

> The hand of the LORD was upon me, and carried me out in the spirit of the LORD, and set me down in the midst of the valley which was full of bones.
> Ezekiel 37:1

If, in the valley of dry bones which Ezekiel saw, some bones only had come together while others remained as they were lying, what would have made the difference? Would it have been that some bones *chose* to rise and others to lie still, and that God waited till he saw what bones chose to rise before he made up his mind regarding them? Or would it not have been *wholly* of God? So it is with regard to dead souls. They do not choose to rise, nor does God wait till he sees some inclination to move amongst some of them before he fixes his plans. No, they rise because God chose them from all eternity. They did not raise themselves, nor did they even desire to rise of themselves.

Take away God's decree, and you take away a sinner's only hope of being saved. Had there been no electing love, there could have been no salvation. And nothing can be more foolish than the idea that God's decree interferes with man's liberty. The only point at which it does interfere is in saving souls. Those that are lost, are lost because God does not interfere with them, but leaves them alone to enjoy their miserable liberty—that is, to remain in the bondage of sin. It is God's electing love that takes off the fetters with which the sinner is bound, that he may draw them to himself with the bands of love. Election draws some to God, but keeps none away. It is a *help*, not a *hindrance*.

# 22 March

And he took bread, and gave thanks, and brake it, and gave unto them, saying, This is my body which is given for you: this do in remembrance of me.
*Luke 22:19*

The Lord's Supper is a full and express remembrance of Jesus. It is a memorial of the Man of Sorrows. It is a memorial of him who was wounded for our transgressions and bruised for our iniquities, upon whom the chastisement of our peace was laid, and by whose stripes we are healed. It is a memorial of the crucified One. It is a monument of bleeding, dying love.

It proclaims the Lamb that was slain. It sets before us his bruised broken body—his shed and sprinkled blood—his face marred more than any man, and his form more than the sons of men. Its simple common elements speak of him who was meek and lowly, as well as of him who poured out his soul unto death. In all its parts it speaks of Jesus—of Jesus alone—of none but Jesus—Immanuel, God with us—Messiah the anointed One—the Beloved of the Father's soul!

It reminds us of his incarnation—his life—his humiliation—his agony—his cross—his death—his grave. It takes us back to the upper chamber in Jerusalem—to the passover table—to Hebron—to Gethsemane—to Gabbatha—to Pilate's hall—to Calvary—to Joseph's tomb. It brings to mind the gracious words of him who spake as never man spake, and into whose lips grace divine was poured (Luke 4:22; John 7:46; Psalm 45:2). It says to us, 'Behold your king! Behold the man! Behold the Lamb of God! Behold my servant, the Branch!'

## 23 March

*He that spared not his own Son, but delivered him up for us all, how shall he not with him also freely give us all things?*
*Romans 8:32*

The apostle here first states a fact, and then he tells us what that fact warrants us to expect from God. He reminds us of what God *has done,* and then infers from this what God *will do.* 'He spared not his own Son, but delivered him up for us all.' *Therefore* there is nothing that he will deny us: 'How shall he not with him also freely give us all things?'

Now, God had every reason to spare his Son, and none to induce him to deliver him up. For, firstly, he was the object of the Father's infinite and unutterable love. 'The Father loveth the Son' (John 3:35). 'This is my beloved Son, in whom I am well pleased' (Matthew 3:17). And whom does an earthly father spare most, but his best beloved child? (Malachi 3:17). Whom is he most unwilling to deliver up to pain or infamy, but the son of his affections? And is not this unwillingness in proportion to the love he bears him? The more that he delights in him, the more does he desire to spare him. If such then be the feeling in the narrow, frozen, selfish soul of man, what must it be in the infinite bosom of the infinite God? Which of all the beings in the universe would he have most wished to spare? Which of them all would he be most reluctant to deliver up? The Son of his love! That Son in whom his soul delighted (Isaiah 42:1)! That Son whom he loved infinitely more than all the angels of heaven!

## 24 March

*He that spared not his own Son, but delivered him up for us all, how shall he not with him also freely give us all things?*
*Romans 8:32*

But you will say, 'It may be so, that he has not spared his Son, but the state of my soul is so bad, my heart so hard and insensible. I am altogether so carnal, sold under sin, that I often despond, and think it impossible that even God can do such a mighty work in me, or effect such a glorious change.'

Ah, and is it thus you reason, with regard either to the power or the willingness of that God who has already given his own Son? Has he given his Son, and do you think, after that, it is too much to hope that he will change your heart? Is the renewing of a single soul a greater work or wonder than the gift of his Son? Give up such dishonouring doubts! Is anything too hard for the God that has parted with Christ? Is anything too much for the love of him who spared not his Son? Has he given his Son, and will he refuse his Holy Spirit? Has he given his Son, and will he refuse to renew you in the spirit of your mind?

Oh, think of this! Ponder the apostle's glorious and resistless argument. Remember that the fact of your being lost, worthless, ungodly, hard-hearted, an enemy, a rebel, did not hinder him from giving his Son. And if they did not hinder that, will they hinder anything? Nay, so far from these being reasons against God's sending Christ, they were the very reasons that led him to send him to save us.

## 25 March

> And the Word was made flesh, and dwelt among us, (and we beheld his glory, the glory as of the only begotten of the Father,) full of grace and truth.
> *John 1:14*

There was nothing great about Bethlehem. It was 'little among the thousands of Judah' (Micah 5:2), perhaps but a shepherd village or small market town. Yet there the great purpose of God became a fact. 'The Word was made flesh.' It is in facts that God's purposes come to us, that we may take hold of them as real things. It is into facts that God translates his truth, that it may be visible, audible, tangible. It is in facts (as in so many seeds) that God embodies his good news, that a little child may grasp them in his hand. So it was with the miracle of our text. God took his eternal purpose and dropped it over Bethlehem in the form of a fact, a little fragment of human history. Over earth, the first promise had been hovering for four thousand years, till at last it rested over Bethlehem, as if it said, 'This is my rest; here will I dwell.'

The city is poor rather than rich. It is not without its attractions, but these are of the more homely kind. Its scenes are not stately; its hills are not lofty; its plains are not wide; its slopes are rocky; it is not like the city of the great King, beautiful for situation, the joy of the whole earth. Yet there 'the Word was made flesh'.

It has no palace nor temple, only an inn for the travellers passing between Hebron and Jerusalem. Its dwellers are not priests nor princes. It is not a sacred city, and is but little noted in history. Yet there, not at Jerusalem, 'the Word was made flesh'.

## 26 March

> And the angel said unto them, Fear not: for, behold, I bring you good tidings of great joy, which shall be to all people. For unto you is born this day in the city of David a Saviour, which is Christ the Lord. And this shall be a sign unto you; Ye shall find the babe wrapped in swaddling clothes, lying in a manger. .
> Luke 2:10–12

The message that comes to us from Bethlehem is a very decided one. It is not a finished one: it was only finished at the cross. But, so far as it goes, it is quite explicit, quite unambiguous. It means love, peace, pardon, eternal life. The lesson taught us at Bethlehem is the lesson of grace—the grace of God, the grace of the Father and of the Son. We may learn much, indeed, as to the way of life, from Bethlehem. It must not, indeed, stand alone. You must associate it with Jerusalem. You must bring the cradle and the cross together. But still it teaches us the first part of the great lesson of peace. It says, though not so fully as Golgotha: God is love. The beginning is not the end, but still it is the beginning. The dawn is not the noon, but still it is the dawn. Bethlehem is not Jerusalem, but still it is Bethlehem. And the Prince of Peace is there. The God of salvation is there. The manifested life is there.

Do not despise Bethlehem. Do not pass it by. Come, see the place where the young child lay. Look at the manger: there is the Lamb for the burnt-offering, the Lamb of God that taketh away the sin of the world. These little tender hands shall yet be torn. These feet, that have not yet trod this rough earth, shall be nailed to the tree. That side shall yet be pierced by a Roman spear. That back shall be scourged. That cheek shall be buffeted and spit upon. That brow shall be crowned with thorns. And all for you! Is not this love? Is it not the great love of God? And in this love is there not life? And in this life is there not salvation, and a kingdom, and a throne?

## 27 March

*What is man, that thou art mindful of him? and the son of man, that thou visitest him?*
*Psalm 8:4*

Lord, what is man! And what is a human heart—the heart even of thy saints when proved and held up to view? 'O heart, heart,' said John Berridge of himself, 'what art thou? A mass of fooleries and absurdities, the vainest, wickedest, craftiest, foolishest thing in nature.' What deep hidden evil, what selfishness, what pride, what harsh tempers, what worldliness come out in a moment, when the stroke goes deep into the soul! How long Job remained steadfast, holding fast his integrity and confidence in God! Stroke after stroke laid him prostrate, yet he gave glory to God in the midst of desolation and sorrow. The inner circle of self had not been reached. But when a loathsome disease drove him to the dunghill, and his friends rose up against him and addressed him as a man marked out by God as guilty, then his faith and patience gave way. The very centre of his being had been reached and probed, and forth came the stream of impatience and unbelief. It takes a sharp arrow and a strongly drawn bow to pierce into the inmost circle, yet God in kindness spares not. The seat of the disease must be reached, and its real nature brought out to the light.

Of all the evils which are thus drawn forth from the heart of the saint, the worst, and yet the commonest, are hard thoughts of God. Yet who would have expected this? Once, indeed, in our unbelieving days our souls were full of these. Our thoughts of God were all evil together. When the Holy Spirit wrought in our hearts the mighty change, the special thing which he accomplished was teaching us to think well of God, showing us how little he had deserved these hard thoughts from us, how much he had deserved the opposite.

## 28 March

> That the trial of your faith, being much more precious than of gold that perisheth, though it be tried with fire, might be found unto praise and honour and glory at the appearing of Jesus Christ.
> *1 Peter 1:7*

Affliction moulds and purifies. Thus it effaces the resemblance of the first Adam and traces in us each lineament of the second, that, 'as we have borne the image of the earthly, we may also bear the image of the heavenly'. 'Oh,' said a saint of other days, 'what I owe to the file, to the hammer, to the furnace of my Lord Jesus!'

Come, then, let us question ourselves and endeavour to ascertain what affliction has been doing for us, and what progress we are making in putting off the old man and in putting on the new. Am I losing my worldliness of spirit and becoming heavenly minded? Am I getting rid of my pride, my passion, my stubbornness, and becoming humble, mild, and teachable? Are all my idols displaced and broken, and my creature comforts do I use as though I used them not? Am I caring less for the honours of time, for man's love, man's smile, man's applause? Am I crucified to the world, and is the world crucified to me by the cross of Christ? Or am I still ashamed of his reproach, and am I half-reluctant to follow him through bad report and through good, through honour and through shame? Do I count it my glory and my joy to walk where he has led the way, to suffer wherein he suffered, to drink of the cup of which he drank, and to be baptized with the baptism wherewith he was baptized?

## 29 March

> That the trial of your faith, being much more precious than of gold that perisheth, though it be tried with fire, might be found unto praise and honour and glory at the appearing of Jesus Christ.
> *1 Peter 1:7*

Affliction is full of warnings. It has many voices, and these of the most various kinds. It speaks counsel, it speaks rebuke, it speaks affection. But it speaks warning too.

Let us hear some of its words of warning. It says, 'Love not the world, neither the things that are in the world. If any man love the world, the love of the Father is not in him' (1 John 2:15). There is no enforcement of this warning so solemn as that which affliction gives. It exposes the world's hollowness and says, 'Love not.' It shows us what a withering gourd its beauty is and says, 'Love not.' It points out to us its hastening doom and says, 'Love not.' It declares the utter impossibility of loving both the world and the Father. 'If any man love the world, the love of the Father is not in him.' 'Know ye not that the friendship of the world is enmity with God?' There can be no companionship between God and the world. They cannot dwell together under the same roof or in the same heart.

It says, 'Take heed, and beware of covetousness' (Luke 12:15). Riches cannot help, neither earthly comfort avail us in the hour of grief. They cannot dry up tears, nor reunite broken bonds. They cannot heal the living, nor bring back the dead. They profit not in the day of darkness. Their vanity and emptiness cannot then be hidden. 'Thou fool, this night thy soul shall be required of thee: then whose shall those things be, which thou hast provided?' It is then we find that we need a 'treasure in the heavens that faileth not'. 'I counsel thee to buy of me gold tried in the fire, that thou mayest be rich.'

## 30 March

> For it became him, for whom are all things, and by whom are all things, in bringing many sons unto glory, to make the captain of their salvation perfect through sufferings.
> *Hebrews 2:10*

To bring many sons unto glory was the end for which the Son of God took flesh and died. This was no common, no inferior object. So vast and worthy did Jehovah deem it, that it pleased him for the attaining of it to 'make the captain of their salvation perfect through sufferings' (Hebrews 2:10). It was an object worthy of the God, 'for whom are all things, and by whom are all things'. It was an object glorious enough to render it 'becoming' in him to make Jesus pass through suffering and death, and to justify the Father in not sparing his only begotten Son. They for whom God has done all this must be very precious in his sight. He must be much in earnest indeed to bless them and to take them to be with him forever. As he so delighted in Enoch that he could no longer bear the separation and the distance, but took him to be with him without tasting death, and long ere he had run the common race of man, so with his saints. He is making haste to bring them to glory, for the day of absence has been long.

The glory which he has in reserve for them must be surpassing glory, for it was to bring them to it that he was willing to bruise his Son and to put him to grief. Eye hath not seen it; ear hath not heard it. It is far beyond what we can comprehend, yet it is all reality. God is not ashamed to be called our God, because he hath prepared for us a city.

# 31 March

> For it became him, for whom are all things, and by whom are all things, in bringing many sons unto glory, to make the captain of their salvation perfect through sufferings.
> *Hebrews 2:10*

We are made partakers of Christ's sufferings. What honour is this! We are baptized with his baptism; we drink of his cup; we are made like him in sorrow as we shall hereafter be made like him in joy! How soothing and sustaining! If reproach and shame and poverty are ours, let us remember that they were his also. If we have to go down to Gethsemane or up to the cross, let us think that he was there before us. It is when keeping our eye on this that we are brought somewhat to realize the feeling of the apostle when he 'rejoiced in his sufferings' for the Church, as filling 'up that which is behind—literally, the leavings of Christ's sufferings—of the afflictions of Christ in my flesh for his body's sake, which is the church' (Colossians 1:24). To be treated better than Christ was is neither what a thoughtful soul could expect, nor what a loving heart could desire.

Suffering is the family lot. The path of sorrow is no unfrequented way. All the saints have trodden it. We can trace their footprints there. It is comforting, nay, it is cheering to keep this in mind. Were we cast fettered into some low dungeon, would it not be consolation to know that many a martyr had been there before us? Would it not be cheering to read their names written with their own hands all round the ancient walls? Such is the solace we may extract from all suffering, for the furnace into which we are cast has been consecrated by many a saint already.

# *April*

JAMES BUCHANAN (1804–1870) was born in Paisley. He was educated at the universities of Glasgow and Edinburgh. In 1828 he became the minister in North Leith, a suburb of Edinburgh. In 1840 he was translated to the High Church (St Giles) in Edinburgh. After the Disruption in 1843 he became the first minister of Free St Stephen's, also in Edinburgh.

Buchanan was appointed Professor of Apologetics at the newly established New College in Edinburgh in 1845. Following the death of Thomas Chalmers, he became Professor of Systematic Theology in 1847.

Buchanan was a Reformed theologian of the old school. He was the author of an extensive range of books and pamphlets. His books entitled *The Office and Work of the Holy Spirit* and *The Doctrine of Justification* are classic examples of the doctrines of grace as taught in Scotland for centuries.

## Sources of daily readings

April 1–28: James Buchanan, *Comfort in Affliction; A series of Meditations* (Edinburgh, 1837).

April 29–30: James Buchanan, in *Free Church Magazine*, Volume I (Edinburgh, 1844).

## Biography

Robert G. Balfour, *Rev. James Buchanan, D.D., LL.D.* in *Disruption Worthies. A memorial of 1843* (Edinburgh, 1876).

# 1 April

*Comfort ye, comfort ye my people, saith your God. Speak ye comfortably to Jerusalem, and cry unto her, that her warfare is accomplished, that her iniquity is pardoned: for she hath received of the Lord's hand double for all her sins.*
*Isaiah 40:1–2*

Mourners in Zion, be comforted! If yours is a life of sorrow, yours also is a religion of hope. If the book of providence seems to you to be 'written within and without', like Ezekiel's roll, in characters of 'lamentation, and mourning, and woe', the Bible is filled with consolation and peace. And the more stormy your passage through this world, the more awful [awe-inspiring] God's judgments, the more severe and confounding your trials and bereavements may be, the more should that blessed book be endeared to your hearts, of which every true disciple will say, with the afflicted Psalmist, *'This is my comfort in mine affliction.'*

It is not one of the least benefits of severe affliction, that it shatters our confidence in every other stay and breaks up our hopes from every other quarter, and leads us, in simplicity, to search the Word of God for comfort. And is it not one of the best recommendations of that precious book, that its characters [letters] become more bright in proportion as all else around us is dark, and that, when all other information becomes insipid or nauseous, its truths are rendered only the more sweet and refreshing by the bitter draught of sorrow. The Bible cannot be known in its excellence, its truths cannot be relished in their sweetness, and its promises cannot be duly appreciated and enjoyed until, by adversity, all other consolation is lost, and all other hopes destroyed; but then, when we carry it with us into the fiery furnace of affliction, like the aromatic plant, which must be burnt before the precious perfume is felt, it emits a refreshing fragrance and is relished in proportion as our sufferings are great.

# 2 April

This is my comfort in my affliction: for thy word hath quickened me.
*Psalm 119:50*

When we feel that we are involved in an inextricable labyrinth of difficulties—when the iron hand of necessity seems to crush us to the earth without leaving one hope of escape—when all seems to be so inevitably fixed and certain, that our prospects on all hands are shut in with dark clouds and we are brought to the very border of despair—surely it is consolatory to reflect that it is not a blind or inexorable fate which oppresses us. Rather, all our present difficulties have been appointed by one who has power to relieve as well as to afflict us, and appointed, too, for reasons which are satisfactory to omniscient wisdom.

And when, again, we contemplate the prevalence of suffering, and the apparently irregular distribution of good and evil in the present world—when we see many in prosperity, while we are ourselves in trouble, and yet are at a loss to discover, in our blindness, the reason for which such unequal measures of prosperity are dealt out—surely we may well allow the consideration of God's infinite rectitude to quiet [silence] our murmurings and to allay the violence of our regret. This is especially so when we are so ignorant both of our own character and of theirs, and so ill qualified to judge of the treatment which is best for us, and so well assured that the principles of God's government shall not be fully developed, and the whole results of his dealings with us shall not be ascertained until this temporary scene of trial and discipline shall have passed away and given place to that eternal state, in which the issues of time will be fully disclosed, and where God shall be justified when he speaks, and clear when he gives his final judgment (Psalm 51:4).

# 3 April

For he doth not afflict willingly nor grieve the children of men.
*Lamentations 3:33*

The Bible unquestionably confirms the testimony of nature and conscience in respect to the present state of trial. It acknowledges the existence of sorrow and suffering under the government of a most wise and benevolent God. It declares that, notwithstanding the moral faculties which God has given to us and the moral indications which the course of providence affords, good and evil are not here dealt out according to the strict measure of desert [what we deserve].

And the reason which it assigns for the sufferings that prevail in the world is the prevalence of sin, while it attributes the irregular distribution of good and evil to the nature of the present state, as one of respite and trial for an eternal state after death. Had its communications stopped at this point, it would have confirmed our worst fears and deepened our most distressing thoughts, for, when revealing (as it does) the benevolence of God, it declares, notwithstanding, that even under his government, sin must be connected with suffering. And when it points to an eternal state, where the principles of his holy and righteous administration shall have their ultimate issue and be more fully unfolded, how can we avoid the apprehension that we are obnoxious [exposed] to the displeasure of our almighty Judge and in danger of an eternal state of retribution from his righteous hand?

# 4 April

Wherefore doth a living man complain, a man for the punishment of his sins?
*Lamentations 3:39*

There are difficulties in which our relation to God and our prospects under his government are involved, because they shut us all up to the doctrine of the cross, and because they will lead us to the only source of sound and abiding consolation—the love of God in Jesus Christ our Lord. We shall find that every such difficulty vanishes, every doubt is repressed, and every fear destroyed, when that love is apprehended and believed.

But meantime, I beseech you, do not hesitate to receive the testimony of God respecting your state and character and prospects, and do not turn away in disgust because they seem dark and appalling in the light of Scripture. True, they *are* dark and appalling indeed, but is it not your interest to know the real state of the case. Is it possible that God can err in the estimate which he forms of your character, or can deceive you as to the fate which, under his own government, awaits unforgiven guilt? From whom—if not from God—can you expect to have such information as shall render your present and future condition, and his plans and intentions with regard to you, intelligible and certain? And although you must feel the statements of Scripture respecting your guilt and your deserts to be humiliating and painful in the extreme, yet does not your own observation (so far as it extends) concur with the testimony of Scripture in regard to the present state? And do not your own consciences suggest many anxious forebodings respecting the future, the same in kind with those which the Bible sanctions and certifies?

# 5 April

For God so loved the world, that he gave his only begotten Son, that whosoever believeth in him should not perish, but have everlasting life.
*John 3:16*

God loved the world. The plan of our salvation proceeded from the spontaneous love of God, *that* being the source of every blessing which this salvation includes, and of every hope which it warrants or inspires.

Let us meditate on the nature of this love. It is not the mere general benevolence which delights in the diffusion of happiness among the obedient subjects of the divine government. And it is not the mere sentiment of compassion with which a benevolent being may be supposed to regard the misery of his apostate creatures, and which might lead him to pity their case, even while he punished their guilt. It is not a mere passive emotion in the divine mind, but an active and operative love, which prompts the purpose and forms the plan of relieving them.

It is the attribute of *mercy*—mercy that not only relieves the wretchedness, but pardons the guilt of its objects, and which allows not even the most aggravated sinfulness to be a bar to the communication of its blessings. Heaven itself affords no exemplification [instance] of this attribute, for no sin has ever been forgiven there, and this world is the theatre which God has selected for the manifestation of the glory of his character as 'the Lord God, merciful and gracious … forgiving iniquity and transgression and sin'.

# 6 April

For God so loved the world, that he gave his only begotten Son, that whosoever believeth in him should not perish, but have everlasting life.
*John 3:16*

And in what circumstances was this love displayed? When the world was in a state of rebellion against him. When the human character had been totally changed from its pristine innocence, and had become the very reverse of his own. When, instead of being the object of men's supreme reverence and affection, he was the object of their enmity and dread. When the holy attributes of his nature, and the moral principles of his government, and the righteous precepts of his law were all alike distasteful to their depraved minds. When his sole prerogative, as the Governor and Judge of the world, had been carelessly forgotten, or daringly denied. When the sublime temple of nature, at whose altar they should have worshipped the one living and true God, was filled with the shrines of idolatry where his supremacy was virtually denied or divided amongst a multitude of false gods. And when the more sacred temple of the human heart (where God desired to dwell, and to be ministered unto by a train of holy affections) had become a chamber of imagery, filled with a host of wicked passions—a temple, indeed, of spiritual idolatry, where the best of all homage, that of man's affections, was rendered, if not to idols of gold and silver, yet to the wealth, and honours and pleasures of the world. When, in one word, God's character was hated by man, and man's character odious to God—yet, even then, 'God so loved the world'.

# 7 April

> For God sent not his Son into the world to condemn the world; but that the world through him might be saved.
> *John 3:17*

And what was the measure of that love which he felt, and which the scheme of redemption unfolds? What man, what angel, what seraph, will undertake to measure it, when this one clause is added, 'God so loved the world, that he gave his only begotten Son'?

To comprehend the full import of such words, we must be able to enter into those feelings of ineffable love with which the Father regards his only begotten Son—a Son, the same in substance, and equal in power and glory with himself, and possessing, along with the divine attributes of almighty power and omniscient wisdom, a character in all respects the same as his own—a character of unspotted holiness and infinite benevolence and love. A Son, too, held in honour and high estimation in heaven, where angels and seraphim adored him as their Creator and Lord, and who, from the beginning, was 'his delight, rejoicing always before him'.

Mysterious and incomprehensible (to our limited capacity) as many parts of this sublime subject may appear, at least we cannot fail to be convinced that no form of words could possibly express a greater amount of love than the simple statement that 'God so loved the world, that he gave his only begotten Son'.

This love will be still farther enhanced in our estimation if we consider the benevolent design of God in giving his Son and the beneficial results of that gift to his believing people. It was that they who believe *might not perish*.

# 8 April

In this was manifested the love of God toward us, because that God sent his only begotten Son into the world, that we might live through him.
*1 John 4:9*

It may be asked, 'Why did God give up his only begotten Son?' What necessity existed for so costly a sacrifice? Might not the mere intimation of his kind intentions towards us, conveyed through one of his commissioned, servants, have served to remove our fears and to establish for us a ground of hope?

Had God been a being of mere compassion, and had we been regarded in no other light than as the objects of his pity, this course might perhaps have been adopted, although we should thus have been deprived of the noblest proof of the strength and ardour of that affection which burned in the divine mind towards us. But, besides being a God of mercy, he is also the moral governor and judge of men, and, besides being the objects of his pity, we were the responsible subjects of his government, and amenable to punishment for our crimes. As his moral government was to continue for ever, and wherever it extends throughout the universe, it is based on the principles of rectitude and retribution, it was necessary to guard against any dishonour being put on that law, which is a transcript of his own holy character, and the rule of his universal and eternal jurisprudence. Hence God would not cancel its threatenings nor relax its authority, nor mitigate its requirements, *even when he had formed the purpose of saving the sinful,* but, on the contrary, made the manifestation of his forgiving mercy the occasion of a brighter display of the holiness and justice both of his character and law.

# 9 April

In this was manifested the love of God toward us, because that God sent his only begotten Son into the world, that we might live through him.
*1 John 4:9*

For this purpose of saving the sinful, he entered into a covenant with his only begotten Son—choosing him as the substitute of the guilty whom he designed to save, laying upon him the responsibility of their guilt and exacting from him the penalty which they had incurred, and engaging, in return, to impute to them the merit of his sufferings and obedience and to deal *with them* according to *his* deserts. And this was done, that while his forgiving mercy was manifested in giving up his Son and, for his sake, receiving his people into favour, his equity might be displayed and his law magnified and made honourable by the vicarious sufferings and death of their surety. As no proof of his love could be greater than the act of giving up his Son, so, surely, no proof of his holiness and stronger than what arise from his *not sparing* that Son when he stood in the room of the guilty.

What greater honour could, in the nature of things, be paid to the law, than what was implied in the voluntary submission of God's own Son to its demands! What a spectacle to men and angels—the Son of God submitting to that law in his own person, acknowledging the justice of its threatenings by enduring them and the equity of its precepts by obeying them, and declaring his holy determination to uphold its authority and to establish it for ever, even at the very time when his love prompted him to deliver his people from its condemning power!

## 10 April

And brought them out, and said, Sirs, what must I do to be saved? And they said, Believe on the Lord Jesus Christ, and thou shalt be saved, and thy house.
Acts 16:30–31

When a thoughtful mind, especially in the season of affliction or in the prospect of death, considers its relation to God and its eternal prospects, it can hardly fail to be impressed with the transcendent importance of that question: 'What must I do to he saved?' If the inquirer betakes himself to the Bible with the view of obtaining satisfactory information on this momentous subject, he finds God's own answer to that question, in these memorable words, 'Believe on the Lord Jesus Christ and thou shalt be saved.' These words are few and simple, but they contain the sum and substance of the gospel message; they teach him to believe the record which God hath given respecting his Son, and, believing that record, to place his personal trust and dependence on Christ as an all-sufficient Saviour, able to save *unto the uttermost* all that come unto God by him.

But when this plain and simple answer is given to his question, the anxious inquirer is apt to be staggered and perplexed by its very simplicity. He is not prepared to find that every bar has been taken out of the way, and that he is at liberty to repair to Christ at once as his Saviour. He is surprised, and begins to doubt whether he has understood the message in the sense in which God would have him to understand it.

## 11 April

And the LORD passed by before him, and proclaimed, The LORD, The LORD God, merciful and gracious, longsuffering, and abundant in goodness and truth, keeping mercy for thousands, forgiving iniquity and transgression and sin, and

that will by no means clear the guilty; visiting the iniquity of the fathers upon the children, and upon the children's children, unto the third and to the fourth generation.
*Exodus 34:6–7*

To an inquirer in these circumstances nothing can be more useful than to set before him a clear view of the warrant of faith, or of the ground on which he is encouraged—at once, and without any delay—to believe on the Lord Jesus Christ, and to come to him for pardon and peace.

The first ground on which the most disconsolate inquirer may be encouraged to return to God through Christ, without delay, is the character of God as it is revealed in his Word. That character is set forth in Scripture in variety of aspects, which are all fitted to conciliate the love and to secure the confidence of sinners. Let every serious inquirer consider the testimony of God in this matter: 'The LORD descended in the cloud, and stood with him there, and proclaimed the name of the LORD. And the LORD passed by before him, and proclaimed, The LORD, The LORD God, merciful and gracious, longsuffering, and abundant in goodness and truth, keeping mercy for thousands.' It follows, indeed, that he 'will by no means clear the guilty; visiting the iniquity of the fathers upon the children, and upon the children's children, unto the third and to the fourth generation'.

How far the last words of this sublime passage should affect the faith and hope of a sinner under the Christian dispensation will be considered hereafter. Meanwhile, let us give due weight to the former part of the passage, in which God's love and mercy are declared with a fulness and variety of expression which leave no room for unbelieving doubt or suspicion.

# 12 April

Mercy and truth are met together; righteousness and peace have kissed each other.
*Psalm 85:10*

The unanimous testimony of the law, the Psalms, the prophets of the Old Testament, the evangelists and the apostles of the New, bears witness to God's character, as a being of manifold mercies, whose very name is *love*. Grace and mercy, indeed, are not the sole attributes of God. And the sinner who would fondly cling to these, may be repelled by the reflection that, merciful as God is, he is also holy, and just; that he is declared, both by the voice of conscience, and by his own revealed Word, to be the avenger of sin; and that, as such, he cannot be regarded by any sinner without alarm and terror. All this is true, and were it overlooked or forgotten, we should entertain a very partial and delusive idea of the divine character.

It is equally true that unassisted reason can discover no method of reconciling the exercise of mercy with the claims of justice, and no ground of confidence in God, such as would warrant the hope of safety for a sinner. But in God's *revealed character*, justice and mercy meet together, righteousness and peace kiss each other. We are under no necessity of forgetting any attribute of his nature or of adopting a partial view of his character for the sake of deriving peace and comfort from it: we can regard it in all his holiness, and yet feel that we are safe.

# 13 April

Hath God forgotten to be gracious? hath he in anger shut up his tender mercies? Selah. And I said, This is my infirmity: but I will remember the years of the right hand of the most High.
*Psalm 77:9–10*

God's declared satisfaction with the redemption of Christ affords a warrant and encouragement to the sinner, such as should banish all the fears which even a correct and scriptural sense of God's holiness and justice may have awakened in his mind. That he should have a deep and abiding sense of God's holiness and justice, is no more than Scripture requires and the state of the case demands. That a sense of God's justice combined with a sense of his own guilt should awaken fear and terror, is equally plain, but he will thereby be only the better qualified for coming to God as he is revealed in the gospel.

Under this impression, let us turn again to the first passage formerly quoted, a passage in which the whole character of God is revealed—first, as infinitely merciful, and secondly, as strictly holy and just. On reading that passage, the sinner may be disposed to say, 'Oh, how sweet and encouraging is the first part of it: the Lord God, merciful and gracious, long-suffering, and abundant in goodness and truth, keeping mercy for thousands.' This is sweet! It is as cool water to the parched ground: would that it had ended here! But when I proceed, I find it written that he will 'by no means clear the guilty; visiting the iniquity of the fathers upon the children, and upon the children's children, unto the third and fourth generations'. This damps my rising hopes, it sinks my very spirit within me; for am *I* not guilty? And if he will by no means clear the guilty, what avails it *me* that he is merciful and gracious? I am irrecoverably ruined and undone.

# 14 April

God was in Christ, reconciling the world unto himself, not imputing their trespasses unto them; and hath committed unto us the word of reconciliation.
2 Corinthians 5:19

How, then, may a sinner extricate himself from this perplexity that God will not clear the guilty? How may he obtain relief, when he cannot deny his own guilt and dares not dispute God's justice? Is there one sinner who feels that, if his guilt were out of the way, he would willingly go to God, as the Lord God merciful and gracious, and who is debarred only by a sense of divine justice? Let him look to the cross of Christ, and he will see the barrier removed. *There* God's character is displayed in all its attributes, and these attributes are seen to be perfectly harmonious. Truth meets with mercy, and righteousness with peace, and the Lord is beheld as at once the 'just God'. and yet 'the Saviour'.

In the cross, the love and mercy of God appear in the gift of his own Son, and his justice is at once displayed and satisfied by the atonement which was there required and rendered. By the substitution of Christ as our Redeemer in our room, and by the infliction of that punishment on him, which our sins had deserved, the law was magnified and made honourable—and the reason for punishment having been removed, God's justice is satisfied, and now 'God is in Christ reconciling the world unto himself, and not imputing unto them their trespasses'. He has declared his satisfaction with the work of the Redeemer, and now, on the ground of that great propitiation, he gives to every sinner the liberty of free access to his throne.

# 15 April

> Incline your ear, and come unto me: hear, and your soul shall live; and I will make an everlasting covenant with you, even the sure mercies of David.
> *Isaiah 55:3*

Remembering, then, God's gracious and merciful character, and his declared satisfaction with Christ's redemption as the ground of pardon, let us consider the language in which he now speaks to sinners from the mercy seat, and we shall find in his invitations a full warrant for confidence and trust.

Both God and Christ invite sinners to draw nigh, in such terms as leave no room and no apology for refusing. These invitations are frequently repeated, and given in every variety of form, the best fitted to remove our doubts and secure our confidence. They are addressed to *sinners as such* and to *all* sinners, without exception, to whom the gospel is sent, insomuch that it may well be said that if there be a man on earth who is *not* a sinner, to him only are they not applicable—but to every man that is a sinner, *and just because he is a sinner*, they are addressed.

Let us listen, then, to the gracious terms in which God speaks to sinners from the mercy seat, and let us listen to them as if God spoke to us alone: 'Ho, every one that thirsteth, come ye to the waters, and he that hath no money; come ye, buy, and eat; yea, come, buy wine and milk without money and without price. ... Incline your ear, and come unto me: hear, and your soul shall live; and I will make an everlasting covenant with you, even the sure mercies of David.'

## 16 April

All that the Father giveth me shall come to me; and him that cometh to me I will in no wise cast out.
*John 6:37*

Besides the revealed character of God and his declared satisfaction with the Redeemer's work, and his free and affectionate invitations to sinners, another ground of encouragement may be found in the assurance which he has given of success, confirmed, as that assurance is, by the recorded experience of all who have ever put God's faithfulness to the proof. God's assurance is, that every one that cometh shall be made welcome, and thus we read in that precious Scripture, 'Him that cometh to me I will in nowise cast out.'

This glorious truth rests on God's faithfulness, and should be received with all trust on his bare and simple word, but it is confirmed and illustrated by the experience of every sinner that has at any time ventured on the faith of God's word to come to him. No such sinner has ever been cast out. Every believer can set to his seal that God is true. If we ask any Christian friend whom we know, whether he has ever had occasion to doubt God's faithfulness to his promise, or to repent of his going to God in Christ on the strength of his testimony, he will tell us, 'Never.' God was more gracious to him, the more he trusted in God. He drew nigh and was made welcome. He has never had reason to regret that he took God at his word. His only regret is that he was so long faithless and unbelieving.

## 17 April

But without faith it is impossible to please him: for he that cometh to God must believe that he is, and that he is a rewarder of them that diligently seek him.
*Hebrews 11:6*

The revealed Word is the *only* warrant of faith. We must come to God on the ground of Bible testimony, if we come at all. It is amply sufficient to justify and to encourage us in venturing to come, and if we believe not Moses and the prophets, if we believe not God speaking in the Word, 'neither would we believe though one should rise from the dead'.

And, let it be observed, this has been the warrant of faith from the beginning—the sole and sufficient ground on which any sinner was ever prevailed with to betake himself to Christ. It was on the strength of God's testimony that the apostles believed—that the confessors and martyrs of the primitive Church believed—that each and every Christian, since the foundation of the Church was laid, first formed his resolution to cast himself on the forgiving mercy of God.

Ask any Christian friend, 'Had *you* any special revelation? Were you told that *your* name was in the book of life?' Or, 'What encouraged you to come to Christ?' And he will answer, 'I had no revelation, but that which is in your hands. I had no insight into the secrets of God's decrees, but I read the Bible. I heard God speaking to sinners in the Word. I knew myself to be a sinner and that God spoke to me. I believed his Word, because I judged him faithful that had promised. I came to him on the warrant of his own invitation, and I have found, in my blessed experience, that "there failed not ought of any good thing which the Lord had spoken"—all came to pass.'

# 18 April

Come unto me, all ye that labour and are heavy laden, and I will give you rest.
*Matthew 11:28*

There is now no room for hesitation or delay. He has spoken graciously to me. He has invited me to draw nigh. He has commanded me to seek his face. He has charged me, at the peril of condemnation, to betake myself to Christ as my Saviour. And I venture, 'Lord, I believe, help thou mine unbelief.'

Oh! When the poor sufferer, stunned and confounded by the heavy strokes of providence, or lacerated by the keener strokes of conviction in his soul, is almost distracted by the terrors of the Lord, is it not a comfort to him in his affliction that Jesus himself has said, 'Come unto me all ye that *labour and are heavy laden,* and I will give you rest,' and, 'Him that cometh to me, I will *in no wise* cast out'?

He calls us to come to him with our burden—let it be the burden of guilt, or the burden of sorrow, or the burden of fear—to come and lay it down at the foot of his cross. And lest the disconsolate spirit should fear that he will not be made welcome, Jesus assures him, that he will in no wise cast him out. Oh, how sweet and consoling that invitation and this assurance to those who are sensible of their condition as sinners and as sufferers! And how should we respond to it, if not in the language of the apostle? To whom, Lord, can we go but unto *thee,* thou hast the words of eternal life.

# 19 April

> We have also a more sure word of prophecy; whereunto ye do well that ye take heed, as unto a light that shineth in a dark place, until the day dawn, and the day star arise in your hearts.
> *2 Peter 1:19*

But what bond subsists betwixt God and man? What is the ground or warrant of that confidence which we draw from the consideration of God's eternal subsistence, in respect to our immortal state? The bond which connects God with man, the ground and warrant of our confidence, is his word. It is plainly implied in this promise, that God's word, the word which he has spoken for the comfort of his people, shall endure, and shall have its accomplishment after the mountains have departed, and the hills have been removed.

God gives his simple word as our guarantee for eternity! In the midst of all our fears he interposes his promise, and that must be our stay! And is it not sufficient? His word is immutable as God himself. By his word the world was created. By his word the world will be dissolved. And by the same word, his people will be sustained amidst all changes. That is a bond of security which time cannot invalidate, nor death impair, nor the wreck of universal nature destroy—for, says the apostle, we are born 'not of corruptible seed, but of incorruptible, by the word of God, which liveth and abideth for ever'. And then, as if to meet the very fears which a sense of our frailty awakens, he adds, 'All flesh is as grass, and all the glory of man as the flower of grass. The grass withereth, and the flower thereof falleth away: but the word of the Lord endureth for ever. And this is the word which by the gospel is preached unto you.'

# 20 April

*For the mountains shall depart, and the hills be removed; but my kindness shall not depart from thee, neither shall the covenant of my peace be removed, saith the* LORD *that hath mercy on thee.*
*Isaiah 54:10*

It is the covenant of grace which is here spoken of. It is mentioned in connection with God's kindness, and he speaks as a forgiving father: 'My covenant shall not depart,' saith the Lord that hath mercy on thee. Blessed be God! It is not of the covenant of works that he has spoken these unchangeable words, otherwise we might well call upon the hills and the mountains to fall upon us, and hide us from his wrath. The covenant of works is called 'the ministration of death', 'the ministration of condemnation', but it is added that it was a ministration which was to be done away. But the covenant here spoken of is 'the ministration of the spirit', 'the ministration of righteousness', 'the everlasting covenant', of which the apostle says, 'If that which is done away was glorious, much more that which remaineth is glorious.'

It is a covenant of redemption. God here speaks as the redeemer of his people, 'For a small moment have I forsaken thee; but with great mercies will I gather thee. In a little wrath I hid my face from thee for a moment; but with everlasting kindness will I have mercy on thee, saith the LORD thy Redeemer.'

# 21 April

Come now, and let us reason together, saith the LORD: though your sins be as scarlet, they shall be as white as snow; though they be red like crimson, they shall be as wool.
*Isaiah 1:18*

He is exalted, as a Saviour, to give repentance and the remission of sins. He has the power of dispensing pardon, and who will question his willingness to exercise it? Did he undertake the work of redemption and humble himself, and become obedient unto death, even the death of the cross, that he might accomplish it, and is he unwilling freely to bestow the pardon which he so painfully procured? Was his soul exceeding sorrowful, even unto death, that sin might be forgiven?

And now that he has passed into the heavens, crowned with victory, will he withhold the fruits of his triumph? Has he addressed to every sinner who hears the gospel the most tender invitations, and called them, in accents of strong persuasion, to come to him? And will any one sinner, however guilty or forlorn, be coldly received or sternly repulsed when, taking Christ's own word for his warrant, he looks up to him in prayer? Oh, little do we know the tenderness of his heart, and the freeness of his grace, if we can for one instant entertain these dark suspicions! 'The blood of Jesus Christ cleanseth from all sin.' 'Come now, and let us reason together, saith the LORD: though your sins be as scarlet, they shall be as white as snow; though they be red like crimson, they shall be as wool.' 'Come unto me, all ye that labour and are heavy laden, and I will give you rest.' 'Whosoever will, let him take the water of life freely.'

# 22 April

> For we have not an high priest which cannot be touched with the feeling of our infirmities; but was in all points tempted like as we are, yet without sin.
> *Hebrews 4:15*

He is also represented as our advocate or intercessor with the Father. He stands engaged to plead our cause in heaven. On earth he prayed for his disciples, and prays for them still. Ere yet he left the world, he remembered their sad estate, the trials which were yet before them, and the dangers by which they should be surrounded, and he offered up for them and for us that touching prayer, 'And now I am no more in the world, but these are in the world, and I come to thee. Holy Father, keep through thine own name those whom thou hast given me.' 'I pray not that thou shouldest take them out of the world, but that thou shouldest keep them from the evil.' 'Sanctify them through thy truth.' 'Father, I will that they also, whom thou hast given me, be with me where I am; that they may behold my glory.'

Is any mourner so disconsolate that he cannot pray? So bowed down to the earth by the pressure of sorrow that he cannot venture to lift his eye to the throne? Let him hear the Redeemer's prayer for him, and take courage, and let him remember that, such as he was when he uttered that prayer on earth, such is he still in heaven.

# 23 April

For whom the Lord loveth he chasteneth, and scourgeth every son whom he receiveth.
*Hebrews 12:6*

The general design of all the afflictions, with which any of God's people are visited in the present state, is their progressive sanctification and final perfection. This is evident from the whole scope and tenor of Scripture, wherein the necessity and usefulness of affliction, for this end, are frequently stated in very emphatic terms, and illustrated by apposite examples. 'This is the will of God concerning you,' says the apostle, 'even your sanctification.' And this, being the grand object of God's design in Scripture, is also the end of all his dealings in providence. It is not only said that 'affliction ... yieldeth the peaceable fruit of righteousness', but that God chastens us, not for his pleasure but 'for our profit, that we might be partakers of his holiness'.

That this is the design of all the afflictions with which we are visited may well serve to reconcile us to them, even when they are most frequent and most severe. For, to a mind that is sensible of its own high capacity and of its best interests, what object can appear so truly great or desirable as this? A progressive and ultimately a perfect conformity, through the sanctification of its powers, to the very image and character of God. That man, who is capable of such a resemblance, is the very highest proof of his dignity as a rational and moral being. That God designs such a resemblance is the noblest proof of his affection—for what higher gift could he bestow than a character similar to his own?

# 24 April

> I am he that liveth, and was dead; and, behold, I am alive for evermore, Amen; and have the keys of hell and of death.
> *Revelation 1:18*

The power of death being in the hands of the Redeemer, the duration of human life is, in every instance, determined by him. And none, therefore, ought to entertain the thought either that death is, in one case, unduly premature, or, in another, unduly delayed. None live, either for a longer or for a shorter period than infinite wisdom has assigned to them. And as reason teaches that to his appointment we must submit, however unwilling—it being irresistible, and far beyond our control—so, as Christians, we should learn to acquiesce in it cheerfully, as the appointment of one who cannot err. That the determined hour had arrived is a reflection that should serve to banish every useless regret. But that this hour was fixed by one in whose wisdom we confide, and of whose interest in our welfare we have the strongest assurance, is a thought which should not only induce resignation but inspire comfort and peace.

For when death does seize any of our friends, whether in the ordinary course of disease and decay, or by violence or accident, how consolatory to the mourning relatives is the thought that it came at the bidding of the Saviour, and that it has not arrived without his sanction and appointment!

# 25 April

> And I said unto him, Sir, thou knowest. And he said to me, These are they which came out of great tribulation, and have washed their robes, and made them white in the blood of the Lamb.
> *Revelation 7:14*

The blood of Christ, shed for the remission of sins, was the sole ground of their acceptance. That blood, sprinkled on their consciences, was the means of purging them from dead works to serve the living God. And to the efficacy of that blood are to be ascribed not only all the peace and holiness which they acquired on earth, but also their exaltation to glory and their blessedness in heaven. This is strongly intimated in the word 'therefore': 'Therefore are they now before the throne of God.'

They did not rise to glory on the ground of their own merit, or by the strength of their own virtue. On the contrary, they were, like ourselves, guilty, and 'miserable, and poor, and blind and naked'. But, feeling their own guilt and danger, they repaired to the cross of Christ, and in his blood a propitiation for sin and a ground of hope was presented, on which they reposed in the humble confidence of faith. 'Therefore are they now before the throne', and with mingled emotions of humility and gratitude they cast their crowns at his feet, and ascribe salvation to their God, and to the Lamb, for ever and ever.

The work of redeeming mercy, which is their song in the house of their pilgrimage, is still the theme of their song in heaven. Not of themselves but to the Lamb do they ascribe the glories of their present state. 'Unto him that loved us, and washed us from our sins in his own blood, and hath made us kings and priests unto God and his Father; to him be glory and dominion for ever and ever. Amen.'

## 26 April

Thou wilt shew me the path of life: in thy presence is fulness of joy; at thy right hand there are pleasures for evermore.
*Psalm 16:11*

Let us, as the disciples of Christ, think much on our everlasting hopes, and never forget, amidst the cares and distresses and drudgery of the world, that we have immortal spirits within us and a glorious inheritance before us. This will animate us to persevere in the Christian course, unseduced by the temptations, and undeterred by the ridicule, of the world. It will give to the poor man an ennobling estimate of himself, such as may preserve him from debasing habits or a servile spirit, and will cheer the toils and troubles of life with a consolation which the worldling never knew.

The exceeding glory of this prospect, indeed, is apt to stagger the faith of many who, feeling their own insignificance and deploring their own vileness, can hardly believe that such a destiny awaits them. But is the predicted glory more wonderful than what God hath already wrought? Is it more wonderful that we should be exalted to heaven than that the Son of God should have descended from it? His humiliation being the groundwork, can we wonder at the glorious superstructure which shall be reared upon it? Nay, is not some such glorious result *necessary* to render that complete and credible which has already been done? For what worthy end was the sacrifice of Christ offered, unless some grand result of that sacrifice remains yet to be revealed? Heaven is but a suitable sequel to the scheme of redemption—a scene of glory bearing a due proportion to the work of Gethsemane and Calvary—an end that shall at once explain and justify the marvellous means by which it was accomplished!

# 27 April

Therefore we are always confident, knowing that, whilst we are at home in the body, we are absent from the Lord: (for we walk by faith, not by sight): we are confident, I say, and willing rather to be absent from the body, and to be present with the Lord.
*2 Corinthians 5:6–8*

Such a change of new life may have been really wrought, and yet there may be seasons in the lives of sincere Christians, in which they cannot so clearly discern the evidence as to derive comfort from the persuasion that they have been converted—seasons of spiritual darkness when their views are clouded (it may be) by unbelief, or seasons of backsliding when they have reason to mourn over resolutions which have been forgotten, vows that have been broken, and obligations, both of duty and of gratitude, which have been shamefully violated—or seasons of spiritual insensibility, when they have so far fallen from the state of spiritual health as to be almost tempted to question whether they have ever been quickened into spiritual life.

At such seasons, it is not wonderful that they cannot, with a good conscience, use the language of the apostle. But dark as their present state is, it does not follow that they are shut out from hope. It is true that they cannot discern in their own troubled spirits those marks of grace which are the evidences of conversion and the earnests of glory, and we cannot, therefore, in these circumstances, direct them to look inward on the frame of their own spirits with any hope of their thereby obtaining relief. No, but we can—and we do—bid every downcast believer to look out of himself to Christ's cross and to God's mercy seat. And we do so with the greater confidence just because he has been brought to feel that he has nothing else to depend on.

# 28 April

> Is any among you afflicted? let him pray. Is any merry? let him sing psalms.
> *James 5:13*

Oh, how many Christians have had reason to acknowledge the blessed effect of affliction, in renewing their communion with God, and reviving their decayed devotion!

Are there not many who can testify from their own experience that, while they were prosperous, the spirit of devotion became imperceptibly more languid in their bosoms. Instead of frequently enjoying prayer as a delightful privilege, they were gradually losing their relish for it, and when they did observe it, it was observed in a cold and formal manner. And they were not sensible of the length to which they had proceeded in spiritual declension till, by some severe stroke of affliction, they were thrown on the resources of a piety too decayed to afford them either support or consolation—and were thus, for the first time, apprised of a danger unperceived till then?

Can they not remember what deep humiliation, what earnest desires, and what fervent supplications were produced by that affliction and the discoveries which it enabled them to make? And are they not sensible [aware] that it was in prayer they found their consolation—when, with their eyes opened to the reality of their condition, they besought the Lord with tears? Indeed, one of the greatest benefits of severe affliction, in the case of God's people, is that it awakens them to greater ardour and diligence in prayer. And such is the elevating and sanctifying effect of earnest prayer, that if affliction were productive of no other benefit, this alone might well compensate for all the loss which is sustained and all the pain which is inflicted, even by the severest dispensations of providence.

## 29 April

Whereby are given unto us exceeding great and precious promises: that by these ye might be partakers of the divine nature, having escaped the corruption that is in the world through lust.
*2 Peter 1:4*

Are you dying creatures, and do you stand in need of life? 'This is the promise that he hath promised us, even eternal life' (1 John

2:25). 'This is the record, that God hath given to us eternal life, and that this life is in his Son.' So rich and various are the promises of God in the Word! They contain 'all things that pertain to life and godliness' (2 Peter 1:3), and are so great and precious, that 'by these ye may be partakers of the divine nature'.

It may seem that many of these promises belong only to converted people, and it is certain that they will be fulfilled and enjoyed only in the experience of believers. Those who stagger at the promise through unbelief, or 'who stumble at the word, being disobedient', shall not obtain the blessings of which we speak. But these promises are, nevertheless, exhibited and proposed to all in the gospel, and are expressly addressed, in many instances, to the unbelieving and unthankful, for it is with us as it was with the Jews. To them pertained the promises, yet many of them forfeited the blessing through unbelief, and the apostle says, 'Let *us* therefore fear, lest, a promise being left us of entering into his rest, any of you should seem to come short of it. For unto us was the gospel preached, as well as unto them: but the word preached did not profit them, not being mixed with faith in them that heard it.' (Hebrews 4:1–2). The promises are really addressed to many who will never experience their fulfilment, for is not Christ *proposed* to all as a Saviour—and Christ, too, in all his fulness? And are not all the promises of God yea and amen in Christ Jesus?

# 30 April

Let the wicked forsake his way, and the unrighteous man his thoughts: and let him return unto the LORD, and he will have mercy upon him; and to our God, for he will abundantly pardon.
*Isaiah 55:7*

To whatever class of gospel hearers, then, you belong, and whatever may be your present character or frame of mind, God's call is addressed to you—he speaks to you in the language of invitation and entreaty, and in that gracious call you may find a sufficient warrant of hope.

But you are not left to draw your encouragement by way of inference merely from the call and invitation of the gospel. It comes to you accompanied with exceeding great and precious promises—promises in which God's faithfulness is absolutely pledged, and which you may confidently plead in prayer. These promises are the very marrow of the gospel, and include in them every blessing which we need for time and eternity. It is not one privilege only that is promised, but all the privileges of the covenant—not a partial, but a full and complete salvation, comprising all that Christ purchased and all that the Spirit imparts. Consider that it is what your soul needs, and see if you cannot find it in one or other of these promises. Are you guilty, and do not stand in need of pardon? God's promise runs in these terms: 'Return unto the LORD, and he will have mercy upon you; and to our God, for he will abundantly pardon' (Isaiah 55:7). 'Come now, and let us reason together, saith the LORD: though your sins be as scarlet, they shall be as white as snow; though they be red like crimson, they shall be as wool' (Isaiah 1:18).

# May

ANDREW BONAR (1810–1892) was born in Edinburgh and underwent his classical and theological training at the university there. In 1838 he was inducted to his first congregation at Collace in Perthshire. He visited Palestine in 1839 with McCheyne and two other ministers as a member of the Church of Scotland's mission of enquiry to the Jews.

Bonar had become close friends with Robert Murray McCheyne in Edinburgh and McCheyne was a frequent visitor to Collace, where his preaching at Communion seasons marked the heyday of evangelical preaching in the district. The friendship was cut short by McCheyne's early death, and it fell to Andrew Bonar to write the biography of McCheyne—a classic of religious biography which has remained in print ever since then.

In 1856 Bonar moved to Glasgow as minister of the Finnieston Free Church. His labours there were also signally blessed. He authored many books, many of which were renowned for their practical content.

## Sources of daily readings

May 1–8: Andrew Bonar, *From Strength to Strength: Four addresses to young believers* (London, 1882).

May 9–23: *Sheaves after Harvest: A group of addresses by Dr A.A. Bonar. Edited by his daughters* (London, 1936).

May 24–31 Andrew Bonar, *The Gospel Pointing to the Person of Christ* (Kelso, 1861).

## Biography

Marjory Bonar, *Reminiscences of Andrew A. Bonar, D.D.* (London, 1895)

# 1 May

And Moses took the blood, and sprinkled it on the people, and said, Behold the blood of the covenant, which the LORD hath made with you concerning all these words.
*Exodus 24:8*

Let us now look all round and upward. See the immediate and wondrous effect of the blood of atonement sprinkled on the altar, the people, and the book of the covenant!

A most magnificent type is presented to our view. Perhaps there is not any grander type in the Old Testament anywhere. The hill Sinai had been one mass of clouds and smoke and darkness, but no sooner was the blood sprinkled in the manner we have been observing, than the whole scene changed. The clouds forthwith melted away, till not a trace of them, not even a vapour, was to be seen. Moses and the seventy elders were called to come up the hill, and they found all was light and sunshine and peace. They looked up to the sky above them, and they saw as it were a pavement of deep blue sapphire, and the whole 'body of heaven in clearness', cleared of every cloud and bright with radiancy and glory. The sun had burst forth and poured its flood of beams over all.

What a change from yesterday! And all because the blood had been sprinkled. Surely we may say that this scene is nothing less than a visible proclamation (so to speak) of that verse which God afterwards spoke with his own lips: 'I have blotted out, as a thick cloud, thy transgressions, and, as a cloud, thy sins: return unto me; for I have redeemed thee.' (Isaiah 44:22).

# 2 May

And Moses took the blood, and sprinkled it on the people, and said, Behold the blood of the covenant, which the LORD hath made with you concerning all these words.
*Exodus 24:8*

Perhaps someone says, 'I know the power of the blood, but I sometimes wonder, if death were coming, if I should be able to meet it calmly.' We assure you, dear friend, that this same blood will carry you through the veil in perfect peace. The same blood that enables you to commune with the Master in prayer and the communion table, will enable you to pass calmly into his presence and be in eternal fellowship face to face with all who have been washed like you.

Perhaps another says, 'There are other scenes awaiting us, and when we think of Christ's coming again, we know not how we shall meet him.' Let me assure you that the moment he appears in yonder sky (and the day is very near: do you not often say, 'Lord Jesus, come quickly'?), two things we shall see in a light in which we never saw them before. We shall see our High Priest wearing his robes of priesthood, and as we gaze on his person shall realize as we never did before the value of his atoning blood. We shall feel that there is room for blood. We shall feel that there is room for nothing but confidence and joy. And in that same moment our Brother and Redeemer will look upon us with a countenance of ineffable delight and love. We shall be ravished with the sight of the King in his beauty. We sometimes sing:

> One look of Jesus as he is
> Will strike all sins for ever dead

But not less confidently may we say one to the other—

> One look of Jesus as he is
> Will strike all fear for ever dead.

# 3 May

And Moses went into the midst of the cloud, and gat him up into the mount: and Moses was in the mount forty days and forty nights.
*Exodus 24:18*

What a season these forty days and forty nights up there! And yet the time would pass quickly on. Light was pouring into the mind of Moses under the teaching of that divine teacher, and perhaps the lessons were relieved now and then by a burst of holy song from delighted angels who watched, desiring to look into these things, in full sympathy with this favoured guest in the pavilion of their God. How quickly the time would pass in such communion! Is it not so with you when you get near to the Lord?

Before Moses was allowed to leave that pavilion, just as his time of communion was closing, the Lord handed to his guest a parting gift. And be you sure that if you get into communion with God he will not let you away without a parting gift. What was the gift he gave to Moses? The Law rewritten on two tables of stone. He handed these to him to take with him and place safely in the ark. When you have been in communion with God you will find that the Lord has dealt very much thus with you. He will write the law (that blessed law, holy and just and good, which was in the heart of Christ, Psalm 40:8) upon your heart deeper than ever. As the fruit of communion, you will find the Holy Spirit has made your conscience more tender, your heart more loving, and your life more holy—your whole soul and being, thought, word and deed more like your Lord and Master. Most blessed result, surely, of communion with him!

# 4 May

> That which we have seen and heard declare we unto you, that ye also may have fellowship with us: and truly our fellowship is with the Father, and with his Son Jesus Christ.
> *1 John 1:3*

Who is here that says, 'I am not one of God's people, but I wish to be among them. How can I join the company?' We reply by asking, 'How was Moses able to go up and remain in the presence of that glory?' Here is the secret of it. Moses wore a garment sprinkled with blood, the blood of sacrifice offered at the foot of the hill. His garment having been sprinkled with that blood at the foot of the hill, he was able to go before the Holy One.

Fellow sinner, it is the blood that takes a sinner into communion with God. Fellow sinner, you have no right to any blessing at all till you have used the sprinkled blood. Do you say, 'I have a right to the sunshine.' No! The sun was created to shine upon holy Adam, unfallen man. You say, 'I have a right to the air I breathe.' No! It was created to be inhaled by holy creatures. 'I have a right to the water out of those gushing springs.' No! They were created for unfallen man. But there is one thing you *have* a right to, namely the blood. It is for sinners. Angels have no right to it; they are holy. You have a right to it, if you are a sinner, and you are welcome to it this night. You are not only welcome; more than this, you are entreated to let it be sprinkled on your conscience. And then you shall not only be cleansed from all sin but also you shall join the Apostle John in the joy of that communion in which he wishes us all to share, declaring that he writes in order that 'ye also may have fellowship with us: and truly our fellowship is with the Father, and with his Son Jesus Christ', and so 'your joy may be full' (1 John 1:3–4).

## 5 May

> When the even was come, there came a rich man of Arimathaea, named Joseph, who also himself was Jesus' disciple: he went to Pilate, and begged the body of Jesus. Then Pilate commanded the body to be delivered.
> *Matthew 27:57–58*

We speak of Joseph's empty tomb as an expression for the work of Christ accomplished and complete. Joseph's deed was recorded by the Holy Spirit, and so he teaches the Church in all generations.

But the day will come when he will get a still higher reward. That reward will be given when the Lord comes. For, according to his promise, he will confess before his Father those who have confessed him before men (Matthew 10:32). Your confession, as well as that of Joseph and Nicodemus, will ensure the same reward. On that day the Lord will call forth Joseph by name, and present him to the Father: 'Father, this is the man who, in that dark hour, when there was not a disciple to own me at the cross, or give me the last rites of sepulture, risked name and wealth, and honour and life, that he might show love to me, who had not a place where to lay my head.' On that day the Father will bring out one of the brightest of his crowns, and put it upon the head of Joseph, who confessed Christ in the hour of danger and reproach.

Young men, you may well covet that great reward. Gird up your loins and confess him in the place where you carry on your calling day by day. Confess Christ by deeds more than by words, and you will win the reward.

## 6 May

> Wherefore the LORD God of Israel saith, I said indeed that thy house, and the house of thy father, should walk before

me for ever: but now the LORD saith, Be it far from me; for them that honour me I will honour, and they that despise me shall be lightly esteemed.
*1 Samuel 2:30*

If any of you during the summer find yourself in Ayrshire, you might take a stroll in the neighbourhood of Muirkirk, and there stand on the spot where John Brown of Priesthill was martyred. You will see his monument there, and read these words inscribed: 'Them that honour me I will honour, and they that despise me shall be lightly esteemed.' The name of his murderer is infamous throughout all Scotland to this hour; but the memory of the martyred disciple has a high place in every heart. Honour God, and he will honour you.

Christian friends, this one action of this man Joseph was of an amazing importance. You cannot tell the importance of one action of yours for Christ. But be sure to notice: that one act came out of a daily life of faith and love. Is there one here tonight who ventures to say, 'It is difficult for me to confess Christ. I should be excused if you knew all the circumstances'? My reply to such is simple. You cannot be in circumstances more difficult than those of Joseph, and he confessed Christ notwithstanding. You are not called to risk life, as well as position and good name. What can you allege as an excuse? You may say, 'There are peculiar difficulties.' 1 John 5:4 gives the reply: 'This is the victory that overcometh the world, even our faith'—our looking unto Jesus. Busy men, busy mothers, young men and maidens, all alike, will find victory here.

# 7 May

He must increase, but I must decrease.
*John 3:30*

'He must increase' is the test of true discipleship. No man is a disciple of Christ until Christ has got a very high place in his heart. An awakened sinner is by no means necessarily a disciple. Many are awakened, many have deep convictions of sin and misery, and draw back to perdition and are, more than before, children of hell. When I was in America, last summer, I happened to tell how Mr McCheyne once said that some persons who were awakened in the Dundee revival of 1840–41 went no further than conviction, and became the bitterest enemies of the cause of God and revival. Another man was once awakened and in deep conviction. He never came to Christ, and he is now one of our bitterest enemies.

Are any of you trusting to conviction? Conviction is not Christ. Conviction ought to send you to the cross, but it is not Christ. God sent John the Baptist to awaken the people, but not to leave them under conviction, and so he preached two things very specially: Christ the Son of God, and Christ the Lamb of God. These two things must have a very high place in your soul if you are really a disciple. You are not a disciple till you have come with your load of sin and laid that load of sin upon the Lamb of God, who is the Son of God. Then you begin to be a disciple, but never till then. You may go back into the world, and sink deeper in sin than ever, if you have not thus given Christ the supreme place.

# 8 May

He must increase, but I must decrease.
*John 3:30*

Ponder much over our text. You may return to it every day of your life. It is found in the same blessed chapter where that text occurs: 'God so loved the world'. Read on till you come to this 30th verse, 'He must increase, and I must decrease.'

Test your religion by this text. Some men have a great deal of religiousness. They pray much in their own way, and give full attention to all public and family duties. But there may be nothing of Christ in all this. There may be nothing but self in their religion. Brother, is Christ the foundation stone of your religion? Christ in his atoning sacrifice? Christ: Prophet, Priest, and King? An old minister says, 'I am jealous of the way in which some use Christ. They use him as a medicine to heal their diseases, but they scarcely can be said to use him as food and feast.' When a man finds Christ crucified to be meat and drink to his soul, he is giving Christ his proper place. 'My flesh is meat indeed, and my blood is drink indeed' (John 6:55).

That was a memorable sermon which the martyr Lambert preached in the midst of the flames. When lifted up on the halberds of the soldiers, the smoke and the fire did not hinder him uttering his soul's joy, 'None but Christ! None but Christ!' And thus he passed into glory. May you and I be found so doing in life and death, to the praise and glory of him who declares, 'Behold, my servant … shall be exalted and extolled, and be very high.'

# 9 May

And Hezekiah commanded to offer the burnt offering upon the altar. And when the burnt offering began, the song of the LORD began also with the trumpets, and with the instruments ordained by David king of Israel.
*2 Chronicles 29:27*

There is a very beautiful incident—I do not know if it is often noticed—in the second Book of Chronicles, chapter 29, in the history of King Hezekiah. He was led to appoint certain arrangements in what regard to what we should call the psalmody of the temple, and one of them is thus stated: 'When the burnt offering began, the song of the Lord began also' (verse 27).

He appointed that every morning when the sacrifice should be offered, they should sing and blow the trumpets, that all Jerusalem might know that the atoning sacrifice was now presented on Israel's altar. When the offering began, then the song of the Lord began. Again, you see there that true praise begins when the sinner's eye rests upon the sacrifice, when the guilty conscience has felt the power of the atoning blood, and when the sinner's vacant heart has been filled with the person of the great Sacrifice, the great Atoner himself.

We said a little while ago that praise is to be offered continually. It is so written (Hebrews 13:15): 'continually'. We should count it our privilege to be in this continual frame of praise. Does not the 119th Psalm, verse 164, put it in this way? 'Seven times a day do I praise thee.' David says in another psalm, 'Evening, and morning, and at noon, will I pray, and cry aloud.' But here it is: 'I will praise thee seven times a day,' as if he would even go beyond the other limit in the matter of praise. At all events, we are to be praising continually. There is no need to fear that we shall want matter, and yet is it not a fact that we do not keep up the freshness of our new song as years go on? And why is this? Is it not because we are not getting a fresh view of the Lamb of God?

# 10 May

And at midnight Paul and Silas prayed, and sang praises unto God: and the prisoners heard them.
*Acts 16:25*

See the honour God put upon true praise rendered to himself! Prayer must be followed by praise. Prayer by itself (the Lord seems to say) is very well, but he wants praise; he must have the harp as well as the golden vial full of odour. We must now have both, as well as those that stand before the Lamb.

And in the prison of Philippi, what do we find? There were Paul and Silas praying. Yes, but they sang praises, and the emphasis is put upon the praises. For it is said the prisoners heard them, or more correctly—at least, more emphatically—it is, 'And the prisoners were listening.' You can, as it were, see them awaking and expressing wonder to each other, and putting their ear to the door of their cell. The prisoners were listening! Songs in a prison! Such songs—songs of Zion—had never been heard there before. It was then that the earthquake shook the prison, and the Lord came down and converted the jailer, a man memorable in the church of God, and who will be memorable till the Lord comes. Praise is pleasant to the Lord, as well as pleasing to us.

But again praise is good, it is sanctifying. There is something in it tending to build up the soul in sanctification. How could it be otherwise? Praise is the element of heaven. If so, in this praise there must be much of heaven.

# 11 May

> Although the fig tree shall not blossom, neither shall fruit be in the vines; the labour of the olive shall fail, and the fields shall yield no meat; the flock shall be cut off from the fold, and there shall be no herd in the stalls: yet I will rejoice in the LORD, I will joy in the God of my salvation..
> *Habakkuk 3:17–18*

Are you afflicted? You could not do wrong in singing praise. It is told us of a Welsh girl that her father had died, and the mother came out of the room weeping. The child said, 'Mother, what is the matter?' 'Oh, what shall I do, my child? Oh, what shall I do?' 'Mother, what is the matter?' 'Your father is dead, child, and what shall I do?' The child looked up in the mother's face, and said, 'Mother, praise the Lord, praise the Lord!' The mother was reproved; she went away and she tried to praise. She began to praise the Lord for what was left, and as she began to praise the Lord for what was left to her she soon found that the burden of her heart was lifted. The Lord was left; the Lord with all his grace was still her possession.

She was in the position of Habakkuk, who sings, 'Though the fig tree shall not blossom, neither shall fruit be in the vines; the labour of the olive shall fail, and the fields shall yield no meat; the flock shall be cut off from the fold, and there shall be no herd in the stalls: yet I will rejoice in the Lord, I will joy in the God of my salvation.' And then he inscribed his song, 'To the chief singer on my stringed instruments.' Was not that a pattern for us? Afflicted one, praise the Lord, and tell your afflicted friends to try praise to the Lord.

## 12 May

> And when the day of Pentecost was fully come, they were all with one accord in one place.
> *Acts 2:1*

The hour for morning prayer (the third hour) was near, and the 120 disciples repair to the temple. They cannot keep to themselves what they have got. Some think that the multitude came together to them at their upper room building, but it is more likely that they went to the temple. At any rate, they are found surrounded by Jews of all nations under heaven, all full of amazement and bewildered with surprise.

But turn from them and look at the twelve. Peter, in their name, rises up. What composed boldness there is in him! He is calm, yet full of zeal and fervour. He speaks, and nothing could be plainer than the language used. It is clear, plain, and distinct. The words used everybody can understand. But, oh, how authoritatively and surely he gives forth his testimony to Christ risen and ascended, and calls on all to hear and obey, and the great multitude are awed as he speaks.

Oh, for such a day of power to us! Oh, for such a coming of the Holy Spirit to every minister, to every worker! We long for this. We look for this. And in passing, notice there is not a syllable in all Scripture that intimates that when the Spirit fills a man, he shouts. When the Spirit fills a man, he is calm. Notice that! What did Christ do? No noisy shout did he send forth: he did not cry, nor lift up, nor cause his voice to be heard in the streets (Isaiah 42:2). For the Spirit comes calmly and gently, though with overwhelming power, enabling the man to bear witness for the Lord.

# 13 May

> Then they that gladly received his word were baptized: and the same day there were added unto them about three thousand souls.
> *Acts 2:41*

'They gladly received his word.' How speedily the message of salvation enters in, opening the heart to hear! We have not time to dwell upon particulars, but look now at the Pentecostal first fruits. Look at that goodly company, three thousand souls. They go away praising God. They go home to eat their meat with gladness and singleness of heart. Observe their brotherly kindness, their fellowship with the apostles, their liberality and unselfishness, and other graces. And there is one specified that we are surprised at. They 'continued in prayer'. They had got what they prayed for during the ten days. Yet they are praying on! Three thousand souls is a good beginning, but it is only a beginning. They pray on, and what we hear next is, souls were daily added to the Church, of such as should be saved.

We must continue in prayer if we are to get an outpouring of the Spirit. Christ says there are some things which we shall not get unless we pray and fast—yes, 'prayer and fasting'. We must control the flesh and abstain from whatever hinders direct fellowship with God. We must leave other things untouched, that we may give ourselves to prayer for a time. Do that often and bring down a blessing. Leave off other reading. Leave off other employments. Give up some of your work, and pray down the Spirit that we may have a great Pentecostal blessing. Our only hope is in the Holy Spirit.

# 14 May

> Now when they heard this, they were pricked in their heart, and said unto Peter and to the rest of the apostles, Men and brethren, what shall we do?
> Acts 2:37

'He will reprove the world of sin ... because they believe not on me.' The word 'reprove' is an old English word which is the same meaning as 'convince' (see Job 6:25; Psalm 50:21). The Spirit convinces—that is, he gives to the soul a sight and a sense of sin. Just as at the great day, in which Enoch's prophecy declares that the Lord as Judge will 'convince all that are ungodly ... of all their ungodly deeds ... and of all their hard speeches', so now, when the Spirit comes into the soul he makes the sinner see and feel the tremendous evil of sin.

The Spirit shows the sinner that by his unbelief he was all along virtually refusing to take pardon for his sins, thrusting the Saviour from him and saying, 'Away with him! Away with him! Trouble me not!' He was resolving to go up to the judgment seat with all his guilt upon him. And thus he was refusing peremptorily to part with his corruptions and his sinful nature, he was determining to remain unholy and impure, for there is no beginning of holiness until sin is pardoned.

Oh, what an abyss of evil is revealed to the sinner in the hour when the Spirit convinces him, as Christ says, 'of sin, because he believes not on me'! No wonder the three thousand souls (men, women and children) on the day of Pentecost so cried out in fear and anguish of heart, when the Spirit silently, but with almighty power, showed this sin of unbelief and charged it home on each, while Peter pointed to the crucified Son of God.

# 15 May

Now when they heard this, they were pricked in their heart, and said unto Peter and to the rest of the apostles, Men and brethren, what shall we do?
*Acts 2:37*

Reader, have you ever felt your need of salvation? Have you ever sought it, as one who must obtain it—or perish? When a sinner is first brought to feel sin to be a burden—when he feels wrath abiding upon his soul, and that his whole past life has been a life without God—his question is, 'What must I do to be saved? Is it possible that my sin can ever be forgiven by a God who is angry with the wicked every day?' The awakened publican's cry is, 'O God, be merciful to me!' And this cry finds God in the very attitude of grace, proclaiming his name, 'the Lord, the Lord God, merciful', and pointing to the Saviour on the throne of grace, where we may obtain mercy.

You must come as a sinner. You must come with nothing but sin. On the day of atonement, the priest in Israel who came forward to the mercy seat laid down nothing but sin on that blood-sprinkled lid. He showed a sinner's way of coming to the Lord, and yet he brought nothing whatever but sin, to be laid down there. So the sinner, in coming to the mercy seat, brings nothing but sin. He confesses the sin he was born with, 'Behold! I was shapen in iniquity,' and lays it down on the sprinkled blood. He confesses his inheritance of corruption from Adam, and lays it down on that mercy seat.

## 16 May

And when he is come, he will reprove the world of sin, and of righteousness, and of judgment: of sin, because they believe not on me.
*John 16:8–9*

You come, wholly as a sinner. Nothing can be more deeply solemnising than this: to have such a burden to lay down there—to have nothing else than a burden of this kind—and to lay all this on the Lord Jesus Christ! How humbling, how fitted to lay the sinner in the dust, is the view this gives of his utter guilt and vileness! And yet, nothing is more inviting, for it is with sin he comes, and as a sinner, and the Lord Jesus meets the sin and the sinner. Is there then any room for delay? Any ground for excuse for hesitating to come at once?

Reader, have you ever laid to heart that this is the truth, as to the state in which a sinner comes to the mercy seat for pardon? Is it true that the greatness of your sins needs be no hindrance to your acceptance, if only you are now willing with all your heart to turn from sin to God? Yes, it is true. It was for sinners the mercy seat was made. It was for sinners the blood was shed. 'This is my blood of the new testament, which is shed for many for the remission of sins' (Matthew 26:28). 'They that be whole need not a physician, but they that are sick. ... I am not come to call the righteous, but sinners to repentance' (Matthew 9:12–13).

# 17 May

*And when he is come, he will reprove the world of sin, and of righteousness, and of judgment: of sin, because they believe not on me.*
*John 16:8–9*

When, at any time, you have heard Christ in all his fulness pressed upon your acceptance—when you have been invited without delay, to draw near with a true heart, in full assurance of faith—is it not true that secretly you may have been raising some such difficulty as this? 'Oh, but I am such a sinner! I cannot expect to be received just as I am. I must wait till I have mended my life, and then I will come. I must wait till I have prayed longer, and then I will come. I must wait till I have had deeper convictions of sin, and then I may hope that the Lord will receive me if I come.'

Is this your view of the way of salvation? If it is, you are surely all in the wrong. Is it not just as if you were to say, 'I cannot go to God just now, for I am a poor, vile, guilty sinner, with no good thing about me at all—a poor beggar, who has nothing to give for salvation. But I shall wait till I have something to recommend me, and then I shall go'?

Dear reader, would this be a free salvation? You want to pay for salvation, but God offers you salvation without money and without price. 'Ho, every one that thirsteth, come ye to the waters, and he that hath no money; come ye, buy, and eat; yea, come, buy wine and milk without money and without price' (Isaiah 55:1). 'Whosoever will, let him take the water of life freely' (Revelation 22:17).

# 18 May

And the Pharisees and scribes murmured, saying, This man receiveth sinners, and eateth with them.
*Luke 15:2*

When a sinner is once truly awakened by the Spirit of God to see the awful ruin of his condition, he then feels that, so far from it being a comfort to him, the very thing that is the likeliest to drive him to despair would be to tell him that he must wait till he finds some good thing in him to recommend him before he could hope for pardon from an angry God. The Lord shows us a more excellent way. Glorious truth! Spoken of Jesus by those who were stumbled by its very glory: 'This man receiveth sinners.' In the gospel call, so far as any ground of acceptance is concerned, the Lord has no respect to the sinner's state at all, as to whether it be better or whether it be worse. The only question is, 'Art thou willing?' The invitation is, 'Whosoever will.'

The sinner who comes in faith to the mercy seat is immediately received. The priest who thus confessed and spread out his sin, found God at that spot where the seven-times sprinkled blood lay, waiting to be gracious. There never was seen the flash of angry lightning over the mercy seat. There never was heard one faint murmur of Sinai thunder there. There was, on the contrary, the bright and glorious cloud that cast its mild rays, sweeter than setting sun ever did, over the sinner who had on that spot spoken out his soul's guilt and left it on the blood.

God looked on the atoning blood, and pointing to it, seemed to say, 'I am well pleased therein, and therefore spare this sinner.'

# 19 May

*Whom God hath set forth to be a propitiation through faith in his blood, to declare his righteousness for the remission of sins that are past, through the forbearance of God.*
*Romans 3:25*

God saw his justice satisfied, because fully met by that setting forth of death for the guilty. Bending over it, it was as if he bent over his beloved Son, in whom he is ever well pleased. The sinner, too, fixed his eye on the same atonement that lay on that mercy seat and, after having so confessed his sinfulness, stood gazing on the blood, as if to say, 'Lord, there is my death for each sin. There is my satisfaction. There is my propitiation. There is thy law's demand. I do not seek aught inconsistent with thy perfect righteousness!'

And this is the position of a believing soul. His eye is on Jesus. His ear hears the testimony that, because of the blood, God has given us eternal life (1 John 5:11). His soul says, 'Christ is the end of the law for righteousness to me.' He is told, 'Him hath God set forth to be a propitiation', and he believes it and holds it up to God. God owns it as enough, and is at peace with him.

Reader, have you ever laid to heart that this is the truth concerning the blood of Christ—that there is immediate pardon for every sinner believing in it and resting upon it? The broken law proclaims that the wages of sin is death. The sinner's hope is not a hope procured upon any other terms. If it were so, where or when for a moment would the sinner be safe? It would be but saying, 'Peace, peace,' while the law said there was no peace. No. Salvation is not an unrighteous compromise between the law and the gospel.

# 20 May

But now in Christ Jesus ye who sometimes were far off are made nigh by the blood of Christ.
*Ephesians 2:13*

Here is peace for the guilty, rest for the weary. Behold this blood! Behold, in what it has done in all generations, the power of that blood to bring far-off sinners nigh! Behold that mercy seat, where the precious atonement blood is sprinkled! There God is waiting to be gracious, waiting to meet you. There, and there only, the holy One can meet with the guilty, and be reconciled. There is salvation to the uttermost, to all who will draw near.

That blood offers immediate forgiveness. It is the plea which God himself, with whom we have to do, has furnished to the perishing sinner. Will he not accept his own plea? 'The precious blood of Christ, as of a lamb without blemish and without spot: who verily was foreordained before the foundation of the world, but was manifest in these last times for you, who by him do believe in God, that raised him up from the dead, and gave him glory; that your faith and hope might be in God' (1 Peter 1:19–21). Will he not recognise the preciousness and power of the blood of his beloved Son, when it is held up in faith by the believing soul? (Read 1 John 1:7; Colossians 1:12–15; Ephesians 2:12–15; Hebrews 12:24).

Is a sinner's appeal to the blood of Jesus his only ground of acceptance? Yes, the one and only ground. The great thing that has created a difference between the soul now believing, and other souls still in sin, is that the eye of the believing one has been fixed upon the atonement. Others see not the power of the blood, and so have no plea with God.

# 21 May

> Unto you therefore which believe he is precious: but unto them which be disobedient, the stone which the builders disallowed, the same is made the head of the corner.
> *1 Peter 2:7*

But is there, then, no hope that we are in Christ unless we possess the full assurance? We do not say so, though we believe that this question has often been used as a refuge from the guilt of not resting with full confidence on the blood of Christ. By reason of the weakness of their faith and the strength of corruption within, the holiest of men are often found walking in darkness. But what we plead for is this, that if a child of God be not kept in peace as regards his acceptance, it is not for the want of something in Christ but because of his own want of faith to take freely what has been so freely given—and that all such doubts and fears regarding the fulness of Christ, whatever be the humbled and exercised look they may assume, while they are the believer's misery, are no less truly the believer's sin.

How precious, then, this way of acceptance! We need no more than this for immediate and present pardon. The crucified and risen Jesus, and nothing else, brings us nigh to God. The crucified and risen Jesus, apart from all besides, reconciles us to God. The crucified and risen Christ is the end of the law for righteousness to every one that believeth. He has borne an awful testimony that the wages of sin is death, and has thus opened the way of salvation for the very chief of sinners, the very basest and vilest of men.

# 22 May

> Purge me with hyssop, and I shall be clean: wash me, and I shall be whiter than snow.
> *Psalm 51:9*

Reader, have you ever felt this blood of Christ to be precious blood? Have you been convinced of sin, and convinced of righteousness? Have you ever felt God's holy justice in requiring such a sacrifice, and his holy love in providing it, not sparing his only begotten Son? Have you ever felt the necessity for that blood being shed, and sprinkled upon your soul before you could be pardoned? It is the blood, and the blood alone, which maketh atonement for the soul. It was to this blood of Christ, seen by faith through the types of the ceremonial law, that David was looking in the fifty-first Psalm when, in bitterness for his guilt, he cried, 'Purge me with hyssop, and I shall be clean: wash me, and I shall be whiter than snow.'

Has the insupportable burden of sin ever thus fixed your eye upon that blood whence alone pardon and relief can come? Or are you yet easy-minded about the state of your soul? Does your conscience tell you that it would make no material difference to you if you were to be told that now there was to be no longer any access to the mercy seat for you? Dear reader, think what you are doing! Is in a fancy? Is the wrath of God a vain imagination? If these were matters of little consequence, if they were as small matters as you now think them, would God have given his only begotten Son, that whosoever believeth on him, should not perish, but have everlasting life?

## 23 May

> How shall we escape, if we neglect so great salvation; which at the first began to be spoken by the Lord, and was confirmed unto us by them that heard him.
> *Hebrews 2:3*

You do not deny that you are a sinner—by nature dead in trespasses and sins, a child of wrath, even as others (Ephesians 2:1, 3). How, then, do you expect to be saved? Are you not neglecting the great and the only salvation? How shall you escape? (See Hebrews 2:3).

'He that despised Moses' law died without mercy under two or three witnesses: of how much sorer punishment, suppose ye, shall he be thought worthy, who hath trodden under foot the Son of God, and hath counted the blood of the covenant, wherewith he was sanctified, an unholy thing, and hath done despite unto the Spirit of grace?' (Hebrews 10:28–29).

The blood was always upon the mercy seat. It was there, night and day, summer and winter, year after year. So Jesus is. He is never unable or unwilling to receive one coming sinner. Do you ask, 'Who are they who would be welcome?' He answers, 'Him that cometh' (John 6:37). Every sinner, of every kind and character, great and small, young and old, are welcome. Nicodemus came to Jesus by night—and he was welcome. The woman that feared to be seen touched him—and was cured. All the publicans and sinners drew near to him—and he stood in the midst. 'Him that cometh to me,' said he, 'I will in no wise cast out.'

And who must come? All that would not perish for ever. For 'there is none other name under heaven given among men, whereby we must be saved' (Acts 4:12).

## 24 May

*Who his own self bare our sins in his own body on the tree, that we, being dead to sins, should live unto righteousness: by whose stripes ye were healed.*
*1 Peter 2:24*

Right views of sin have a tendency to lead us to right views of the person of the Saviour. But the converse also is true: right views of the Saviour's person lead to right views of sin. It is in Christ, the Son of God substituted for the sinner, that we see the abyss of evil in our sin, and that we become aware that sin is so clamorous for wrath as to be silenced only by the interposed person of the Son of God.

But turn aside again. Approach an infant newly born drawing its first breath in this fallen world. There is sin in that soul. And small as the sin may seem when compared with that of sinners who have lived forty or seventy years, yet even the sin of that infant is such an evil as nothing can remedy but the blood of the Son of God. If the sin of that infant is to be forgiven, the Son of God must 'pour out his soul unto death' in its behalf.

Set before you any one of your own acts of disobedience, selecting those which may, in your judgment, appear the smallest and slightest. Yet that act was sin—such an act that, ere it can be forgiven and you received into favour, Godhead must he moved! God the Son must rise from his place on the Father's bosom and haste to your rescue.

## 25 May

> Who his own self bare our sins in his own body on the tree, that we, being dead to sins, should live unto righteousness: by whose stripes ye were healed.
> 1 Peter 2:24

Less than the atonement through Christ would be insufficient; less than this would be entirely useless. For the abyss is bottomless. No angel's strength could bear the burden of the wrath due to your one sin, while certainly no angel's love could endure the trial of interposing as your substitute. Sin is something that only God can deal with—a mysteriously tremendous evil.

These lessons are taught us when we fix our attention, not on the mere blessing of forgiveness, but also on the person who brings it. If we were to adopt another plan, too commonly pursued, and merely speak of salvation a work done and finished well—or as a door opened at which the vilest may come in, or as a free invitation to the chief of sinners—we might in that case miss altogether the clear light cast on sin by the gospel. But on the other hand, connect all with the person—and in this case with the divine nature of the person—show that here is the work of God in our nature, God occupying our law-room. Show that here is the door of access opened, but only in consequence of almighty love shedding the blood of the beloved Son, heaven's Isaac. Show that here is a free invitation to the vilest, but that it is thus free only because the Saviour who came was creator of all conditions, and pay the last mite. Show all this, and forthwith the light of the cross is cast on sin, and you see it to be an infinite evil, an evil understood by God alone.

# 26 May

> In the last day, that great day of the feast, Jesus stood and cried, saying, If any man thirst, let him come unto me, and drink.
> *John 7:37*

'How am I to cross that mountain?' says an anxious soul, pointing to the doctrine of electing love. 'How am I to find myself among the number of the elect?' 'And,' says another, 'if you cannot assure me that the blood of Christ was intended as much for me as for Peter or Paul, Mary Magdalene or Mary of Bethany, how can I rest on it?' Another, yet more bold, comes forward and declares that, 'If Christ did not die alike for all men, and bear all sinners alike on his heart when he died, then there is no truth sufficient for a sinner seeking salvation to rest upon.'

Now, to all those travellers who would willingly (if they could) find out that there is no such mountain as electing love because they fancy it is an insuperable one, we say at once: the person of the Lord Jesus stands in front of that glorious mountain whose top touches heaven, and you have to do with his person ere you set a foot on that mountain.

Our warrant for believing in Christ is simply this, that he cries to the children of men, 'To you, O men, I call.' And he bids them all come in the first place to himself. Come and see this person (Proverbs 8:4). 'If any man thirst, let him come unto me, and drink' (John 7:37). 'Come unto me, all ye that labour and are heavy laden' (Matthew 11:28), ye that are toiling up that mountain with a load on your souls that almost crushes you at every step.

## 27 May

> As far as the east is from the west, so far hath he removed our transgressions from us.
> Psalm 103:12

No one could be supposed to have seen the Alps, if he tells you that all he saw was some rocky ridges of hills which his eye felt no strain in looking to. The Alps are not such hills: they tower to the clouds. Equally true it is that no one can be considered as having really seen sin, who never saw it to be very great; or to have got real rest to his soul, who has not seen the Saviour to be very great. Indeed, a very great salvation is needed in order to give any true peace to a soul truly awakened; such salvation as is discovered when the soul discovers the person of the Saviour. Then it sings, 'Jehovah is my strength and song; he also has become my salvation' (Isaiah 12:2). In Jehovah is the Rock of ages.

For such a state of soul only one thing can avail, namely, the discovery which the Spirit makes to the man in conversion, the discovery of Christ's full sacrifice for sin. Therein may be seen a propitiation as full and efficacious as conscience craves, because it was wrought out by him who is God-man. Therein may be seen the whole person of the Saviour presented to the soul as the object to be embraced, and that person associated with the merit of all he has done and suffered. Nay more: every act and suffering of that glorious person confronts the case of every sinner.

# 28 May

> As far as the east is from the west, so far hath he removed our transgressions from us.
> *Psalm 103:12*

Oh, inconceivable fulness for us in him, whatever be the special sin which our conscience at any moment is feeling! Only let us ever keep Christ himself in view, Christ clothed to the foot in that garment of active and passive righteousness.

It is thus we get the sea with all its multitudinous waves (see Isaiah 48:18) to flow up every creek and sweep round every bay. His person being such, his work completely fits into the soul's necessities. And all this is so great, that not only does it affect us negatively—not only does this full view of Christ remove every tremor from the soul—it works besides into the heart a positive bestowal of bliss.

It is like sometimes in nature, when every breath of wind is so lulled asleep that not a leaf moves on the bough of any tree, the sun is shedding his parting ray on the still foliage, and the sea rests as if it had become a pavement of crystal. This is peace in nature. Your heart feels, amid such a scene, not only the absence of whatever might create alarm or disquiet, but the presence also of some elements of positive enjoyment, as if there were an infusion of bliss in the scene. Now infinitely more is this the case in the kingdom of grace. The presence of Christ in the heart (the Spirit there testifying of Christ) lulls fear to sleep, and while he makes disquiet almost an impossibility, never fails to bring in positive delight and bliss.

## 29 May

Surely he hath borne our griefs, and carried our sorrows: yet we did esteem him stricken, smitten of God, and afflicted.
*Isaiah 53:4*

Union to Christ's person is a fact in the case of every believer, and ought therefore to be a constant subject of meditation to every believer. Now, this union realised leads to a realising of the person. Hence, in the Lord's Supper, it is always important for the communicant to ask with Paul, 'The cup of blessing which we bless, is it not the communion of the blood of Christ? The bread which we break, is it not the communion of the body of Christ?' (1 Corinthians 10:16).

That ordinance, so rich in blessing and in blessed suggestions, is fitted always to bring us back to a fresh and present realising of the person of Jesus, by bringing us to a remembrance of our union to that person. Can we think of union to him, and not go on to ask, 'Who is this to whom I am united? Who is this that is my husband? Who is this that is far more mine than the husband is the wife's? What is his heart? What is his hand of might? Where are his possessions? Where are the proofs of his love? Are his glories bursting on my view?'

Undoubtedly it mellows and matures the character of saints to be much occupied with their Lord's person, but as undoubtedly it quickens their sense of obligation, and keeps alive love and gratitude, to be thus ever in contact with a personal Saviour. Ideas, however noble, may leave our souls comparatively dry, and they will always leave us infinitely less affected in our conscience, than when we meet our God in his personality.

# 30 May

*His mouth is most sweet: yea, he is altogether lovely. This is my beloved, and this is my friend, O daughters of Jerusalem.*
*Song of Solomon 5:16*

Many saints seem to be little aware how much of grace there is in the knowledge of the person of Jesus. It would singularly benefit some of these, who have lived much on what they know *about* Jesus, to try for a week the more blessed and fruitful way of dealing directly with *himself*. There are treasures in the person of him whose doctrines they believe, if only they could use them. A great philosopher says on another subject what we may accommodate to this, 'A man may believe in the work and person of Christ for twenty years, and only in the twenty-first—in some great moment—is he astonished at the rich substance of his belief—the rich warmth of this naphtha-spring.' He adds to his ideas a person. And exchanges knowledge about a truth for knowledge of him that is true—yes, exchanges opinions for a deep joy in the living One, a joy which nothing earthly gave nor can destroy.

By this looking to the person, the believer's holiness, or growth in grace, is advanced in a threefold way. For this looking to the person leads to communion, to a realising of his life for us, to imitation—all which conform the soul to his likeness.

Communion with him is one result, and a sanctifying result. When we dwell on the Saviour's person, we are in his company. Faith places us by his side and shows us his glory, until what we see makes our heart burn within us.

# 31 May

> Thine eyes shall see the king in his beauty: they shall behold the land that is very far off.
> Isaiah 33:17

Art thou a weary pilgrim? Walk on a little longer with thine eye still toward the right hand of the Majesty on high, for soon thou shalt see 'the king in his beauty'. Hast thou been vexed, like righteous Lot, from day to day, in seeing and learning earth's wickedness? Hast thou been saddened by witnessing death ravaging families, and removing some of thine own dearest ones? Hast thou but dimly descried amid thy tears the form of him who walked on the sea at midnight to reassure his dejected and trembling disciples? Hast thou often been disappointed when thou didst think thou hadst got a look of things within the veil, that would for ever turn thine eyes from beholding vanity? Be of good cheer. 'Thine eyes shall see the king in his beauty.' Thy heaven shall consist in seeing him as he is—knowing him as he knoweth thee.

Among all the rewards offered to those who overcome by the Captain of Salvation (when, after a sixty years' absence, he visited his suffering disciple in Patmos face to face), none is so magnificent, none so soul-filling, as that wherein he offers himself in his glory. In this promised reward he may be said to offer us himself at the time when all his own reward has been bestowed, and when himself has been anointed with the oil of gladness above his fellows.

# June

Hugh Martin (1822–1885) was born in Aberdeen and underwent his university studies at Marischal College in that city. He was a renowned mathematician and became a member of the London Mathematical Society. He maintained his interest in this subject and at a later stage in his life he acted as an examiner in Mathematics at the University of Edinburgh.

After teaching at Gordon's Hospital (now Robert Gordon's College) in Aberdeen for a time, he was inducted to the Free Church charge of Panbride near Carnoustie, Angus, in 1844. He remained in Panbride until 1858 when he was translated to the Free Greyfriars congregation in Edinburgh. Poor health forced him to take early retirement from the ministry in 1865.

Hugh Martin was a frequent and able speaker at the General Assembly of the Free Church of Scotland. He was prominent in contending against the emerging Higher Criticism of the Bible and against the movement to introduce unscriptural forms of worship into the Free Church.

Martin's literary output included many contributions to the *British and Foreign Evangelical Review* and the *Transactions of the London Mathematical Society*. In addition, he edited the *Watchword* magazine and authored several books, a number of which became classics of Christian literature, such as his commentary on the biblical book of Jonah and *The Atonement*.

## Sources of daily readings

June 1–9: Hugh Martin, *The Prophet Jonah: His character and mission to Nineveh* (London, 1856).

June 9–21: Hugh Martin, *Christ For Us* (Edinburgh, 1998).

June 22–30: Hugh Martin, *The Shadow of Calvary* (Edinburgh, 1875).

## Biographies

*Biographical Introduction* in *Christ for Us* (*op. cit.*).

Douglas Somerset *Life of Hugh Martin* in *The Bulwark: Magazine of the Scottish Reformation Society* (Oct.–Dec. 2008), pp. 14–25.

# 1 June

> But the LORD sent out a great wind into the sea, and there was a mighty tempest in the sea, so that the ship was like to be broken.
> *Jonah 1:4*

The Scriptures, in speaking of natural events, are remarkable for the unfaltering and continual ascription of them to God. 'There arose a great wind,' the vast majority of men would say. Holy Scripture uses this style: 'The Lord sent out a great wind into the sea.'

Hence, according to the same style, those who go down into the sea are said not merely to see great works and wonders, but the works and wonders of the Lord, as in that magnificent—that unrivalled—description of a storm: 'They that go down to the sea in ships, that do business in great waters; these see the works of the Lord, and his wonders in the deep. For he commandeth, and raiseth the stormy wind, which lifteth up the waves thereof. They mount up to the heaven, they go down again to the depths: their soul is melted because of trouble. They reel to and fro, and stagger like a drunken man, and are at their wits' end. Then they cry unto the Lord in their trouble, and he bringeth them out of their distresses. He maketh the storm a calm, so that the waves thereof are still. Then are they glad because they be quiet; so he bringeth them unto their desired haven. Oh that men would praise the Lord for his goodness, and for his wonderful works to the children of men!' (Psalm 107:23–31).

## 2 June

Wherefore they cried unto the LORD, and said, We beseech thee, O LORD, we beseech thee, let us not perish for this man's life, and lay not upon us innocent blood: for thou, O LORD, hast done as it pleased thee.
*Jonah 1:14*

We learn, then, from the conduct of these heathens, how deeply rooted in human nature is the conviction of a God. But we learn also the great worthlessness of prayers wrung out under terror. There is inlaid in human nature a central assurance or conviction of a God. In the case of the ungodly it is allowed, for the most part, to lie utterly dormant and concealed. If imminent and appalling danger forces out some alarmed manifestation of it in some excited cry to God for mercy or protection, there is really as little evidence of grace or virtue in such a prayer as when the warhorse, in the instinct of self-preservation, rears in terror as the gleaming sword flashes round his head. The prayer that is acceptable to God is the prayer of faith, of calm confidence and reliance on the word and love and wisdom and power of a gracious and a reconciled Father.

Oh, there is no 'glory to God', no 'peace on earth' except through the great Advocate and Intercessor, and through the prayer of faith presented in his name! Through him and his infinitely perfect sacrifice, how manifestly does our God appear to us, as no terrific tyrant under whom we must cringe in abject servility; as no flexible fool whom we may flatter into a change of purpose to suit our convenience, or secure our impunity in sin. No! He is the God of infinite love, giving up his Son to die for sinners.

# 3 June

> Then Jonah prayed unto the LORD his God out of the fish's belly.
> *Jonah 2:1*

Thus Jonah—delivered from his guiltiness and evil conscience, reconciled to God in peace, washed from his sins and made again a recognised king and priest, and so recognising and presenting himself before God in his holy temple by faith—offers the sacrifice of thanksgiving. Shut up still in his darksome grave, in the deep, in the shadow of death, we hear him nevertheless singing marvellously—far more marvellously than Paul and Silas in the prison—singing in his darkness, as if he said, 'God is the Lord, which hath shewed us light: bind the sacrifice with cords, even unto the horns of the altar' (Psalm 118:27).

Light! What light has Jonah? He has the light of faith—the light that shineth in the darkness—that lighteth up the shadow of death. And amidst the light, he cometh to God's altar to offer the sacrifice of thanksgiving. He cometh unto God—unto God, his exceeding joy.

You will praise God joyfully, downcast and disquieted believer, when once he shall have given you the deliverance you desire? Your song will begin when God hath done for you all that you ask? Ah, your song in that case shall be grounded in sense, not springing from faith. For observe—while your trial still lasts, while your vexing thorn still goads you, while your much loved hope seems plunged in the depths of ocean and no sensible sign yet appears of it being restored, while there is need of patience, and still there is need of faith—if God gives you warrant for faith, even his promise, is that not ground of immediate thanksgiving?

# 4 June

So the people of Nineveh believed God, and proclaimed a fast, and put on sackcloth, from the greatest of them even to the least of them.
*Jonah 3:5*

The repentance of Nineveh is one of the most singular events in history. A great and proud city suddenly smitten into the most profound humiliation—from the greatest of its inhabitants unto the least of them, from the king on the throne to the meanest citizen—is a spectacle to which, I suppose, history affords no parallel. Cities and countries and communities have oftentimes, with not a little unanimity, given themselves to humiliation and fasting. But there is no event on record that can at all be compared with the fast and the repentance of Nineveh.

And how very great is the encouragement which this holds out to sinners to repent and return unto the Lord with all their heart and with all their soul! A repentance arising only from a regret, however deep, and producing an outward reformation, however valuable, but without a change of heart, will assuredly avail but little. God may not count it utterly of no value in the light or on the platform of time. But in the light of eternity and of the spiritual world, it can profit you nothing.

We must all appear before the judgment seat of Christ. And anticipating that most awful event, it is ours to rend our hearts and not our garments, to seek grace that the tree may be made good, that we may be actually renewed in the spirit of our minds, transformed in the renewing of our minds, renouncing ourselves, and putting on Christ Jesus and living in the Spirit.

# 5 June

> The men of Nineveh shall rise in judgment with this generation, and shall condemn it: because they repented at the preaching of Jonas; and, behold, a greater than Jonas is here.
> *Matthew 12:41*

Behold, a greater than Jonah is here! Jesus was three days and three nights in the heart of the earth. Jonah died and rose again in a figure, a metaphor—a figure carrying in it terrible reality, but stopping short of actual death.

Jesus died and rose again. He suffered, the just for the unjust. In the room of transgressors he stood. In the name of, and as bearing the persons of transgressors he was judged, condemned, avenged upon in all the completeness and terrors of the wages of sin which is death, the wrath and curse of the Lord God Almighty. The arrows of Jehovah pierced him. The curse of the eternal Ruler's broken law descended on him. He tasted the bitterness, yea, the sting of death. His soul was exceeding sorrowful. He poured out his soul unto death. He 'knoweth the power of God's wrath' unto the uttermost. And if the experience of Jonah was a sign and an enforcement conjoined with his message, oh, with what overwhelming urgency may Jesus refer to his experience!

My reader, when Jesus counsels you to repent and flee from the wrath to come, the exhortation comes from one—if we may reverently use, as we may with intense truth use, the saying—comes from one who knows what he is speaking of. Yes, he knoweth that wrath. The tears he sheds over lost souls are prompted, in part, by personal knowledge of the wrath whereinto they are plunging themselves.

# 6 June

> For as Jonas was three days and three nights in the whale's belly; so shall the Son of man be three days and three nights in the heart of the earth.
> *Matthew 12:40*

Christ's death and resurrection are a conjoint sign and seal of his mission from the Father. It is, indeed, in this respect that the Son of man becomes truly that overpowering sign which either blinds and dooms the unbelieving, or finally convinces and illuminates the humble in heart. His person, even after all, would not, without his work—his work of atoning death and justifying resurrection—be such a sign as we have affirmed. His person truly is the sign—but it is so, and that conclusively, because the Son of man was three days and three nights in the heart of the earth.

It was, even from the first, in the view of his sufferings and victory, that any light shone in the promised Deliverer. Save for this—save for the light thrown forward from his coming cross and resurrection-Sabbath—even the divineness of his person and the stainlessness of his character would have been no real light in a world covered with gross darkness; no light into God's purpose of mercy towards it, God's special moral administration in it.

It is in the cross and empty grave that we truly, and for the first time, see light. It is there we see light into our state and case as the sinful subjects of a holy God, the guilty criminals before a righteous Judge, the trembling anticipants of death and eternity. It is there we see light into the infinite saving love of God.

# 7 June

> But we preach Christ crucified, unto the Jews a stumblingblock, and unto the Greeks foolishness.
> *1 Corinthians 1:23*

'We preach Christ crucified, the power of God, and the wisdom of God.' When we preach Christ, we keep this in our own view, we set this in your view: namely, that the Christ whom we preach, whom we press on your acceptance, is the infinite power, the omniscient wisdom of God. In him there is not merely perfect righteousness to justify you from all sin, and infinite love and grace to make that righteousness freely over to you, sinner, enemy though you be (Romans 5:8, 10), but this very Christ is the power of God, the wisdom of God.

Can you fail to see how very thoroughly this meets your case, and shuts you up to an immediate reception of the Saviour? There is a drawing power in the cross, utterly unbounded, able to bring and to save the chief of sinners. Give yourself up unto it: it will bring you into the love of God, into your Father's bosom. There is power in the planetary system, and in the pathless spaces of the stellar heavens. But the power there is limited: God's power could go greatly farther in its efforts than the heavens and the earth give proof of. It cannot go farther than it goes in the cross. *There*, there is not merely a display of power, leaving infinite efforts and effects for God's power to achieve behind and after all. There is all God's very power itself—the power of God, his omnipotence unto salvation.

# 8 June

> But unto them which are called, both Jews and Greeks, Christ the power of God, and the wisdom of God.
> *1 Corinthians 1:24*

There are obstacles in the way of your salvation—your forgiveness, your holiness, your coming unto Jesus, your believing on his name, your walking worthy of his love—obstacles manifold and strong. Are they almighty? One need scarcely seek an answer. Earth and hell and all creation may join their power to destroy you, but their allied forces do not make omnipotence. Finite powers at the uttermost, they fall infinitely short of almightiness. And can almightiness not cope with them? Yea, verily.

But where does almighty power emanate, to overthrow them? In what direction—what line—may I so place myself, as to find omnipotence coming forth to draw me to the Lord? In the line of the cross. In your looking unto Jesus. 'I, when I am lifted up, will draw all men unto me.' Through the blood of the dying Surety, almighty power comes forth on all them that believe.

Yea, and the splendours of omniscient wisdom break around your enlightened spirit also. If it were not so—if God should lay aside his wisdom and make a mere diplomatic stroke of policy in saving sinners, a subtle compromise with the claims of law, a mere trickful appearance and illusion of justice, an exhibition of indulgence without remission of sin, or of proffered remission without shedding of blood, a gift of general, uncovenanted, unmediatorial mercy—there could be no power needed and no power put forth in such a scheme of saving you. But God maintains his wisdom, and glorifies it to the uttermost in the cross. All shall be wisely done. 'My servant shall deal prudently.'

# 9 June

Therefore now, O LORD, take, I beseech thee, my life from me; for it is better for me to die than to live.
*Jonah 4:3*

'*Therefore*, now, O Lord, take, I beseech thee, my life from me; for it is better for me to die than to live.' Most miserable inference! Most painful exclamation! It is the exclamation of a believer, a saint, a man of God. But it is the cry of a soul far aside from its duty. Unable to guide either his mind or his ministry amidst the perplexity which the apparent vacillation or change of purpose on the part of God occasioned, Jonah prefers death to life. He prefers death to the apprehended dishonour of God and the destruction of his own usefulness as God's prophet. Excessive though his grief is—uncontrolled though his feelings are—they are evidently the feelings and the grief of a godly man. An earthly-minded man were incapable of such emotions. Yet are they altogether indefensible and inexcusable.

Our life is in the hands of God and he can threaten the removal of it in a thousand ways, every one of them sufficient to cause a displeased prophet to repent of his rash desire. He had but escaped from a species of living death that had filled him with anguish and extorted from him the most agonising cries for the Lord's pity and deliverance. And how can he forget that God might again plunge him into the jaws of destruction and 'answer his prayer by terrible things in righteousness'?

Very different was the decision of Paul on the question of death or life continued. He had 'a desire to depart and be with Christ.' He felt that *that* was 'far better'. Nevertheless, he saw that it was for the good of the Church that he should abide in the flesh. He was willing, therefore, to die or to live at the pleasure of the Lord.

# 10 June

But what saith it? The word is nigh thee, even in thy mouth, and in thy heart: that is, the word of faith, which we preach.
*Romans 10:8*

'The word is nigh thee; that is, the word of faith.' Now this implies, O sinner, that, Christ's redemption work being perfect, and sealed as such by his resurrection, your salvation work is a work done at a 'word'. That is clearly implied in this persuasive. It has no meaning at all if it does not imply, first of all and above all, that salvation is by grace, seeing all the redemptive work is done already. Ye are saved by grace, through faith. And it is of faith that it might be by grace. But faith needs a word to go upon: 'Be merciful unto me, according to thy word.' 'Remember the word unto thy servant, upon which thou hast caused. me to hope.'

The promise, accordingly, is the word of faith, the word which faith receives, the word which the Spirit uses to generate faith. This is the word on God's part which answers to faith (or, rather, to which faith answers) on man's part, in that great transaction in which reconciliation between the offended God and the alienated sinner is effected by the word of the truth of the gospel.

This 'word', intended of God to be so received in faith unto our actual salvation, is very properly called 'the word of faith'. It is the word which faith proceeds upon as true, the word which kindles and calls up faith itself, and then trusts itself to the faith which it has kindled. This 'word is nigh thee; even in thy mouth and in thine heart.' Such is the testimony of the 'righteousness which is of faith'—none other than the Word, the second person of the Godhead, God incarnate, the Christ of God. And none can be so deeply interested in 'the word of faith' as 'the righteousness which is of faith'.

## 11 June

I acknowledged my sin unto thee, and mine iniquity have I not hid. I said, I will confess my transgressions unto the LORD; and thou forgavest the iniquity of my sin. Selah.
*Psalm 32:5*

The point so strikingly brought out in these words is the connection—the sure and immediate connection—between the confession of sin and its forgiveness. This connection is doctrinally asserted in the memorable declaration: 'If we confess our sins, God is faithful and just to forgive us our sins, and to cleanse us from all unrighteousness.' It is affectingly exemplified in the parable of the prodigal's repentance, for no sooner had he poured into his father's bosom his ingenuous and unreserved acknowledgement of his iniquity, 'Father, I have sinned against heaven, and before thee, and am no more worthy to be called thy son,' than the father immediately, in full and unreserved forgiveness, said to his servants, 'Bring forth the best robe, and put it on him.'

The belief of this connection was evidently the great encouraging consideration that sustained the hope of David's smitten heart in Psalm 51: 'Wash me thoroughly from mine iniquity and cleanse me from my sin cleanse me from my sin. *For* I acknowledge my transgressions: and my sin is ever before me.' And in looking back on his deep exercise of spirit, as recorded in the remarkable and instructive Psalm before us, there was nothing that stood out to his view more prominent or memorable than just that sure and immediate connection between his confession of sin and the forgiveness which the Lord in his grace had so promptly and distinctly given him to experience. 'I said, I will confess my transgressions unto the Lord; and thou forgavest the iniquity of my sin.'

# 12 June

> Knowing this, that our old man is crucified with him, that the body of sin might be destroyed, that henceforth we should not serve sin.
> *Romans 6:6*

Observe that in this manifold communion with Christ the first and leading element is communion with him in his death, in his cross.

And the reason is that it was by his death that he obtained for us that promise and gift of the Spirit, whereby we are united to him and made a new creature in him, called unto his communion or fellowship.

Christ was born for us in the manger, but that does not secure the Spirit for us, though it was a glorious step thereto. For us he was baptized in Jordan. For us he was tempted in the wilderness and triumphed in his temptations. For us he lived and laboured and sorrowed and watched and prayed. For us he agonized in Gethsemane, was apprehended as a malefactor, was led away captive and bound, was stricken and smitten and afflicted and, as a sheep before her shearers is dumb, so he opened not his mouth. And in all this, if the Spirit once come forth and unite us to him, we have communion with him in the merit and spirit of the whole. But if his interposition for us go no further, the door of the Spirit's forthcoming from Christ to us and from the Father through Christ is still locked. It is the cross, the perfect expiation of the cross, that opens that door, for 'Christ hath redeemed us from the curse of the law, being made a curse for us: for it is written, Cursed is every one that hangeth on a tree.'

## 13 June

> Knowing this, that our old man is crucified with him, that the body of sin might be destroyed, that henceforth we should not serve sin.
> Romans 6:6

It is through Jesus Christ and him crucified that the Holy Ghost is shed on us abundantly. The cross is the pathway, the channel, by which the Spirit comes. The cross is the reason why he comes. It is the holy justification of a holy God in sending forth the Spirit to a miserable sinner. See to it that by faith you own this to a miserable sinner. See to it that by faith you own this same reason as your reason for expecting the Spirit. And as by faith you look along by the cross of Christ to your Father's throne, doubt not but there is coming forth unto you abundantly the Spirit of the Son, whereby we cry, 'Abba Father.'

But if it be directly and immediately for and by the cross that the Spirit of Christ cometh to you, then the immediate and first and central communion that you have with Christ is in his cross: ye are crucified with Christ. The cross is yours. His perfect propitiatory sacrifice in all its merit is yours. You are sanctified, cleansed, dedicated unto God, offered up and acceptable unto him by the offering of the body of Christ once for all. This is your fundamental privilege as a believer. On this foundation all your other privileges rest. From this centre all your other privileges flow forth, 'Know ye not, that so many of us as were baptized into Jesus Christ were baptized into his death?'

## 14 June

> Forasmuch then as the children are partakers of flesh and blood, he also himself likewise took part of the same; that through death he might destroy him that had the power of death, that is, the devil.
> *Hebrews 2:14*

How full of material for unbounded hope to the believer is this glory of the humanity of Jesus! If we believe on this glorified Emmanuel, then behold our very brother, flesh of our flesh, bone of our bone, exalted to the highest created glory. This is our nature which has the highest seat in heaven. This is he who, because the children were partakers of flesh and blood, himself also likewise took part of the same, and now, having offered a full sacrifice for sin, he has carried humanity within the veil, even to the holiest of all, to the very throne of God, where he sits infinitely exalted above all creatures. And now he that sanctifieth and they that are sanctified are all of one so that his people shall not stand in the outer court but have a way opened up through all the seraphic hosts of heaven till they come even to his throne, the centre of the glories of the universe, where they shall forever dwell nearest to Emmanuel's person, because they are dear to his heart as the purchase of his agony and pain.

Let your thoughts dwell much upon the covenant glory of Emmanuel and this may, in the hands of him who reveals Jesus and takes of the things that are his and shows them to the soul, be the means of drawing forth all your affection to him as the chiefest among ten thousand and the altogether lovely one.

## 15 June

> What prayer and supplication soever be made by any man, or by all thy people Israel, which shall know every man the plague of his own heart, and spread forth his hands toward this house: then hear thou in heaven thy dwelling place, and forgive, and do, and give to every man according to his ways, whose heart thou knowest.
> *1 Kings 8:38–39*

Let me speak briefly of the cure of heart plagues. The discovery of heart plagues may be effected by examining the life and character of Christ. The cure of them will be found in his death. It is the death of Christ alone that has virtue in it to heal our plagues, to mortify and slay our lusts. All your resolutions, all your wise plans of surmounting and expelling your plagues, will never succeed unless you bring them continually to the cross of Christ. You must have believing communion with a crucified Saviour if you are to mortify the deeds of the body, to crucify he flesh with its affections and lusts. Without this you may change one for another, but you will never aright mortify or vanquish any.

Christ gave himself or us that he might redeem us from all iniquity. There is a secret virtue in his blood, received by faith alone, which powerfully wastes the energy of every plague and sinful habit. Our old man is crucified with him, that the body of sin might be destroyed, that henceforth we should not serve sin. Engrafted into his death we become dead to sin, and sin reigns not in our mortal bodies, that we should obey it in the lusts thereof. Whatever heart plague you have discovered, bring it to the cross of Christ. Despite all deceitful efforts it may make to escape the fiery ordeal, compel it to face and confront the cross of Christ.

# 16 June

> Knowing this, that our old man is crucified with him, that the body of sin might be destroyed, that henceforth we should not serve sin.
> *Romans 6:6*

It is by a believing use of the cross that you are to slay your corruptions or cure your heart plagues. In proportion as you wander in spirit from the cross, your plagues and besetting sins will revive. Your right and adequate return to the cross weakens and mortifies and kills them.

All sanctification is from participating in the power of the cross. It is from communion in the death and resurrection of Christ. It is by being made conformable unto his death. If the body of sin is to be destroyed and you are not henceforth to serve sin, your old man must be crucified with Christ. You must be baptized into his death. You must make his death your own. You must drink of the cup which he drank of and be baptized with the baptism wherewith he was baptized.

Humiliation and holiness can be found by a sinner nowhere but at the cross. And they cannot be carried away from the cross. You must make the cross itself yours if you are to make humiliation and holiness yours. He gave himself, that he might redeem you from all iniquity. He loved you and gave himself for you, that he might cleanse you with the washing of water by the word. He redeemed you by his blood unto himself, that *he* might—that no iniquity might—have dominion over you. His name was called Jesus because he should save his people from their sins.

## 17 June

> Knowing this, that our old man is crucified with him, that the body of sin might be destroyed, that henceforth we should not serve sin.
> *Romans 6:6*

To the cross of Christ therefore they must again and continually come, to exercise fresh and lively faith, and for fresh communion with him in his death. Then once more in believing contemplation, in quiet dependence on the Spirit by that cross, they set before them Jesus Christ manifestly crucified for them. They meditate on the glory of his pardon, the matchless marvel of his love, and his purpose to redeem them from all iniquity and set them free from their love of and bondage to sin. They meditate afresh on the purchase that he has made of all-sufficient grace to conform them to himself, and on the right he has earned as their Saviour to reign as king, to subdue them to himself, to give them repentance unto the acknowledgement of the truth, to deal at his pleasure by his Spirit with their spirit, and to maintain in them a broken and a contrite heart.

When they mix all these meditations with faith, and by faith lay their hearts open to receive all that they thus see Christ's cross obtaining for them, submitting to the power they see that cross fitted and designed to wield over them and in them, then this lively acting of their faith will be found weakening the energy of the old man, and enabling them, in the name of Jesus, in the constraints of his love and in the power of his Spirit, to put sin with its instigations away, to keep themselves from their iniquity, to deny ungodliness and worldly lusts, to put off the old man and to die more and more unto sin, serving not sin but righteousness and God.

# 18 June

*For ye are dead, and your life is hid with Christ in God.*
*Colossians 3:3*

The believing child of God is in possession of eternal life. He is in *present* possession of it. He does not tarry till he enters into glory to be put in possession of everlasting life. He possesses it already. 'He that believeth on the Son of God hath'—even now, while sojourning in this estate of trial and probation—'everlasting life' (John 3:36).

The believer, then, is in present possession of everlasting life. And how great are the glories which this one fact implies! He stands personally in the favour of heaven; he stands well with God—oh, how well!—even as God sees his shield and looks on the face of his anointed one. And in this favour of God—in this good understanding between him and his God—the very life of his soul consists. 'In his favour is life' and 'thy loving kindness is better than life.' He is a son of the King of glory, he is an heir of God, a joint-heir with Christ. He is a member of a spiritual priesthood, of a general assembly of worshippers, officiating daily before the God of the whole earth. He is a king and priest. There is no end of the glorious things that are spoken of the city of God and its citizens. They have a life which, in its character and functions and privileges, and history and prospects, is altogether full of glory.

# 19 June

For ye are dead, and your life is hid with Christ in God.
*Colossians 3:3*

The hidden life is a secure life, it is safe. And oh, how safe, considering where it is laid up; considering with whom we share it! It is laid up in God: 'Your life is hid in God.' It is shared with Christ: 'Hid with Christ in God.' It is hid in God, in the inaccessible depths of Godhead—inaccessible to every eye save the eye of faith, which seeing in the light of God's Word and God's Spirit, enters with safety and penetrates among the things and thoughts of God only wise. This life is hid with God, for 'with thee is the fountain of life' and 'in thy favour is life'. Yea, it is that secret life in God—that unspeakable favour of God—possessed by Emmanuel himself, which believers share. Their life is bound up with Christ, 'hid with Christ in God'.

Yea, more: Christ is their life, for we read that he 'who is our life shall appear'. Christ himself is our life, for all the fulness of the Godhead dwelleth in him, and the fountain of life which Godhead only yields. And seeing that God the Son, in mediatorial fellowship with the Father in our name, enjoys in our name the favour of God—surely, if divine favour is life, Christ, the eminently favoured one, the beloved, must be our life. God has given us eternal life, and this life is in his Son.

Oh, then, draw near, and by Christ, the open door—the door into the deep things of God, the door into the Father's opened heart of love, the door into the otherwise hopelessly concealed mysteries of Godhead unapproachable—behold the overflowing, the exhaustless fulness of your life!

# 20 June

> Blessed be the God and Father of our Lord Jesus Christ, who hath blessed us with all spiritual blessings in heavenly places in Christ.
> *Ephesians 1:3*

The language of the believing soul is, 'The lines are fallen unto me in pleasant places; yea, I have a goodly heritage.' There are other texts of Scripture which also speak of the Christian heritage in its unity: a 'pearl of great price'; 'a kingdom that cannot be moved'; a 'portion'. But this text speaks of the heritage in its multiplicity, as made up of or branching out into a multitude of blessings.

Such is the Lord's ultimate object in saving us. He designs thereby to make his own glory manifest, to make it resplendent and conspicuous. He proposes to give an eternal exhibition of the greatness and glory of his grace, 'that in the ages to come he might shew the exceeding riches of his grace in his kindness toward us through Christ Jesus'. He means to give a revelation to angels of his wisdom, 'to the intent that now unto the principalities and powers in heavenly places might be known by the church the manifold wisdom of God'. Thus there is glory to God in the highest, peace on earth, and good will toward men.

The obtaining of Christ is not the last step but the first. Then, Christ being yours, draw out of his fulness, search and prove his blessings. Press on and prove on. Live on by the faith of the Son of God, while in your experience and enjoyment you are ever learning more and more what riches of grace and truth are laid up in Jesus. Rejoice that they are all your own in Christ, and give thanks unto the Father as in this doxology: 'Blessed be the God and Father of our Lord Jesus Christ, who hath blessed us with all spiritual blessings in heavenly places in Christ.'

# 21 June

Beloved, now are we the sons of God, and it doth not yet appear what we shall be: but we know that, when he shall appear, we shall be like him; for we shall see him as he is.
1 John 3:2

There are included in these words, first, a bold and firm assertion: 'Beloved, now are we the sons of God.' Secondly, we have a candid acknowledgement, a frank admission of an apparent objection: 'It doth not yet appear what we shall be.' Thirdly, there is a triumphant removal of that objection by a bold and firm anticipation, counteracting or counterbalancing it: 'But we know that, when he shall appear, we shall be like him: for we shall see him as he is.'

Our claim of sonship we rest firstly on the Father's love; we prove it by his love to us. In that love we glory as the foundation of our sonship, and to it we call attention as the explanation of our sonship. 'Behold, what manner of love the Father hath bestowed upon us.'

Be very sure also that it is on the peculiar love of God, his special call and personal fellowship with the Son, that you must rest your sonship, if you would distance its security and truth clear from this conflict with sense, shame and sorrow, while the glory, the victory and the joy do not yet appear

But hold by faith to sovereign, gracious, peculiar love. Hear in faith the Father's special, personal call to you, and maintain by faith a personal communion with the Son. Then, though it does not yet appear what you shall be, in that you merely share with the Eternal Son himself as he was in the world, you still may boldly maintain, 'Now are we the sons of God.'

# 22 June

*Then saith he unto them, My soul is exceeding sorrowful, even unto death: tarry ye here, and watch with me.*
*Matthew 26:38*

No language can describe the impression which a statement like this ought to make upon us. The person who is here set before us—the position of prostrate, yea, all but abject supplication—the cry of anguish wrung out from him in the prospect of a stroke about to fall upon him, which he trembles lest his weak, frail human nature should be unable to bear—all these considerations, and each of them, ought to fill us with the liveliest and most inexpressible astonishment.

It is deeply to be feared that too many read the verses before us in a state of mind indefinitely approaching to unconscious yet real infidelity. Is it possible that there could be such an amount of insensibility in any mind that steadily contemplated this scene as an event which really occurred? Could this transaction be viewed with more indifference than it is by multitudes, even though it were announced as a mere fiction? Nay, suppose it were a fiction, it would be a grander one unspeakably than the imagination of the thoughts of any man ever devised.

Oh, it reveals to us the carnality of our minds when we feel that we can meet a fact like this with so little of that adoring wonder and love and praise which reason and conscience tell us it is worthy and fitted to call forth. Truly no truth is more fully proved by experience and observation than that we need the Spirit to take of the things of Christ and show them to us—that we need the Spirit of grace and supplications to be poured upon us ere we can look on him whom we have pierced and mourn.

## 23 June

And he came out, and went, as he was wont, to the mount of Olives; and his disciples also followed him. And when he was at the place, he said unto them, Pray that ye enter not into temptation. And he was withdrawn from them about a stone's cast, and kneeled down, and prayed, saying, Father, if thou be willing, remove this cup from me: nevertheless not my will, but thine, be done.
Luke 22:39–42

That the sorrow of Christ in Gethsemane was of a very intense and terrible description, we have many infallible proofs. The Scriptures testify, recording indeed his own testimony, that he 'began to be very heavy', to be 'sorrowful', to be to be 'sore amazed', and 'sorrowful even unto death'. And these expressions are far from conveying the great force and emphasis of the original.

In confining our attention at present to the consideration of the sorrow of the Lord, to discover what from the Scriptures may be learned of its nature and causes, we ought to feel that we specially require the Spirit of the Lord to rest upon us, the Spirit of knowledge and of the fear of the Lord, that we may not irreverently intrude where angels might tremble to advance, or gaze with presumptuous eye where angels might veil their faces with their wings.

Deep grief, among mere men, is for the most part, generously accounted a sacred thing. Here we have the grief of him who is the ever-blessed God, the sorrow and weakness and fear and trembling of him who is the Lord God omnipotent, the tears and prostrate agonies and cries of one who is now seated on the right hand of the majesty in the heavens, angels and principalities and powers being made subject to him! The sorrows of the garden arose from the prospect and foresight of the sorrows of the cross.

# 24 June

> And being in an agony he prayed more earnestly: and his sweat was as it were great drops of blood falling down to the ground.
> *Luke 22:44*

Can there be any difficulty now in understanding generally what the nature and emphasis of his sorrow must have been? Think of Jesus coming into this terrible position towards the Judge of all—towards his Father and his God—towards him whose approbation and pleasure in him were the light and joy of his life unspeakable! Think of him consenting to have all the sins of myriads imputed to him by his Father: to underlie, that is, the imputation, in his Father's judgment, of every kind and degree and amount of moral evil—every species and circumstance and combination of vile iniquity!

There is a book of reckoning which eternal justice writes in heaven, wherein is entered every charge to which infinite unsparing rectitude, searching with omniscient glance alike the darkness and the light, sees the sons of men become obnoxious. This terrific scroll, so far as the elect of God are concerned in it, was unrolled before the eye of Jesus in Gethsemane, 'the iniquities of us all' which God was now about to lay upon him were therein disclosed, and you have to think of the sorrow with which he should contemplate his becoming responsible and being held of God to be responsible for all that that record charged—his being accounted of God, in his own one person, guilty of all that that record bore! It was hereupon that the Christ who, in prophetic Scripture as in the fortieth Psalm, proclaimed himself the Father's willing covenant servant: 'Lo, I come, in the volume of the book it is written of me; I delight to do thy will, O my God; thy law also is within my heart' (Psalm 40:6).

## 25 June

And he cometh unto the disciples, and findeth them asleep, and saith unto Peter, What, could ye not watch with me one hour?
*Matthew 26:40*

Ah, how was Peter hereby prepared for his greater fall—the others for forsaking Jesus and fleeing—all of them or being guilty of sin and laden with sorrow, till they should be forgiven and restored by a risen Redeemer! Who can trace how very different their conduct and their comfort might have been during that terrific time, had they watched and prayed like Jesus, and as Jesus had enjoined? They escaped with their faith indeed still in life, for the watching and the prayer of him with whom they would not watch, had been for them even more than for himself. They escaped, yet so as by fire.

Even so may you reach heaven at last, if indeed you are Christ's. For if ye are Christ's, the Spirit of Christ dwelleth in you. Otherwise ye could be none of his. And if the Spirit of him that raised up Christ from the dead dwell in you, you are renewed in the spirit of your minds, and the spirit is willing though the flesh is weak, and the Lord will not break his covenant with you. Every true believer, whatsoever may befall him by the way, shall at last appear before God in Zion, and dwell where neither sorrow nor sighing nor sifting can come any more—where the inhabitants shall not say, 'I am sick,' for those that dwell there are forgiven their iniquities, and God shall wipe away all tears from their eyes.

## 26 June

And he cometh unto the disciples, and findeth them asleep, and saith unto Peter, What, could ye not watch with me one hour?
*Matthew 26:40*

How blessed, then, to come into Gethsemane and there to deal in prayer and supplication with that same will of God with which Jesus was so sorrowfully yet so faithfully concerned. You come to give yourself unto the Lord, to surrender your soul and body and love and service to the God of salvation. You do so in Gethsemane. You do so with express reference, in the prayer of faith, to that will of God which Jesus came to do, and for the doing of which a body was prepared him. You learn the topic of your prayer in this garden of the Lord's agony. You lay hold on the will of God and surrender yourself to him. Be assured it is a time of acceptance. Your surrender is accepted in deed and in truth. The Lord cannot reject what is his own, and by this will of God you are sanctified, separated to him as his own, whom he cannot disallow. For the Lord knoweth them that are his.

Is this comfort too high for you? Is it, as it were, meat too strong for thee, O meek and contrite soul, who art in thine own estimation no better than a babe in Christ—glad couldst thou but realise that even that blessed state and character are thine? Still we say to you, come here into Gethsemane and learn from Jesus to pray concerning this same will of God with which all his prayer is conversant.

## 27 June

Watch and pray, that ye enter not into temptation: the spirit indeed is willing, but the flesh is weak.
*Matthew 26:41*

Come, in like manner, to Gethsemane. Come, see the place where the Lord prayed! Here he prayed with supplications and strong crying and tears, wrestling even unto blood. True, he is not here. He is ascended as he said. And his prayers now are glorified, even as his person is. But still, even as the grave is sweetened with the fragrant savour of his burial, and the believer's body there shall rest, still united to Christ, till the resurrection, so now when you enter

Gethsemane, is it not fragrant with the savour and the success of him whose strong crying and tears Gethsemane witnessed? And may you not here continue instant in prayer, united to and in communion with him, and having fellowship in the prayer of him who was here as your forerunner? For in leading you forth as his own sheep, he ever goeth before you. In Gethsemane he goeth before you in prayer. He seeks to associate you there in prayer with himself, that so your failure or success may all rest on his responsibility.

Wilt thou not, O my soul, agree with the suppliant sufferer, thy Saviour, in this most blessed proposal to watch and pray with him? Oh, why shouldest thou refuse? For how great shall be thy gain! Thy prayer now placed on the same footing with his, resting on the same promise and covenant, embracing the self-same theme, cast in the same mould, directed to the same aim, prompted by the same Spirit of the Son crying, Abba Father, and risked upon the same destiny and issue: your prayer with his, bound up and identified with his, cannot but be heard, as his was heard in that he feared.

## 28 June

> And while he yet spake, lo, Judas, one of the twelve, came, and with him a great multitude with swords and staves, from the chief priests and elders of the people.
> *Matthew 26:47*

Pause then, O my soul, and contemplate and improve this great sight of the Substitute and Saviour of sinners arrested and surrendering to the hands of justice. It is sin that makes him liable to this arrest, and it is the wages of sin—it is death—that pursues him relentlessly unto the end.

And how, O sinful soul, shalt thou escape? If these things be done in the green tree, what shall be done in the dry? If this judgment and arrest begin on the Son of God, how shalt thou be allowed to go at large? Thy sins are many: they are legion. Each one of them has power to awaken a relentless prosecutor, who will never slumber till he hail thee to the bar and judgment seat of God. All may be smooth and quiet with thee now, but be sure thy sin will find thee out. And then, whither wilt thou flee? 'Whither shall I go from thy Spirit, or whither shall I flee from thy presence? If I ascend into heaven thou art there; if I make my bed in hell, behold thou art there. If I take the wings of the morning and dwell in the uttermost parts of the sea, even there thy right hand shall hold me. If I say, surely the darkness shall cover me, even the night shall be light about me. For there is not a word upon my tongue, but lo, O Lord, thou knowest it altogether. Thou hast beset me behind and before, and laid thine hand upon me.'

# 29 June

> And while he yet spake, lo, Judas, one of the twelve, came, and with him a great multitude with swords and staves, from the chief priests and elders of the people.
> *Matthew 26:47*

O my trembling soul, thou hast no escape from this warrant that is gone out from the Judge of all against thee. Though thou dig into hell, thence will his hand take thee. Though thou climb up to heaven, thence will he take thee down. Though thou hide thyself on the top of Carmel, he will search and take thee out thence. And though thou be hid from his sight in the bottom of the sea, thence would he command the serpent to arrest and bring thee forth into his sight. Yea, in vain, even in the awful end, wouldst thou call upon the mountains and the rocks to fall on thee and hide thee from the face of the Lamb.

Men and brethren, what shall we do? Agree with thine adversary quickly, whiles thou art in the way with him, lest at any time the adversary deliver thee to the judge, and the judge deliver thee to the officer, and thou be cast into prison.

But thou art guilty. Thy conscience tells thee so, and tells thee that thou oughtest to be arrested and hailed to the bar of God. Yea, verily! But is there not a shield? Is there not a plea? Might it not be well to arrest thyself and surrender? Oh, that I could but get the counsel of the Wonderful, the Counsellor, you say! Oh, that I might live in the redemption and freedom purchased by the arrested, the self-surrendered Substitute! Oh, that I were verily among the number whom Jesus shields with that omnipotent demand, 'Let these go their way.'

## 30 June

> For I know that in me (that is, in my flesh,) dwelleth no good thing: for to will is present with me; but how to perform that which is good I find not.
> *Romans 7:18*

Who among us feel painfully a law in our members warring against the law of our mind, and bringing us into captivity to the law of sin which is in our members, so that we cry, as the Lord is witness, 'O wretched man that I am! Who shall deliver me from the body of this death?' Let us thank God through Jesus Christ our Lord. Let us bear in mind that he was bound for us, but was a captive only that he might lead captivity captive.

Let us seek grace more and more that, being delivered out of the hands of our enemies, we may serve God in holiness and in righteousness all the days of our life. Let us wrestle against that law of sin and death that would lead us into bondage. Let us never yield, but vindicate our freedom as freely forgiven and fully justified and unchangeably adopted children of God through the work and merit of him who was fettered that ye might be free. And let us anticipate the time of our full deliverance into the glorious liberty of the sons of God, when Jesus shall come again and verify in its ultimate and grandest form his glorious triumph, as with his risen saints and all his angels he answereth for the last time the call of Israel: 'Arise, O Lord, thou and the ark of thy strength: let thine enemies be scattered and let them that hate thee flee before thee,' while once more, yea, more gloriously than ever, the chariots of the Lord shall be twenty thousand, thousands of angels, the Lord among them as on Sinai and the host of the redeemed, from all ages and dispensations shall exclaim, 'O Lord, thou hast ascended on high; thou hast carried captivity captive.'

# July

JOHN DUNCAN (1796–1870), also known as 'Rabbi' Duncan, was born in Aberdeen and attended university in that city. While studying theology, he questioned the most fundamental truths of the Christian faith and became a practical atheist. César Malan, the famous preacher from Geneva, visited Scotland in 1826, and his conversations with John Duncan were the means of the young Scotsman's conversion.

In 1830 John Duncan was appointed to preach in the rural charge of Persie in Perthshire. In the summer of the following year he was engaged as the English-speaking assistant to the minister of Duke Street Gaelic Chapel in Glasgow, where his work was to deliver an English lecture every Sabbath afternoon. He was formally ordained to the ministry in 1836 when he became the first minister of the Milton Parish Church in the Cowcaddens area of Glasgow, a church which was built for him through the liberal donations of friends who appreciated his profound preaching. Five years later he became the first Scottish missionary among the Jews when he was sent to Budapest, Hungary.

John Duncan had a great flair for languages and after the Disruption in 1843 he was appointed as Professor of Oriental Languages at New College, Edinburgh. His love for Hebrew and his lifelong interest in the Jewish people led to him being familiarly called 'Rabbi' Duncan. His annual speeches about the Mission to the Jews were regarded as a highlight of the General Assembly of the Free Church.

Duncan was not only a man of great learning but also of intense devotion. His preaching, and especially his Communion sermons and addresses, were highly valued.

## Sources of daily readings

July 1–12: James S. Sinclair (ed.), *Rich Gleanings after the Vintage from 'Rabbi' Duncan* (London, 1925).

July 13–31: David Brown (ed.), *The late Rev. John Duncan, LL.D. In the pulpit and at the communion table* (Edinburgh, 1874; reprinted as *Pulpit and Communion Table* by Free Presbyterian Publications, 1969).

## Biography

David Brown, *Life of the Late John Duncan, D.D.* (Edinburgh, 1872; reprinted as *The Life of Rabbi Duncan* by Free Presbyterian Publications, 1986).

# 1 July

We have thought of thy lovingkindness, O God, in the midst of thy temple.
*Psalm 48:9*

The subject of the meditation was the lovingkindness of Jehovah. That is an ample subject. We cannot at present even look at it all. Let us, in order to enter into what is meant, look at that bright display of it which is brought by the circumstances immediately under our view, that great and wondrous lovingkindness which we are about to commemorate. The death of the Lord we are about to show forth, and in that death there are many subjects of believing contemplation. Let us look at it in this one: his death is lovingkindness. It is the lovingkindness of God the Father, the Son, and the Holy Ghost.

It is the lovingkindness of Jehovah the Father. 'Herein is love, not that we loved God, but that he loved us, and sent his Son to be the propitiation for our sins.' In that wondrous verse there are many subjects. It is love to those who did not love: Jehovah's love is wondrous because it is to those who did not love. And wondrous it is in wisdom, as maintaining the honour of all his perfections and of his violated law, giving his Son to be the propitiation, thus at once loving sinners, the violators of the law, and yet honouring and maintaining all the interests of that holy, just and good law, the emblem and expression of his own holy, just and good nature.

We see here, then, justice and equity maintained, but the main expression—what is presented to us especially—is love.

# 2 July

And as it is appointed unto men once to die, but after this the judgment: so Christ was once offered to bear the sins of many; and unto them that look for him shall he appear the second time without sin unto salvation.
*Hebrews 9:27–28*

The first appearing of Christ, *with* sin, and his second appearing, *without* sin, unto salvation. This is the other pair of things with which the Apostle compares death and judgment. '*As* it is appointed unto men once to die, but after this the judgment: *so* Christ was once offered to bear the sins of many; and unto them that look for him shall he appear the second time, without sin, unto salvation.' Amidst all the deaths that have taken place, there is one that stands out distinct and pre-eminent above them all.

*We* die, because we are sinners. We die, because we sinned in the first of men. We die, having added innumerable actual transgressions, sin having abounded. But there died one who was holy, harmless, undefiled, and separate from sinners, one who did no violence, neither was deceit found in his mouth, one of whom the heavenly Father proclaimed, 'This is my beloved Son, in whom I am well pleased,' and one who was not involved in the guilt of Adam's transgression, for he came not by ordinary generation. 'Forasmuch as the children are partakers of flesh and blood, he also himself likewise took part of the same.' 'God sent forth his Son, made of a woman.' But he came not—he did not enter, as we do—by connection with Adam, for he had divine being eternally. He existed from eternity as the coequal Son in the bosom of the Father. Nor did he take our flesh by ordinary generation, and so incur the guilt of our flesh by ordinary Adam's first sin.

# 3 July

> Watch and pray, that ye enter not into temptation: the spirit indeed is willing, but the flesh is weak.
> *Matthew 26:41*

After supper is ended comes the garden, Gethsemane's garden. And from it comes a lesson, a lesson which is best learned just in Gethsemane itself, where its strongest motives are. 'Watch and pray, that ye enter not into temptation.'

Jesus, when about to enter this garden, took three of the disciples with him: Peter and James and John. He told them before he took a few steps forward from them, 'My soul is exceeding sorrowful, even unto death,' and wanted them to watch till he came. And all the three fell asleep. We are not to be harder on them than Jesus himself was concerning this. He said, 'The spirit indeed is willing, but the flesh is weak.'

It pleased the Lord to bruise him, to put him to grief, and the very atmosphere perhaps, with the excessive sorrow after great joy and long watching, overcame them. They had not forsaken him, as they did afterwards, but still they were not awake. He sought comforters; he sought them to watch and pray, but they did not. Oh, what reliance shall we put on the intercession of the saints when Peter and James and John fall asleep, while our Lord goes alone to bear our burden and drink our cup? Not the zeal of Peter, not the integrity of James, and not the bright, burning, pure love of John, can keep them awake.

'Watch and pray, that ye enter not into temptation.' Temptation will come after the Supper—it came to Judas, and it came to Peter—and we are called to watch and pray that we enter not into temptation.

# 4 July

> And for this cause he is the mediator of the new testament, that by means of death, for the redemption of the transgressions that were under the first testament, they which are called might receive the promise of eternal inheritance.
> *Hebrews 9:15*

'Broken for you', sinner: for you. And why? 'He is therefore the mediator of the new covenant, that by means of death, for the redemption of the *transgressions* that were under the first covenant.' It is for transgressors. For transgressors, but all Jerusalem and all the nation were transgressors. It is for transgressors, but it was for John leaning on Jesus' bosom. It was for Peter to whom had been revealed these things. It was for all the others who had forsaken all and followed Jesus. For transgressors, but for *such* transgressors: for those who had received Jesus' words, and had known that he came out from God and believed that he had sent him. And not for those present only, but according to the prayer of intercession, 'for them also which shall believe on me through their word'.

What a feast is provided! It begins at Jerusalem and goes out to the ends of the earth, for 'Jerusalem which is above is free, which is the mother of us all'. 'In this mountain will the Lord of hosts make unto all people a feast of fat things.' And, as precious as it is, and as costly as it is, it required the mission, the incarnation, the obedience, and the perfecting of the obedience by the atoning death of the Son of God. It is given heartily. 'Eat, O friends; drink, yea, drink abundantly, O beloved!' Receive and be blessed, and let him who is at the head of the Table have the enjoyment of that privilege of which he tells us in the words preserved by Paul, 'It is more blessed to give than to receive.'

## 5 July

But my God shall supply all your need according to his riches in glory by Christ Jesus.
*Philippians 4:19*

My God shall supply all your need, all your wants. They are very great. The world could not supply all your wants. The world could supply none of them—at least, none of the greatest of them. All that supply would leave you poor and destitute. You have learned—defectively learned, but learned—that it would profit you nothing, though you were to gain the whole world, and lose your own soul. You have learned that the world is a poor world, and that it is not only poor, but that 'all that is in the world, the lust of the flesh, and the lust of the eyes, and the pride of life, is not of the Father, but is of the world'. You have lost it; you should realise that you have lost it. If it was counted gain for you, it is among the things which you have counted loss, the 'all things' which, that you might win Christ, and be found in him, you have lost. It passeth away, and the fashion thereof. Transitory world, let it go! World that is not of the Father, let it go! Count it loss; count the loss of it gain!

Now, may 'the Lord direct your hearts into the love of God, and into the patient waiting for Christ' and come, that ye may abound in love more and more one toward another and toward all men, to the end he may establish your hearts unblameable and unreproveable before him in love.

## 6 July

Elect according to the foreknowledge of God the Father, through sanctification of the Spirit, unto obedience and sprinkling of the blood of Jesus Christ: Grace unto you, and peace, be multiplied.
*1 Peter 1:2*

What is this foreknowledge? Is it the foreknowledge of anything in God's elect, distinguishing them naturally from others? Nay, 'hath not the potter power over the clay, of the same lump to make one vessel to honour, and another unto dishonour?' Of the *same lump*. Is it the foreknowledge of what now distinguishes them? The foreknowledge of faith, and repentance, and perseverance to the end? Nay, the apostle Paul says such things as these: 'According as he hath chosen us in him before the foundation of the world, that we should be holy and without blame before him in love'; 'Whom he did foreknow, he also did predestinate to be conformed to the image of his Son.' God hath chosen his people to be holy, to be conformed to the image of his Son, we read, and therefore not in consequence of foreknowledge of the holiness, of the conformity. Not good works foreseen as the cause of election, because good works are declared to be the end of election: 'Good works which God hath before ordained that we should walk in them.' 'By grace are ye saved through faith; not of works, lest any man should boast.' Not *of* them, but *unto* them.

The foreknowledge of God, there, is just his scheme of redemption. God has not only chosen certain persons, but chosen them to be saved in a special way, commonly called the covenant of grace. No man—no unsanctified, disobedient man, unsprinkled with the blood of Jesus—may presume to go and read in God's secrets. God has not told the names of his elect to be saved. But he has told the name of one elect: the elect Saviour.

# 7 July

> To an inheritance incorruptible, and undefiled, and that fadeth not away, reserved in heaven for you.
> *1 Peter 1:4*

Children of God, what a Father you have got! What an elder brother! What an inheritance! What a lively hope!

Ye may well endure trials—ye may think it not strange even concerning fiery trials. Be not over cast down or over heavy. When in heaviness, seek to look in the direction of the Father and the risen Saviour and the inheritance. And so, if the heaviness be not gone, the great joy will support the heart, so as it will go gladly under a heavy load.

And as for others, are there those here that are fatherless, godless? For the godless are fatherless. They have a father, but, ah, what a father! 'Ye', said Christ to Christless Jews—and Christless Scotch people are the same, 'are of your father the devil.' A bad father! What inheritance have ye? What beauty hath it? What stamina hath it? What pure beauty is in it? What unfading bloom of excellence? How long will it last? Will you take your glory down to the grave with you, down below the grave into the lower places? A bad father! A bad inheritance! 'The wages of sin is death.'

And Christ sends the gospel. He who sent Paul, sends the gospel ministry and the gospel message to you. To what end? 'To open your eyes, and to turn you from darkness to light, and from the power of Satan unto God; that you may obtain the forgiveness of sins, and inheritance among all them that are sanctified through faith which is in Christ.'

# 8 July

> That the trial of your faith, being much more precious than of gold that perisheth, though it be tried with fire, might be found unto praise and honour and glory at the appearing of Jesus Christ.
> 1 Peter 1:7

Faith in Jesus Christ is precious faith—both the faith concerning Christ and the faith in Christ. The faith of a penitent, confiding heart, wrought by the renewal of the Holy Ghost, that faith is exceeding precious. It is precious in its author, being a divine production; it is precious in its object; it is precious in its fruits and effects. It is the principle of the Christian's life: 'The life that I live in the flesh I live by the faith of the Son of God.' It is the faith which contemplates the blessed light of God. It is the faith which, opening the mouth wide that God may fill it, tastes that God is gracious. It is the faith which, waiting on God and obtaining strength, mounts up with wings like eagles—runs and is not weary—and walks, and is not faint. Consider the glorious examples of it in the worthies of old, of which we read in Hebrews 11.

Now this faith is counterfeited by hypocrites and self-deceivers—they substitute other things for it. And true believers, the faith, as it is in them, is not only imperfect, but mixed with much error and with many evils. Taking the new man, the precious faith, as wrought by the Spirit of God, is pure gold, nothing but pure gold.

# 9 July

> Whom having not seen, ye love; in whom, though now ye see him not, yet believing, ye rejoice with joy unspeakable and full of glory.
> *1 Peter 1:8*

Do we love Jesus? Or do we not? What is the centre of our Christianity, considered objectively and subjectively?

Objectively, is it the Lord Jesus Christ himself? Are we acquainted with him? Have we ever heard—not with the external ear—not his voice personally, but his voice as the sheep hear it? 'His mouth is most sweet.' Is it so to us? Is it Jesus—not this thing or the other thing belonging to him, but Jesus himself—that we love, and them in their own place because of that belonging? Is it Jesus of Nazareth whom we love? The one whose life is written by the four evangelists, is it him whom we love? Whom we love, with a love that is given to none other—with a love which is which is peculiar to him as being what the Father is not to us and the Holy Spirit is not—God in our nature, in whom all our religious affections and all our human affections meet together harmoniously.

Subjectively. Having Christ for its object, what is our religion subjectively? Is it the heart's love? Is it notion? Is it trust? True, trust is important, but the question here is love. If it be faith, is it faith that worketh by love? In short, is our religion, being faith in Christ, the response of a loving heart, a heart at the same time blaming and mourning its own littleness, yet still the response of a loving heart to the living heart—to the love which in the heart of God and Christ hath a length and breadth and depth and height which surpass knowledge?

# 10 July

Receiving the end of your faith, even the salvation of your souls.
*1 Peter 1:9*

'The salvation of your souls.' Our souls are precious. They are ourselves—a principal part of ourselves, at least, and that on which the felicity or misery of the whole man depends. 'What is a man profited, if he gain the whole world, and lose his own soul? Or what shall a man give in exchange for his soul?' That is, suppose the man sold it, what would he buy it back again with? Some of you more advanced young people have been taught a little of bookkeeping. Here is a question for you to solve at your leisure. 'What is a man profited?' Profit and loss, and if the whole world be on the profit side and the soul lost on the loss side, strike the balance. Then if the soul be lost, what shall it be bought back again with? It is so precious.

But our souls are lost—our souls have been lost. If we see and feel it not in some becoming degree, some such as leads us above all things to value the Saviour of the lost, then we have no part in Christ, for 'he comes to seek and to save that which was lost' and none other. If I think I am not among the lost, Christ is no Saviour for me. But whether we believe it or not, our souls are lost.

## 11 July

> O taste and see that the LORD is good: blessed is the man that trusteth in him.
> *Psalm 34:8*

Have we tasted that the Lord is gracious? If we have, let us cleave close to him. Let us seek evermore that the Lord would give us this sweet, this nourishing, word of his grace and grace of his word.

There may be some here who have not tasted that the Lord is gracious; who yet in some way believe that the Lord is gracious; who don't deny the testimony of the Word or the testimony of Christians who have tasted that the Lord is gracious; who believe that Jesus is the Christ, that Christianity is true, that Christianity and Christians are a reality; who believe that the Lord is gracious and that there are men who have tasted the sweetness of his grace—but yet they themselves have never tasted that the Lord is gracious.

Now, how long, oh how long, shall the meat which is set before you on the gospel table, and which you are saying is very good—you are quite sure is very good—be left untested by you? Christ, you are sure, is very good, and you believe there are men who have tasted—men who, you cannot doubt, belong to the Lord, own his grace, and have tasted that the Lord is gracious. Well, why will you never do this: taste? You are there looking at the table, perhaps you are looking and thinking, 'Oh that I had it!' 'Whosoever will, let him take.' 'O taste and see that God is good.' May the Lord so incline and enable you!

# 12 July

> Jesus saith unto him, I am the way, the truth, and the life: no man cometh unto the Father, but by me.
> *John 14:6*

Jesus says, 'I am the way and the truth and the life.' This is a false and lying world. It is false in sentiment—putting evil for good, darkness for light—calling good evil, and evil good. It is also a world destitute of the truth in substance and reality. It is a vain world, and vanity is untrue, unreal.

Jesus is the truth—the truth of all right sentiment and of all reality. God in Christ is the very truth. Christ is the true God and eternal life. He is true and real man, holy man. He is true out and out. He is the incarnate, personal truth. Now, 'he grew up before Jehovah as a tender plant, and as a root out of a dry ground'. And truth thus sprang out of the earth when Jesus was born, and righteousness, looking down on truth, acquiesced. 'I do always the things that please him.' 'This is my beloved Son, in whom I am well pleased.'

'God is in Christ reconciling the world unto himself, not imputing their trespasses unto them.' Christ was standing in the room and stead of sinners. And what he was—what he was as the incarnate Son and Holy One of God—and what he did, was in the room and stead of sinners given to him, of sinners believing on him—was for us men and our redemption. Not for himself was he incarnate, for he had no need of the incarnation as the eternal Son of God; not for himself, but for a sinful world, did he spring out of the earth. Truth sprang out of the earth; and righteousness looks down from heaven on him, and through him on sinners believing on him.

## 13 July

*My beloved is mine, and I am his: he feedeth among the lilies.*
*Song of Solomon 2:16*

There is this want [lack] and that want. Sometimes it is, 'Oh, my little faith! Lord increase my faith,' and so of all other graces. But 'the Lord God is a sun and shield; the Lord will give grace and glory; no good thing will he withhold from them that walk uprightly'.

Ah, to live on the promise, we need to live by the promiser! Have you learned, or are you learning, what it is to be 'strong in the Lord, and in the power of his might', to be 'strong in the grace that is in Christ Jesus'? 'My beloved is mine, and I am his.' I cannot say much about my graces. If they are anything at all, I owe them to the Lord. Not unto us, not unto us, but unto thy name give glory. I have little in possession, but I leave all in the hands of my Lord. Though I have it not, I have it in him, because he has it and he is mine.

Well, believer, if your beloved is yours, he is yours with all he is and with all he has. And if you are his, all your wants are his in one sense: they are in one sense his possession, that he may supply all your need out of his riches in glory.

Ah, then, the beloved should be very precious, both because of what he is in himself and what he is to you. And then ought you to seek, that 'musing, the fire may burn', that with the highest affection you may say, 'My beloved is mine, and I am his.'

## 14 July

*Not by works of righteousness which we have done, but according to his mercy he saved us, by the washing of regeneration, and renewing of the Holy Ghost.*
*Titus 3:5*

We come with the guilt of our sin to Christ, who died for sins, the just for the unjust. And we come with our sinful nature to Christ, that our old man may be crucified, and that by the Spirit of life in Christ Jesus there may be found the new man.

Well, he receives us with all our guilt, and that is the worst in a certain point of view, for our sinfulness is removed when once our guilt is removed 'by the washing of regeneration and renewing of the Holy Ghost' by the Spirit of grace. But for the removal of our guilt, the incarnation, the humiliation, the obedience, the death of the Son of God was needed. Well, we come with all that. We come with our ignorance to him as Prophet, to be taught the lessons of his Word by the inward instruction of his Spirit, to be taught 'by his Word and Spirit'—not different things, but through his word *by* his Spirit. We come with all our guilt to him as Priest. And we come with all our remaining stubbornness to him as King, to rule and govern and mightily defend.

But while the love in this conjugal relation is a peculiar love—'Husbands, love your wives; wives, love your husbands'—it takes different directions in the place of husband and wife. Thus, the husband provides for the household. And so [does] Jesus. Therefore, married to the Lord, you don't live on your own fortune—you have nothing without him.

# 15 July

> My beloved spake, and said unto me, Rise up, my love, my fair one, and come away.
> *Song of Solomon 2:10*

Now, is he your beloved? Is he? Whether you can say, 'He is mine, and I am his,' or not, is he your beloved? What think you of the gospel offer of Christ? Does your heart lie with it? Does your desire lie with it? What think you of Christ freely offered in the gospel? If you cannot say, 'My Beloved is mine, and I am his,' do you say, 'Oh, he is lovely, and I cannot but love him'?

Is your heart with the gospel offer, yea or nay? 'Yes, I would like to hear it again.' Is your heart with him who is offered in the gospel? Do you like the offer of Christ? Or do you mean to use it? Or do you mean to let him stand a little longer, 'his head filled with dew, and his locks with the drops of the night', before you listen to him?

Do you want to be called a little longer? Do you want not to accept yet? Do you want to be neither off nor on? Ah, tempt him not! He hath dignity, and he is aware of his dignity. In every one of his gospel offers there is infinite condescension, and it is not because he is ignorant of his own worth that he has continued to beseech you so long, but because he is long-suffering, not willing that any should perish. And do you say, 'I'll try his long-suffering a little longer—I don't want to break with him, to give him nay, but I don't want to give him a direct yes'? Then how you abuse him! And if you should never have an offer of Jesus Christ more, would it be doing you any injustice?

# 16 July

> Though I speak with the tongues of men and of angels, and have not charity, I am become as sounding brass, or a tinkling cymbal.
> *1 Corinthians 13:1*

What a noble grace is love! God is love. What says he in the law? 'Thou shalt love.' What says he in the gospel? 'God so loved.' The apostle, though he determined to know nothing among the Corinthians save Jesus Christ, and him crucified, yet knew here how to preach many a good sermon from that simple text, 'Christ crucified'. He preached love, which is the sum of the gospel. From which this lesson is to be taken, 'If God so loved, we should love.'

Love—the greatest of all the graces, greater than faith, greater than hope. The believer has his eye on a heaven of rest; it is a heaven of love. Love is the fruit that grows on this stem of faith and hope. There shall be no need of faith's telescope where all is seen. There shall be no need of hope's flight where there is the possession of all conceivable good, the full enjoying of God to all eternity.

Hast thou this love? If thou hast it not, thou art nothing. Cast up what thou hast, but possess what thou mayest, if thou hast not love thou art nothing and art getting nothing. It is a poor life, that—to be nothing, and to be nothing profited. And if thou hast it not, what shall be the end of these things? Most assuredly, not that thou shalt be admitted into heaven, to turn God's heaven into another hell.

## 17 July

> Thy kingdom come. Thy will be done in earth, as it is in heaven.
> Matthew 6:10

Jesus in Gethsemane had taken the cup which the Father there put into his hands, after praying thrice, 'If this cup may not pass away from me, except I drink it, thy will be done.' The humanity of the incarnate God shrank from the taking of the cup, and yet obedientially he did take it—voluntarily, obedientially. Remember that though it was not the eternal Godhead that suffered but the humanity, it was a *person* and not a *nature* that suffered—God-man. Though it was not the Godhead, which cannot suffer, but the humanity, *he* was crucified in weakness, and he took the cup in great weakness. He fell on his face, and his sweat was like great drops of blood falling down to the ground. 'There appeared unto him an angel from heaven, strengthening him.'

O what a scene was that! What a wonderful mystery, when he took that cup! Ah, what a wondrous cry! 'Father, if it be possible!' His human soul looked at the possibilities to the omnipotent God, with whom all things are possible, and he said, 'If this be possible, if, with the salvation of the Church, it be possible; if the Church can be saved without my drinking this cup, let it pass from me.' If it had been possible to shun the cup, he would have shunned it. That was his will, if it were possible. But if not, 'Not my will, but thine, be done.'

## 18 July

And the Word was made flesh, and dwelt among us, (and we beheld his glory, the glory as of the only begotten of the Father,) full of grace and truth.
*John 1:14*

Oh, it is miserably little that I know of Jesus Christ—miserably little! But with this I sum up all the brightness of the beatific glory—the being with Christ where he is, and beholding his glory. Ah yes!

And so we see that, however different the life of sight in the glorified is from the life of faith in the justified, their principle is the same: beholding the glory of Christ—beholding the glory of Christ by faith here, and there beholding and saying that the half, that the thousandth part, had not been told us. This is the one thing which constitutes the sameness of grace and glory—the beholding of Christ.

Ah, what an object this is for faith to gaze on—his glory as exhibited in Scripture testimony! But what an object, when we gaze not only with unveiled face—for that the apostle says is the privilege of faith—but in immediate presence! And if the sight of Christ be so transforming here, what will the sight of Christ be there, through eternal ages! Ah, this is what will never tire a saint! This is what never tires the eye of faith now. Ah, it is tired sometimes, and what it then sees may appear very insipid even to him to whom Christ is most precious. But sight never will tire. His beauty, his excellence, his glory—an eternity does not waste it, so as it becomes insipid.

## 19 July

> For ye are bought with a price: therefore glorify God in your body, and in your spirit, which are God's.
> *1 Corinthians 6:20*

Whose are we? Are we our own still? Do we hold ourselves our own? Do we feel as if we were our own? Do we act as if we were our own? Whose will is the rule of our conduct? Our own or Christ's? Whose cause do we make ours? Our own or Christ's? On whose interests are we oftenest and most ardently looking? Our own or Christ's? Where would we be most willingly? Would we be where Christ is—here in his ordinances, or above in his personal presence? Or would we be where Christ is not? What troubles us most? Is it dishonour to Christ? What pleases us most? Is it glory given to Christ? What glory do we give to him? How do we give it? Is it with our spirits and with our bodies?

If we are not Christ's, whose are we? Our own? And if we be our own, we have a poor proprietor—a poor proprietor! What are we to make of ourselves? How are we to dispose of ourselves? How are we to get through life? 'Oh,' you say, 'that can be managed.' Well, but at death, and at the judgment seat, and throughout eternity, how are we to manage for ourselves, if we be our own? Ah, but if we should present the claim to be our own, there is one that will scoff and mock! 'Thine own! Poor deluded one! Thou art mine.' You have heard of 'the god of this world', of 'the spirit that now worketh in the children of disobedience'.

# 20 July

> How excellent is thy lovingkindness, O God! therefore the children of men put their trust under the shadow of thy wings.
> *Psalm 36:8*

'How excellent is thy lovingkindness, O God!' What meat is there for human souls to feed on? The lovingkindness of the Lord—on *that* a soul can feed. It is spiritual food for a human soul, that is a spirit. And the spirit born of the Spirit can and does feed on it. 'How excellent is thy lovingkindness, O God!' 'We will remember thy love more than wine.' 'Therefore the children of men put their trust under the shadow of thy wings.'

Preserved by thee, and loaded with temporal benefits, they not only receive them as being thy creatures, they receive them on the ground of Jehovah's faithfulness, and so put their trust in thee. 'They shall be abundantly satisfied with the fatness of thy house.' Thy house, the church of the living God.

Well, this church, this house of God, has its fatness: 'the fatness of thy house'. The kingdom of heaven is set forth under the parable of a feast. 'My oxen and fatlings are killed.' And Christ explains his meaning in words which I need but repeat to you. 'My flesh is meat indeed, and my blood is drink indeed.' You who have tasted therein, will you not all say, 'Amen! Indeed, indeed, indeed!'

'They shall be abundantly satisfied.' Well, is he not a bountiful God? Is he not bountiful in the provisions of his providence and in the provisions of his grace? And are we not a foolish people and unwise? And have we not cause for ourselves and others to take up these words, 'O that men would praise the Lord for his goodness, and for his wonderful works to the children of men!'

# 21 July

Who hath delivered us from the power of darkness, and hath translated us into the kingdom of his dear Son.
*Colossians 1:13*

Hath he drawn me? Hath he drawn thee? From what, to what? From what has he drawn? Has he drawn from this world and from its prince? All that he draws, he draws from that quarter—all fuel for the eternal burnings, and he draws to make pillars in the temple of his God. He draws, turning men 'from darkness to light, and from the power of Satan unto God, that they may receive forgiveness of sins, and inheritance among them which are sanctified'.

Has he drawn you? Drawn you out of darkness into light, out of Satan's kingdom into his own kingdom? Drawn you from the present evil world, drawn you from all its sentiments, likings and dislikings, wishes, efforts? Drawn you, not grudgingly, out of its society? A man may be drawn away out of the world into a convent, and carry the world with him in the shape of the love of it—his body drawn, his carcase drawn, his unwilling soul held back by the beloved world, to which he is crucified, not crucified to all its godless sentiments, to all its selfish ways, to all its vain honours, by being drawn to the Crucified.

Has he drawn you from yourself? That requires the most drawing force of any, to draw man from himself. Has he drawn you from all your own sentiments, from all your own willings, from all your virtues and from all your sins, from your religions and irreligions, from your fancied good and real evil—drawn you away from all?

# 22 July

But God forbid that I should glory, save in the cross of our Lord Jesus Christ, by whom the world is crucified unto me, and I unto the world.
*Galatians 6:14*

Have you nothing now but him? 'God forbid that I should glory, save in the cross of our Lord Jesus Christ.' The apostle did not say, 'God forbid that I should glory,' leaving out the cross of Christ from the causes of his glory, but 'God forbid that I should glory, *save* in the cross of our Lord Jesus Christ.' Mistake not that!

You say, 'We put it in among the causes of our glorying. God forbid that I should glory if it has not a place.'

That's not it. 'God forbid that I should glory, *save* in the cross of our Lord Jesus Christ.' So it is. 'By whom the world is crucified unto me, and I unto the world.' I was not crucified. Christ, Christ crucified, that's the object drawing—drawn to *it*—drawn away from all that is not Christ, drawn to Christ—drawn to him in his person, covenant engagements, work, gospel, law, grace, authority—drawn to him as your Prophet, and Priest, and King—as all your salvation and all your desire.

Are you being drawn? Drawn more and more? If Christ has begun drawing you, sure I am he has not finished drawing you. We are not so near Jesus as we should be, as we must be, as, if we are under his drawing, we shall be. All who have been drawn are being drawn still. And all who have been drawn and are being drawn are approximating, are coming to Christ. They have heard him who says, 'Come!' And they have set out to go to him, and they're going, going. And he is always saying, 'Come, come!' and they're coming and getting nearer.

## 23 July

*Then will I teach transgressors thy ways; and sinners shall be converted unto thee.*
*Psalm 51:13*

'Sinners shall be converted unto thee.' These words show that the conversion of a sinner is possible. Sinner, the lost God may be returned to, the averted face may be turned toward God. There is such a thing as the conversion of a sinner, else you must be eternally godless, and therefore eternally unholy and unhappy. True, by the way by which man went out he cannot come in again. God drove out the man from Eden, and placed cherubim with a flaming sword to keep the way. If you would come back to God in Eden, you must meet the cherub's sword. That would be death.

But 'who is this that engageth his heart to approach unto God?' There is one who met the sword, against whom Jehovah's sword awoke. He 'finished transgression, made an end of sin, and brought in everlasting righteousness', and he is now 'exalted to be a Prince and a Saviour, for to give repentance and forgiveness of sins'. He was sent to seek and to save, and he sent Paul, even as now he sends his servants, 'to open men's eyes, and to turn them from darkness unto light, and from the power of Satan unto God'. And he whom Jesus thus sent went and preached everywhere 'that men should repent, and bring forth fruits meet for repentance'. You see what the sinner needs is, back to God—back to God.

## 24 July

*Testifying both to the Jews, and also to the Greeks, repentance toward God, and faith toward our Lord Jesus Christ.*
*Acts 20:21*

You must be converted, or you cannot go to heaven, for while God could not bear to have your presence there, no more could you bear to have God's presence there. A holy God and an unholy sinner, an angry God and a guilty sinner, would not make a happy heaven together. It is not possible. You must be converted. You must go back to God. You must be restored to his favour. You must be renewed in his image. You must be employed in his service. You must find your happiness in him. God made you for that, and without that you cannot be blessed while you are man, but the fall will terminate in everlasting misery.

You were alienated from God by the fall, but that alienation is greatly strengthened. You were born in sin, brought forth in iniquity, but every day you continue in sin your natural alienation is increased, for if one sin destroyed man's moral nature, every sin strengthens man's depravity. And the longer you continue in sin, the less you care about going back to God, about being converted. You go to other things for happiness, and perhaps for a time you find it. Your depraved appetite getting that which is congenial to it, you are made happy for a moment. You can suppose a man ignorantly taking sweet poison, and being pleased with it, although it would destroy his body. So the sinner is pleased with the sweet poison of sin, although it will destroy his soul.

# 25 July

> Return, ye backsliding children, and I will heal your backslidings. Behold, we come unto thee; for thou art the LORD our God.
> *Jeremiah 3:22*

Why are sinners unwilling to be converted? One cause is the love of sin, the preference of sin to Christ, the preference of sin to pardon and salvation. Along with pardon, God says, 'A new heart also will I give you,' and the sinner does not want a new heart—he likes the old one better. God says, 'From all your idols and filthiness will I cleanse you,' and the sinner does not want to be so cleansed.

The love of sin: 'This is the condemnation, that light is come into the world, and men loved darkness rather than light, because their deeds were evil.' Light was in the world, and darkness came into it. But light again, brighter than the primeval, shone into the world. And why is it, then, that they who have gone away won't come back again? Because they love the darkness better. And that is the condemnation. It is not Adam's fall, but—if we perish under the gospel—it is that we preferred sin to salvation by Christ. There are other sufficient reasons for it, but this is one reason why we need not complain of Adam's fall, when we prefer continuance in the state into which it brought us to salvation by Christ.

Another cause is diabolical darkness. 'If our gospel be hid, it is hid to them that are lost, in whom the god of this world hath blinded the minds of them which believe not.'

# 26 July

> And therefore will the LORD wait, that he may be gracious unto you, and therefore will he be exalted, that he may have mercy upon you: for the LORD is a God of judgment: blessed are all they that wait for him.
> *Isaiah 30:18*

The sinner, when he turns to God in Christ, sees what? He sees a reconciled God. I don't say, at first, a God reconciled to *him*, but a reconciled God. He sees a God waiting to be gracious, and exalted to shew mercy. He sees a God who is a just God and a Saviour. He sees a God who, in wonderful wisdom, has devised and provided a way of escape, even a plan of salvation, in which his whole perfections—his holiness, justice, goodness, truth, and mercy—meet harmoniously in the pardoning of the chief of sinners.

Sinner, wilt thou turn? Wilt thou turn so far as to turn thy face to look on a reconciled God? Don't say, 'I cannot call him my God.' Ah, do not confound faith with assurance! Do not confound turning to God with what comes upon return to God, and comes more and more upon return to and close walking with God!

Will you seek to turn so as to behold the way into the holiest of all opened? Will you try to think wherein the dealing of God towards you, a sinner, distinguishes you from the devil, a sinner? Wherein is God's dealing with you, who have sinned like Satan, different from his dealing with Satan? With you it is not only a dealing of long-suffering, it is a dealing of extended grace. And will you turn so far as to look at that?

# 27 July

> Remember, O LORD, what is come upon us: consider, and behold our reproach.
> *Lamentations 5:21*

The conversion of a sinner unto God is a possible thing. It is a very difficult thing, but a possible thing. Of sinners, all away from God, there are degrees of sinfulness. Even while the latent depravity of mankind is complete, the growth of this root of bitterness is in some, more; in some, less. Yet so as the conversion of the least sinner is very difficult, and the conversion of the greatest sinner is possible. Of the least sinner [it is] so difficult, that it is only by omnipotent grace that it is possible. And therefore, from the very consideration that it is by omnipotent grace, the conversion of the chief of sinners is possible. Say not then, oh sinner, 'My conversion is impossible.' Say, 'My conversion is the alternative of my damnation. My damnation is inevitable if I am not converted, but my conversion, through God's grace, is a possible thing.' 'Sinners shall be converted unto thee.'

And here, if there is any one whose heart is so far turned as that he prefers conversion to damnation, then it is very likely that he will be struck with the difficulty of conversion. For he who truly prefers conversion to damnation is beginning to essay [attempt] conversion, and he who essays it finds its difficulty. No man knows that, as a mere theory, as a mere doctrine. But when a man tries conversion, when he essays obedience to the command of God, 'Make you a new heart', he finds that he cannot change his own heart. But then in that position there is encouragement from this, that whatever God may do with the sinner, 'sinners shall be converted'.

# 28 July

> Testifying both to the Jews, and also to the Greeks, repentance toward God, and faith toward our Lord Jesus Christ.
> Acts 20:21

Conversion is unto God. 'Sinners shall be converted *unto thee*.' Now, I suppose there is not a thing about conversion that sinners, even in some seriousness about complying with God's call to turn, are more apt to go astray upon than this, of conversion being unto God. Sinners convinced of sin find their need of conversion, and they endeavour to turn from sin to righteousness, from sin to duty, from their evil ways to good ways. That is very common, because it comes more home to natural conscience.

The knowledge of sin is by the law. Therefore, when the conscience is enlightened concerning sin, the sinner turns to the law. Nor do I speak of this with thorough disapprobation—far from it! And yet, those who essay it, if God has begun a work of grace in their souls, in the very attempt will find disappointment. In seeking to turn from sin unto duty, they will find this out, that 'the law is holy, and the commandment holy, and just, and good', but they are 'carnal, sold under sin'. And so they will be brought at last to this: 'Unless God interposes, I am lost. True, I am welcome back again; true, coming to God by Christ I shall be received—but I cannot.' The sinner first of all finds that he is insufficient for duty, then says, 'I will come to Christ,' but finds that he is as insufficient for that as for the other. He is so far brought off seeking to turn from sin unto duty, and then seeks to turn from sin unto Christ, when he finds himself just unable to do that.

# 29 July

> Testifying both to the Jews, and also to the Greeks, repentance toward God, and faith toward our Lord Jesus Christ.
> *Acts 20:21*

But, blessed be God! He is triune—Father, Son, and Holy Ghost. And so the sinner is brought to the need of a salvation altogether of God—of the Father in his eternal purpose and love, of the Son in his redeeming work, and of the Spirit as the applier of the redemption purchased by Christ. He is shut up to Jehovah, God. 'Sinners shall be converted *unto thee.*'

'Repentance unto life is a saving grace, whereby a sinner, out of a true sense of his sin, and apprehension of the mercy of God in Christ, doth, with grief and hatred of his sin, turn from it *unto God.*'[2] It is not said, 'doth turn from sin unto duty, from sin unto holiness,' but 'doth turn from it *unto God!*' When we turned from God, what was it to? To sin. And there is a sinner turning, and what is he to turn from? From sin. And what is he to turn unto? Unto God. It is a very solemn thing, that. But it was by turning from God that we turned to sin. And turn we as we like, till we turn to God we are godless. We turn from unconcern to concern—very good. We turn from thoughtlessness to careful thought—so far, exceedingly good.

---

[2] Part of the answer to Westminster Shorter Catechism question 87: *What is repentance unto life?*

But observe, we are in a godless state in the midst of that, and continue in a godless state till we turn to God.

## 30 July

*The voice of him that crieth in the wilderness, Prepare ye the way of the LORD, make straight in the desert a highway for our God.*
*Isaiah 40:3*

This is the voice of one crying in the wilderness, 'Prepare ye the way of Jehovah, make straight in the desert a highway for our God.' The hope of Israel had come at last. 'When the fulness of the time was come, God sent forth his Son, made of a woman, made under the law, to redeem them that were under the law.' And the voice which had sounded by the mouths of all the holy prophets which had been since the world began, now sounded with more distinctness and more emphasis, whilst with the finger John the precursor pointed and said, 'Behold the Lamb of God!'

Look in the first place at that which he takes away: 'the sin of the world'. The whole world is in the sin. It involves me, it involves thee, it involves each individual. But behold the Lamb of God! 'Behold the Lamb of God, which taketh away the sin of the world!' He was in the world, but he was not of the world. He comes into this world from the God against whom this world transgressed. And what may the world expect he comes to do? When God sent his Son into this sinful world, on what other errand could it be but to condemn the world? Ah no! 'God sent not his Son into the world to condemn the world, but that the world through him might be saved.' Oh, what a visitor! How rightly might John point to him! How rightly may we all listen to John's short but pithy declaration, 'Behold the Lamb of God, which taketh away the sin of the world!'

# 31 July

The next day John seeth Jesus coming unto him, and saith, Behold the Lamb of God, which taketh away the sin of the world.
*John 1:29*

We are by nature all of us of the world; we are all in the world's sin. We have been speaking about the world's sin, but oh, friends, it's *my* sin! I am one of this world, and I am in its sin. The world is all sinful together, but sinners must be saved out of it one by one. As regards the application of the salvation, sin is taken away from sinners of that world individually. You and I then, being sinners, and in the world's sin, we would need to be beholding the Lamb of God. And oh that we had these objects together in our minds this day, the one would not distract the other—the world's sin, and our individual sin, and the Lamb of God! Oh to see both! And to see the latter highest and brightest! To behold our sin, so that its dark face may commend to us the glorious one! To feel our own sin, that we, in reference to the world's sin in us individually, may find what has to be taken away, and look to him who does take sin away, that so sin may not be slight in our esteem, but the Lamb of God more precious—seeing his merit transcending our demerit infinitely and absorbing it! And accordingly, seeing and knowing and believing that in our case sin hath abounded, but that in the Lamb of God who taketh away the sin of the world grace hath superabounded; seeing that sin hath reigned unto death over us, but that grace reigns through righteousness unto eternal life by Jesus Christ our Lord.

# *August*

THOMAS CHALMERS (1780–1847) was born in Anstruther, Fife and attended lectures at the University of St Andrews. He was licensed as a preacher of the gospel in 1799 and in 1803 he was inducted to the village charge of Kilmany in Fife. Chalmers was an unconverted man when he began his ministry, but during his time in Kilmany he underwent a saving change and thereafter was foremost among the evangelical ministers of the Church of Scotland.

He was translated to the Tron Church, Glasgow, in 1815 and then in 1819 to the newly erected parish of St John's, also in that city. In these charges he dealt with religious and social issues that were particularly relevant in a large city. In 1823 he was appointed as Professor of Moral Philosophy at the University of St Andrews and five years later as Professor of Systematic Theology in Edinburgh.

Within the Church of Scotland Thomas Chalmers became a powerful leader of the 'Evangelical' party, which was mainly expressed in the fight against the so-called patronage laws. He was at the forefront of the process that culminated in the Disruption of 1843.

After the Disruption, he became the first Principal of the New College of the Free Church. Chalmers was a man of great intellectual ability and he proved to be particularly effective in many areas of church life. He is rightly counted among the great men in the history of the Scottish Church.

## Sources of daily readings

August 1–8: Thomas Chalmers, *Sermons preached in the Tron Church, Glasgow* (Glasgow, 1819).

August 9–25: Thomas Chalmers, *Lectures on the Epistle of Paul the Apostle to the Romans, Vols I, II and III* (Glasgow, 1842).

August 26–31: William Hanna (ed.), *Posthumous Works of the Rev. Thomas Chalmers, D.D., LL.D*, Vol. I, *Daily Scripture Readings, Vol. I*, (Edinburgh, 1852).

## Biography

William Hanna, *Memoirs of Thomas Chalmers, D.D., LL.D.* (Edinburgh, 1854).

## 1 August

For thus saith the LORD unto the house of Israel, Seek ye me, and ye shall live.
*Amos 5:4*

Though, to the natural eye, the doctrine of Christ be not plain, the way is plain by which we arrive at it. Though, ere we see the things of Christ, the Spirit must take of them and show them unto us, yet this Spirit deals out such admonitions to all that—if we follow them—he will not cease to enlarge and to extend his teaching till we have obtained a saving illumination. He is given to those who obey him. He abandons those who resist him.

When conscience tells us to read and to pray and to reform, it is he who is prompting this faculty. It is he who is sending through this organ the whispers of his own voice to the ear of the inner man. If we go along with the movement, he will follow it up by other movements. He will visit him who is the willing subject of his first influences by higher demonstrations. He will carry forward his own work in the heart of that man who, while acting upon the suggestions of his own moral sense, is in fact acting in conformity to the warnings of this kind and faithful monitor. So that the Holy Spirit will connect his very first impulses on the mind of that inquirer who, under the reign of earnestness, has set himself to read his Bible, and to knock with importunity at the door of heaven, and to forsake the evil of his ways, and to turn him to the practice of all that he knows to be right. The Spirit will connect these incipient measures of a seeker after Zion with the acquirement of wisdom and revelation in the knowledge of Christ.

# 2 August

> Then said one unto him, Lord, are there few that be saved? And he said unto them, Strive to enter in at the strait gate: for many, I say unto you, will seek to enter in, and shall not be able.
> *Luke 13:23–24*

Let it not be said, then, that because the doctrine of Christ is shrouded in mystery to the general eye of the world, it is such a mystery as renders it inaccessible to the men of the world. Even to them does the trumpet of invitation blow a certain sound. They may not yet see the arcana [mysterious things] of the temple, but they may see the road which leads to the temple. If they are never to obtain admission there, it is not because they cannot, but because they will not come to it. 'Ye will not come to me,' says the Saviour, 'that ye might have life.'

Reading and prayer and reformation, these are all obvious things. And it is the neglect of these obvious things which involves them in the guilt and the ruin of those who neglect the great salvation. This salvation is to be found of those who seek after it. The knowledge of God and of Jesus Christ, which is life everlasting, is a knowledge open and acquirable to all. And on the day of judgment, there will not be found a single instance of a man condemned because of unbelief, who sought to the uttermost of his opportunities, and evinced the earnestness of his desire after peace with God by doing all that he might have done, and by being all that he might have done and by being all that he might have been.

Be assured, then, that it will be for want of seeking if you do not find. It will be for want of learning, if you are not taught. It will be for want of obedience to the movements of your own conscience if the Holy Ghost, who prompts and who stimulates the conscience to all its movements, be not poured upon you in one large and convincing manifestation.

# 3 August

For there is one God, and one mediator between God and men, the man Christ Jesus.
*1 Timothy 2:5*

By putting the Mediator away from you—by reckoning on a state of safety and acceptance without him—what is the ground upon which, in reference to God, you actually put yourselves?

We speak not at present of the danger of persisting in such an attitude of independence—of it being one of those refuges of treachery in which the good man of the world is often to be found—of it being a state wherein peace, when there is no peace, lulls him by its flatteries into a deceitful repose. We are not at present saying how ruinous it is to rest a security upon an imposing exterior, when in fact the heart is not right in the sight of God and while the reproving eye of him who judgeth not as man judgeth is upon him, or how poisonous is the unction that comes upon the soul from those praises which, upon the mere exhibition of the social virtues, are rung and circulated through society.

But, in addition the danger, let us insist upon the guilt of thus casting the offered Mediator away from us. It implies, in the most direct possible way, a sentiment of the sufficiency of our own righteousness. It is expressly saying of our obedience that it is good enough for God. It is presumptuously thinking that what pleases the world may please the maker of it, even though he himself has declared it to be a world lying in wickedness.

# 4 August

And a man shall be as an hiding place from the wind, and a covert from the tempest; as rivers of water in a dry place, as the shadow of a great rock in a weary land.
*Isaiah 32:2*

There lieth a great gulf between God and the whole of this alienated world. And after looking round amongst all the men of all its generations, we may say, in the language of the text, that there is not a daysman [mediator] betwixt us who can lay his hand upon both.

What we aim at, as the effect all these observations, is that you should feel your only security to be in the revealed and the offered Mediator, that you should seek to him as your only effectual hiding place. He alone, in the whole range of universal being, is able to lay his hand upon you and shield yon from the justice of the Almighty, and to lay his hand upon God and stay the fury of the avenger. By him the deep atonement has been rendered. By him the mystery has been accomplished, which angels desired to look into. By him such a sacrifice for sin has been offered as that, in the acceptance of the sinner, every attribute of the divinity is exalted and the throne of the Majesty in the heavens, though turned into a throne of grace, is still upheld in all its firmness and in all its glory. Through the unchangeable priesthood of Christ the vilest of sinners may draw nigh and receive of that mercy which has met with truth, and of that peace which is in close alliance with righteousness. And without one perfection of the Godhead being surrendered by this act of forgiveness, all are made to receive a higher and more wondrous manifestation.

# 5 August

But not as the offence, so also is the free gift. For if through the offence of one many be dead, much more the grace of God, and the gift by grace, which is by one man, Jesus Christ, hath abounded unto many.
*Romans 5:15*

When no man could redeem his neighbour from the grave, God himself found out a ransom. When not one of the beings whom he had formed could offer an adequate expiation, then did the Lord of hosts awaken the sword of vengeance against his fellow. When there was no messenger among the angels who surrounded his throne that could both proclaim and purchase peace for a guilty world, then did God manifest in the flesh descend in shrouded majesty amongst our earthly tabernacles, and pour out his soul unto the death for us and purchase the church by his own blood. And bursting away from the grave which could not hold him, he ascended to the throne of his appointed mediatorship. And now he—the first and the last, who was dead and is alive, and maketh intercession or transgressors—is able to save to the uttermost all who come unto God through him. And standing in the breach between a holy God and the sinners who have offended him, he makes reconciliation and lays his hand upon them both.

But it is not enough that the Mediator should be appointed by God, he must be accepted by man. And to incite our acceptance he holds forth every kind and constraining argument. He casts abroad, over the whole face of the world, one wide and universal assurance of welcome. 'Whosoever cometh unto me shall not be cast out.' 'Come unto me all ye who labour and are heavy laden, and I shall give you rest.' Where sin hath abounded, grace hath much more abounded.

# 6 August

Wherefore he is able also to save them to the uttermost that come unto God by him, seeing he ever liveth to make intercession for them.
*Hebrews 7:25*

The path of access to Christ is open and free of every obstacle which kept fearful and guilty man at an impracticable distance from the jealous and unpacified Lawgiver. He hath put aside the obstacle, and now stands in its place. Let us only go in the way of the gospel and we shall find nothing between us and God but the author and finisher of the gospel. On the one hand, Christ beckons to him the approach of man, with every token of truth and of tenderness, and on the other hand, he advocates our cause with God, and fills his mouth with arguments, and pleads that very atonement which was devised in love by the Father, and with the incense of which he was well pleased. And as the fruit of the travail of his soul, Christ claims all who put their trust in him, and thus, laying his hand upon God, turns him altogether from the fierceness of his indignation.

But Jesus Christ is something more than the agent of our justification: he is the agent of our sanctification also. Standing between us and God, he receives from him of that Spirit which is called the promise of the Father, and he pours it forth in free and generous dispensation on those who believe in him.

Without this Spirit there may, in a few of the goodlier specimens of our race, be within us the play of what is kindly in constitutional feeling. But the utter irreligiousness of our nature will remain as entire and as obstinate as ever. The alienation of our desires from God will persist with unsubdued vigour in our bosoms, and sin, in the very essence of its elementary principle, will still lord it over the inner man with all the power of its original ascendancy.

# 7 August

We love him, because he first loved us.
1 John 4:19

As soon as God's love of kindness [kind love] is believed, so soon [then] the love of gratitude springs up in the heart of the believer. As soon as man gives up his fear and his suspicion of God and discerns him to be his friend, so soon does he render him the homage of a willing and affectionate loyalty.

There is not a man who can say, 'I have known and believed the love which God hath to us,' who cannot say also, 'I have loved God because he first loved me.' There has not, we will venture to affirm, been a single example in the whole history of the church of a man who had a real faith in the overtures of peace and of tenderness which are proposed by the gospel, and who did not at the same time exemplify this attribute of the Christian faith, that it 'worketh by love'.

It is thus that the faith which recognizes God—as God in Christ reconciling the world unto himself—lies at the turning point of conversion. In this way, and in this way alone, is there an inlet of communication open to the heart of man for that principle of love to God, which gives all its power and all its character to the new obedience of the gospel. So soon as a man really knows the truth—and no man can be said to know what he does not believe—this truth will enthrone a new affection in his bosom, which will set him free from the dominion of all such affections as are earthly and rebellious.

# 8 August

*But ye, beloved, building up yourselves on your most holy faith, praying in the Holy Ghost.*
*Jude 20*

This suggests a practical direction to Christians for keeping themselves in the love of God. They must keep themselves in the habit and in the exercise of faith. They must hold fast that conviction in their minds, the presence of which is indispensable to the keeping of that affection in their hearts. This is one of the methods recommended by the apostle Jude when he tells his disciples to build themselves up on their most holy faith.

His direction to you is both intelligible and practicable. Keep in view the truths which you have learned. It is just by holding these fast and by building yourself up on their firm certainty that you preserve this affection. Any man versant in [familiar with] the matters of experimental religion knows well what it is when a blight and a barrenness come over the mind and when, under the power of such a visitation, it loses all sensibility towards God. There is, at that time, a hiding of his countenance, and you lose your hold of the manifestation of that love wherewith God loved the world when he sent his only begotten Son into it, that we might live through him.

You will recover a right frame, when you recover your hold of this consideration. If you want to recall the strayed affection to your heart, to recall to your mind the departed object of contemplation, to reinstate the principle of love in your bosom, reinstate faith and it will work by love. It is got at through the medium of believing and trusting. Nor do we know a more summary direction—and, at the same time, a more likely direction—for living a life of holy and heavenly affection, than that you should live a life of faith.

# 9 August

For God, who commanded the light to shine out of darkness, hath shined in our hearts, to give the light of the knowledge of the glory of God in the face of Jesus Christ.
*2 Corinthians 4:6*

When I think of Christ, and think of him as one who has poured out his soul unto the death for me, I feel a confidence in drawing near unto God. When employed in this contemplation, I look to him as a crucified Saviour. But without keeping mine eye for a single moment from off his person—without another exercise of mind, than that by which I look unto Jesus, simply and entirely, as he is set forth unto me—I also behold him at one time as an exalted Saviour, and at another time as a commanding Saviour, and at another time as a strengthening Saviour. In other words, by the mere work of faith in Christ, I bring my heart into contact with all those motives and all those elements of influence which give rise to the new obedience of the gospel.

When the veil betwixt me and the Saviour is withdrawn, when God shines in my heart with the light of the knowledge of his own glory in the face of his Son, when the Spirit taketh of the things of Christ and showeth them unto me, and I am asked which of the things it is that is most fitted to arrest a convicted sinner in the midst of his cries and prayers for deliverance, I would say that it was Christ lifted up on the cross for his offences and pouring out the blood of that mighty expiation, by which the guilt of them all is washed away. This is the rock on which he will build all his hopes of acceptance before God.

# 10 August

Being justified freely by his grace through the redemption that is in Christ Jesus.
*Romans 3:24*

To be justified, here, is not to be *made* righteous but to be *counted* righteous. To be justified by faith expresses to us the way in which an imputed righteousness is made ours. Faith is that act of the recipient by which he lays hold of this privilege. It contributes no more to the merit that is reckoned to us than the hand of the beggar adds any portion to the alms that are conferred upon him. When we look to the righteousness that is made ours by faith, it is well to go altogether out of ourselves, and not to mix up any one personal ingredient—whether of obeying or of believing—with it. The imagination of a merit in faith brings us back to legal ground again, and exposes us to legal distrust and disquietude. In the exercise of faith, the believer's eye looks out on a cheering and a comforting spectacle, and from the object of its external contemplation it fetches homeward all the encouragement which it is fitted to convey.

In a former verse of this epistle, we are said to be justified by grace. It was in love to the world that the whole scheme of another righteousness was devised and executed and offered to man as his plea, both of acquittal and of reward before the God whom he had offended. In another place of the New Testament we read of being justified by Christ, even by him who brought in that righteousness which is unto all and upon all who believe.

# 11 August

Therefore we are buried with him by baptism into death: that like as Christ was raised up from the dead by the glory of the Father, even so we also should walk in newness of life.
*Romans 6:4*

My brethren, The best practical receipt [direction] I can give you for becoming holy is to be steadfast in the faith. Believe that Christ's righteousness is your righteousness, and his graces will become your graces. Believe that you are a pardoned creature, and this will issue in your becoming a purified creature. Take hold of the offered gift of heaven, and you will not only enter after death on the future reversion of heaven's triumphs and heaven's joys, but before death—nay even now—you will enter upon the participation of heaven's feelings and the practice of heaven's moralities.

Go in prayer with the plea of Christ's atonement and his merits, and state in connection with this plea that what you want is that you be adorned with Christ's likeness, and that you be assisted in putting on the virtues which signalised him. And you will find the plea to be omnipotent, and the continued habit of such prayer, applied to all the exigencies of your condition, will enable you to substantiate the example of your Saviour, throughout all the varieties of providence and of history.

In a word, faith is the instrument of sanctification. And when you have learned the use of this instrument, you have learned the way to become holy upon earth now, as well as the way to become eternally happy in heaven hereafter. The believing prayer that God will aid you in this difficulty and counsel you in this perplexity, and enable you to overcome in this trial of charity and patience, and keep up in your heart the principle of godliness amid the urgency of all those seducing influences by which you are surrounded—this you will find to be the sure stepping stone to a right acquittal of yourself in all the given circumstances of your condition in the world.

## 12 August

> Likewise reckon ye also yourselves to be dead indeed unto sin, but alive unto God through Jesus Christ our Lord.
> *Romans 6:11*

When a sinner is bidden to reckon himself dead unto sin, and this phrase is understood personally, he is bidden to reckon himself a saint—to reckon what is not true—and surely this is not the way of causing him to be a saint. But when he is bidden to reckon himself dead unto sin, and this phrase is understood forensically, he is bidden look upon himself as a partaker with Christ in all the privileges and immunities of him on whom the sentence is already discharged and gone by, and to whom, therefore, there is no more condemnation.

But it may be said, might not this be an untruth also? Do I read anywhere in the Bible of Christ dying for me in particular? The apostle is speaking to his converts when he says, 'Reckon yourselves dead unto sin.' But is it competent to address any one individual at random, to reckon himself in this blessed condition of freedom from a penalty, that Christ hath intercepted and absorbed in behalf of all who believe on him? Might not he, in so reckoning, be as effectually working himself up into the belief of a delusive imagination, as if he reckoned he was a new creature—while all the habits and tendencies of the old man still remained with him, in full and unabated operation?

## 13 August

> Likewise reckon ye also yourselves to be dead indeed unto sin, but alive unto God through Jesus Christ our Lord.
> *Romans 6:11*

My brethren, it is no where said in the Bible that Christ died so for me in particular, as that by his simple dying the benefits of his atonement are mine in possession. But it is everywhere said in the Bible that he so died for me in particular, as that by his simple dying, the benefits of his atonement are mine in offer. They are mine if I will. Such terms as 'whosoever' and 'all' and 'any' and 'ho, every one' bring the gospel redemption specifically to my door. And there it stands for acceptance as mine in offer, and ready to become mine in possession on my giving credit to the word of the testimony.

The terms of the gospel message are so constructed that I have just as good a warrant for reckoning myself dead unto sin as if, instead of the announcement that God hath set forth Christ to be a propitiation for the sins of the world through faith in his blood, I had been the only sinner in the world, or I had been singled out by name and by surname and it was stated that God had set forth Christ a propitiation for the sins of me individually, through faith in his blood. The act of reckoning myself dead unto sin through Christ is just the act of receiving the truth of Christ's declaration—according to the terms of the declaration.

## 14 August

For if we have been planted together in the likeness of his death, we shall be also in the likeness of his resurrection: knowing this, that our old man is crucified with him, that the body of sin might be destroyed, that henceforth we should not serve sin.
*Romans 6:5–6*

Mark the apostle's receipt [directions] for holiness. It is not that you reckon yourself already pure, but it is that you reckon yourself already pardoned. It is not that you feel as if the fetters of corruption have as yet been struck off, but that you feel as if altogether lightened and released from the fetters of condemnation, and that you may go forth in the peace and joy of a reconciled creature. And somehow or other this, it would appear, is the way of arriving at the new spirit and the new life of a regenerated creature.

And how it should fall with the efficacy of a charm [delightful object] on a sinner's ear, when told that the first stepping stone towards that character of heaven after which he has been so hopelessly labouring, is to assure himself that all the guilt of his past ungodliness is now done away!—that the ransom of iniquity is paid and that, by a death the pains of which were ever felt, the penalties of that law he so oft has broken shall never reach him! It is indeed levelling the mountains and making the crooked paths straight when such a high way of access is thrown across the gulf of separation that is between sin and sacredness. And never, my brethren, will this transition be made good—never will the sinner know what it is to taste of spiritual joys or to breathe with kindred delight in a spiritual atmosphere—till, buried in another's death and raised in another's righteousness than his own, he can walk with the confident peace of one who knows that he is safe, under the secure and ample canopy of the offered Mediatorship.

# 15 August

> Let not sin therefore reign in your mortal body, that ye should obey it in the lusts thereof.
> *Romans 6:12*

This representation of a believer's state upon earth is in accordance with Scripture. We find the apostle stating that the flesh lusteth against the spirit and the spirit against the flesh, and in such a way too as that the man cannot do what he would. He would serve God more perfectly. He would render him an offering untinctured by the frailty of his fallen nature. He would rise to the seraphic love of the upper paradise, and fain be able to consecrate to the Eternal the homage of a heart so pure that no earthly feculence [dirt] shall be felt adhering to it. But all this he cannot do! And why? Because of a drag that keeps him, with all his soaring aspirations, among the dust of a perishable world. There is a counterpoise of secularity within, that at least damps and represses the sacredness, and it is well that it does not predominate over it. His secularity belongs to the old nature, being so very corrupt that Paul says of it, 'In me, that, in my flesh, there dwelleth no good thing.'

There is a law, then, which warreth against the law of our mind, even while that mind is delighting inwardly in the law of God. The conflict is so exceedingly severe that even they who have the first fruits of the Spirit groan inwardly while waiting for the redemption of the body and for a translation into the glorious liberty of the children of God.

## 16 August

> Neither yield ye your members as instruments of unrighteousness unto sin: but yield yourselves unto God, as those that are alive from the dead, and your members as instruments of righteousness unto God.
> Romans 6:13

Be assured, my brethren, that in proportion to the strength and the simplicity of your determination for God will be the clearness of your Christianity, and the comfort attendant on all its hopes and all its promises. It is the man whose eye is single, whose whole body shall be full of light.

You complain of darkness, do you? See that there be not a want of perfect oneness and willingness and sincerity as to the total yielding of yourself unto God. The entanglement of one wrong and worldly affection may mar your purposes. The influence of one forbidden conformity may do it. To the right following of Christ, there must be the forsaking of all. He must be chosen as the alone master. Nor will he accept of a partial yielding up of yourselves. It must be an entire and unexcepted yielding. Nor is there anything so likely as the doublings [duplicity] of a wavering and undecided purpose to wrap the gospel in obscurity and throw a darkening shroud over all that truth which ministers peace and joy to the believer's soul.

See that in yielding yourselves unto God it be perfect surrender that you make. See that you give yourself wholly over to his service. I am not asking at present how much you can do, but go to the service with the feeling that your all is due and with the honest intention and desire that all shall be done.

# 17 August

> For sin shall not have dominion over you: for ye are not under the law, but under grace.
> *Romans 6:14*

Compare the promise that sin shall not reign over you with the precept of two verses ago, 'Let not sin reign over you,' and it will throw light on a very interesting connection, even on the way in which the precepts of the gospel and the promises of the gospel stand related the one with the other. The promise does not supersede the precept. 'I will give you a new heart and a new spirit,' he says in one place; 'Make you a new heart and a new spirit,' he says in another. 'God worketh in you both to will and to do,' in one place; 'Work out your own salvation,' in another.

It is precisely in the same way that he bids the man of withered hand stretch it forth. The man could not, unless power had been given, but he made the attempt. And he found the power. The attempt, or an act of obedience on the part of the man, was indispensable. The power, or an act of bestowment on the part of God, was also indispensable. They both met, and the performance of the bidden movement was the result of it. Had the man made the attempt without the power, there would have been no stretching forth, or had the man got the power and not made the attempt, there would have been as little of stretching forth. It as the concurrence of the one with the other at the instant that gave rise to the doing of the thing which was required of him.

## 18 August

> But now being made free from sin, and become servants to God, ye have your fruit unto holiness, and the end everlasting life.
> *Romans 6:23*

There are some who are positively afraid of putting forth their hand on the work of the commandments at all till they are qualified for the service of God on sound and evangelical principles. Now, in every case it is right to be always doing what is agreeable to the will of God. There may be a mixture at first of the spirit of bondage. There may be a remainder and taint of the leaven of legalism. There may be so much of nature's corrupt ingredient in it at the outset, that the apostle would say of these babes in Christ who had just set forth on their new career, 'I speak unto you, not as unto spiritual, but as unto carnal.' Yet still it is good to give yourselves over, amid all the crude [unpolished] and embryo and infant conceptions of a young disciple, to the direct service of God. Break loose from your iniquities at this moment! Turn to all that is palpably on the side of God's law! Struggle your way to the performance of what is virtuous, through all those elements of obscurity and disorder which may fluctuate long in the bosom of a convert!

Do plainly what God bids, and on the direct impulse, too, of God's authority, and the fruit of your thus entering upon his service will be the perfecting at length of your own holiness—such a holiness as shall be without spot and wrinkle—purified from the flaw of legal bondage or of mercenary selfishness.

# 19 August

> Wherefore, my brethren, ye also are become dead to the law by the body of Christ; that ye should be married to another, even to him who is raised from the dead, that we should bring forth fruit unto God.
> *Romans 7:4*

Under the law we were bidden to do and live, and the fear of a forfeiture—or the consciousness of having incurred a forfeiture—already infused the spirit of bondage into all our services. Under Christ, we are bidden to live and do. We are put into the secure possession of that which we before had to strive for, and the happy rejoicing creature comes forth at will, with the services of gratitude and of new obedience. Instead of life being given as a return for the work that we render, our work is given as a return for the life that we receive.

And it will further be seen that, whereas a slavish and creeping and jealous selfishness was the principle of all our diligence under the law, it is a free and affectionate generosity which forms the principle of all our diligence under the gospel. In working to the law, it is all for ourselves—even that we may earn a wage or a reward. In working to Christ it is all the freewill offering of love and thankfulness—not in the mercenary spirit of a hireling, but with the buoyant alacrity of an eternally-obliged and devoted friend—because we thus judge, that, as Christ died for all, then were all dead; and he died, that they who live should live no longer to themselves, but unto him who died for them and who rose again.

## 20 August

What shall we say then? Is the law sin? God forbid. Nay, I had not known sin, but by the law: for I had not known lust, except the law had said, Thou shalt not covet.
*Romans 7:7*

It is thus, and on this principle, that God wills you to be holy and just and good, but these are the very attributes which the text gives to the law. It was written first on tables of stone. It is now written by the Holy Ghost on the tablets of your heart. And the process is now that you are made to delight in the law after the inward man—and when released, as you will be by death, from the corruptions of the outward man, heaven will be open for your admission as the only place that is fitted to harbour and to regale you.

You know of gold that it has two functions. With gold you may purchase a privilege, or with gold you may adorn your person. You may not be able to purchase the king's favour with gold, but he may grant you his favour, and when he requires your appearance before him, it is still in gold he may require you to be invested. And thus of the law. It is not by your own righteous conformity thereto that you purchase God's favour, for this been already purchased by the pure gold of the Saviour's righteousness and is presented to all who believe on him. But still, it is with your own personal righteousness that you must be gilded and adorned. It is not the price wherewith you have bought heaven, but it is the attire in which you must enter it.

## 21 August

For we know that the law is spiritual: but I am carnal, sold under sin.
*Romans 7:14*

Peruse with faithful application to your own heart the fifth chapter of Matthew, where, article by article, you have the comparison between a spiritual and what may be called a carnal commandment. You will at once perceive how truly the same individual may say of himself that, when he was in the flesh, touching the righteousness of the law he was blameless—and yet, when advanced and elevated above this state and now in the spirit, he may say, 'O wretched man that I am, who shall deliver me from the law of sin in my members?'

'I am carnal.' It is on the principles just now uttered that Paul may have made this affirmation of himself. The same man who could say of all the good that was done, 'Nevertheless not me but the grace of God that is in me.' Surely this man, who thus knew what he should refer to God's grace and what he should refer to his own separate and unaided self, might, even after this grace had become the habitual visitant or inmate of his heart, still look to his own soul and, conceiving of it as apart or disjoined from the fountain out of which he draws the supplies of its nourishment, he might well say that 'I am carnal'.

Think of a Christian as made up of two ingredients, the one consisting of all that he inherits by nature, the other consisting of all that is superinduced on him by grace. Think of his inward and experimental life as consisting of a struggle between these ingredients, in which the one does habitually—and will at length—ultimately and completely prevail. But the wrong principle belonging properly and primitively [by nature] to the man himself, and the right principle being derived from without through the channel of believing prayer or the exercise of faith in Christ Jesus, how natural is it in these circumstances for every Christian to regard the one as the home article and the other as a foreign article, for which he stands indebted to a fountain that is abroad—and whereunto it is his business to resort perpetually.

## 22 August

Now then it is no more I that do it, but sin that dwelleth in me.
*Romans 7:17*

His soul is ever travelling between his own emptiness and Christ's fulness. And like the apostle before him, when urged with any temptation, he recurs to the expedient of beseeching the Lord earnestly that it might depart from him. And the answer to this petition is remarkable. It does not appear that the temptation was made to depart from him, but it was deprived of its wonted force of ascendancy over him. It was not by the extirpation of the evil but by the counteracting strength of an opposite good that the apostle was kept upright as to his walk, in the midst of all the adverse and corrupt tendencies of his will.

'I will make my grace sufficient for thee,' was the Lord's answer to him. It was not that he did not still feel how in himself he was weak. The weakness of nature remained. 'But in that weakness I will perfect my strength,' says the Saviour.

And so it is, we believe, to the end of our days. There is a felt distinction between the weakness that is in ourselves and the strength that cometh upon us from the upper sanctuary. Even Paul was doomed to the consciousness that he had both a flesh and a mind—one of which would have inclined him wholly to the love of sin, and with the other of which he kept the corrupt tendency that still abode with him in check, and so maintained a conduct agreeable to the law of God.

# 23 August

*He that spared not his own Son, but delivered him up for us all, how shall he not with him also freely give us all things?*
*Romans 8:32*

'For us all.' The apostle may perhaps be confining his regards in this clause to himself and his converts, to those of whom he had this evidence that they were the elect of God—that the gospel had come to them with power and with the Holy Ghost and with much assurance. But, notwithstanding this, we have the authority of other passages for the comfortable truth that Christ tasted death for every man, and so every man who hears of the expiation rendered by this death has a warrant to rejoice therein. He is set forth a propitiation for the sins of the world, and so it is competent for everyone in the world to look unto this propitiation and be at peace. And he gave himself a ransom for all, to be testified in due time. And so might each of you who hears this testimony embrace it for himself, and feel the whole charm [delight] of his deliverance from guilt and from all consequences.

Christ did not so die for all as that all do actually receive the gift of salvation. But he so died for all as that all to whom he is preached have the real and honest offer of salvation. He is not yours in possession till you have laid hold of him by faith. But he is yours in offer. He is as much yours as anything of which you can say, 'I have it for the taking.' You, one and all of you, my brethren, have salvation for the taking, and if it does not indeed belong to you, it is because you do not choose to take it. It is because you have treated it as the worthless thing that you trample it under your feet and will not stoop to seize upon it. All of you are welcome, even now, to salvation, if you are only willing for a whole salvation.

# 24 August

*He that spared not his own Son, but delivered him up for us all, how shall he not with him also freely give us all things?*
*Romans 8:32*

I feel this subject to be inexhaustible. It is not the preciousness of Christ as being himself a gift that the text leads me to expatiate on. It is the goodness of it as a pledge of other gifts. Unspeakable blessing in itself, it is the sure harbinger of every other blessing in its train. It is rich in the promise of things to come, as well as great in the performance of a present stupendous benefit. And along with the full acquittal and the all-perfect righteousness which it brings along with it to the believer now, it affords the best guarantee for all the grace and all the glory that shall afterwards accrue to him.

There are other securities for this than those on which I have insisted, other aspects in which the sure and well-ordered covenant may be regarded, other evolutions of its solidity and strength that might well cause the believer to rejoice it as in a treasure, the whole value of which inestimable, and to delight himself greatly in the abundance of peace and of privilege that with Christ are invariably made over to him. Will God stamp dishonour on this his own great enterprise of the world's redemption? Will he leave unfinished that which he hath so laboriously begun? Will he hold forth the economy of grace as an impotent abortion to the scorn of his enemies, and more especially of him, against whom the Captain our salvation has gone forth on a warfare to root up his empire over the hearts of men and to destroy it? Is not the hostility of Satan to all the designs and doings of our Saviour in itself a guarantee that we, who have run to him for refuge, shall be covered over with his protection and be at length brought out by him in triumph?

# 25 August

*Who shall separate us from the love of Christ? shall tribulation, or distress, or persecution, or famine, or nakedness, or peril, or sword? As it is written, For thy sake we are killed all the day long; we are accounted as sheep for the slaughter. Nay, in all these things we are more than conquerors through him that loved us. For I am persuaded, that neither death, nor life, nor angels, nor principalities, nor powers, nor things present, nor things to come, nor height, nor depth, nor any other creature, shall be able to separate us from the love of God, which is in Christ Jesus our Lord.*
*Romans 8:35–39*

To have the precise understanding of this passage, you should remember that the love of Christ in verse 35, and afterwards the love of God in verse 39, may be understood in two senses—either as signifying his love to us, or our love to him.

The whole context seems to decide for the first of these meanings, as in that part of it which goes before, it is of God's dealings with, and regards to his elect. It is of his being upon their side that the argument is held. It is of the surrender that he made in their behalf, when he gave up his Son unto the death, and with him shall freely give them all things. It is of Christ dying and interceding for our good. It is of the love that is felt in heaven and is pointed downward to earth, and not of the love that is felt on earth and is pointed upward to heaven.

And in that part of the context which follows, it is still of him who loved us that he speaks. Notwithstanding, we shall find, I think, on a narrower examination of the whole passage, that our love to him is embraced therein, though it be his love to us that is more directly and obviously expressed by it.

# 26 August

This shall be the law of the leper in the day of his cleansing:
He shall be brought unto the priest.
*Leviticus 14:2*

Now follows the process of cleansing leprosy, a process devolved likewise on the priest, as well as the prior examination of it was. And we may now, therefore, be on the outlook for analogies with the matter of our salvation by the remedies and applications of the gospel, just as analogies are alleged between the disease of leprosy and the great spiritual disease of sin under which we all labour.

The main analogies suggested by the passage before us are, first, the necessity of a certain state in the sinner ere the atonement of Christ can tell savingly upon him. He must have faith and penitence. It was not till the leper exhibited a certain change of state that orders were given by the priest for a sacrifice. The slain bird and the bird left alive and let loose are supposed to typify respectively the sacrifice of Christ for our sins and his resurrection for our justification. There is great beauty in the conception that the live bird dipped in the blood of the dead one might typify the effect of the sacrifice in giving efficacy to the pleas and intercession of the risen Saviour.

The prescriptions given to him who had been leprous, after the ceremonial of the dead and living birds, might typify the requirements which lie on a believer after Christ had died for his offences and had risen again for his justification, namely that he should cleanse himself from all filthiness of the flesh and spirit, and perfect his holiness in the fear of God.

## 27 August

And when any will offer a meat offering unto the LORD, his offering shall be of fine flour; and he shall pour oil upon it, and put frankincense thereon.
*Leviticus 2:1*

The meat offerings had nothing sacrificial in them. They were expressions of homage and thankfulness, and may therefore be held as typifying the deeds of our new obedience after we had entered into reconciliation through the blood of Christ. A sin offering requires the death of a victim, for without the shedding of blood there is no remission.

Yet these offerings had somewhat of the nature of a sacrifice: a portion of them was burnt upon the altar, the remnant being for Aaron and his sons. And so also our deeds of new obedience are termed sacrifices. They are acceptable to God by Jesus Christ. Associated with him, they are well-pleasing to God, even as what of the meat offering was burned upon the altar was of sweet savour unto the Lord.

Leaven and honey were prohibited from the meat offerings burnt by fire. Yet it would seem as if, with the first-fruits spoken of in verse 12, honey and leaven might be offered, as indeed appears competent from Leviticus 23:17 and 2 Chronicles 30:5, but in this case, of course, they could not be burned on the altar. A meat offering of the first-fruits is distinct from the legal offering of first-fruits required by law, it being voluntary. There was neither leaven nor honey allowed in it, and, accordingly, we read that it is an offering made by fire unto the Lord.

Lord, having received by faith Christ Jesus, our Passover sacrificed for us, let me now purge out this old leaven and keep the feast with the unleavened bread of sincerity and truth.

## 28 August

And of the blue, and purple, and scarlet, they made cloths of service, to do service in the holy place, and made the holy garments for Aaron; as the LORD commanded Moses.
*Exodus 39:1*

The names of the children of Israel borne upon the shoulders of the high priest form a significant emblem of our relation to him who hath taken the mediatorial government upon his shoulders, and who presents our names with acceptance before God. The precious stones set in the breastplate, and each representing one of the tribes of Israel, show forth still more significantly the relation in which the spiritual Israel—the redeemed and the sanctified—stand to their great high priest in the heavens, where he appears for us an advocate and intercessor at the right hand of God.

Oh, give me rightly to consider him who is the Apostle and High Priest of my profession! May I have more faith in him, and then will I have more of feeling and friendship towards him. More especially, let me apply the declarations and promises of the gospel to myself, and then will I take the comfort of thinking that he bears me upon his heart—that the great forerunner within the vail is there to plead for me. Oh that I ventured my all upon him, and kept close by him as the Lord my righteousness! What a blessed peace would then take possession of my heart, and in quietness and in confidence I should have strength.

And what a fit succeeding topic for reflection is supplied by the few but emphatic words of 'Holiness unto the Lord'! Let me never disjoin the peace of the gospel from its holiness. The great high priest in the heavens is holy, and he who sanctifieth and they who are sanctified are all of one.

# 29 August

> And thou shalt make an altar to burn incense upon: of shittim wood shalt thou make it.
> *Exodus 30:1*

The altar of incense was of small dimensions, to be accommodated in the holy place, or placed before the vail, or on the hither side of the vail from the mercy seat and right before it. It was to God the incense of a sweet-smelling savour. And there, accordingly, he met with the high priest—met him in mercy, as from the mercy seat. In meeting him who appeared there for the people, he may be said to have met with all the worshippers of Israel; nor are we aware of a more beautiful symbolic representation than is here set before us.

From Luke 1:10 we learn it to have been the practice for the people to pray without [outside] at the time of incense, that the prayers might rise with acceptance before God. And in Revelation 8:3–4 we read of an angel with a golden censer, who offered incense with the prayers of all saints before the throne. And the smoke of the incense ascended with the prayers of the saints before God.

Heavenly Father, may every prayer of mine ascend to thee, perfumed with the incense of a Saviour's merits. Let me offer no strange incense. Let me trust in nothing but the intercession of Jesus Christ and the virtue of his blood. Let this be my perpetual incense, and Christ's the name in which I pray continually, even that name which is as ointment poured forth.

# 30 August

> Speak unto the children of Israel, and say unto them, When either man or woman shall separate themselves to vow a vow of a Nazarite, to separate themselves unto the LORD.
> *Numbers 6:2*

A Nazarite signifies one who is separated, as Joseph, in Genesis 49:26. And so, previous to the law here described, it may have signified one signalized by his religion among men.

There is atonement made for the defilement contracted by the Nazarites, although it was made up for by the period of consecration beginning anew from the time of the defilement, and the full period of the separation being afterwards to be completed—and the example of restitution not being accepted without a sacrifice. Neither did the fulfilment of this period suspend the necessity of a sin-offering at the close of it. Sin mixes with our best and holiest services, and at all times, for peace to our consciences, we need to have the blood of sprinkling applied to them.

What a beautiful and affecting conclusion we have in this chapter! Oh, may this blessing be realized on me and mine! What a forthgoing of spontaneous affection on the part of God to his own!

My Father in heaven, thus bless me, and rejoice over me for good. Keep me from evil. Cause thy face to shine on me, and be gracious unto me. Manifest thyself unto me, and let me behold thy reconciled countenance, so as to have peace. Oh, may thy name be put in me, and not a name to live while I am dead—but let me have the power as well as the form of godliness.

## 31 August

> Now therefore hearken, O Israel, unto the statutes and unto the judgments, which I teach you, for to do them, that ye may live, and go in and possess the land which the LORD God of your fathers giveth you.
> *Deuteronomy 4:1*

Moses proceeds from giving a narrative to delivering a solemn and earnest exhortation. There were days when the direct influence of such Old Testament addresses on the side of obedience was deafened to my ear by the imagination of an old covenant and the fear, lest by giving way to the obvious effect of such addresses, that I was violating the orthodoxy of the New Testament and allowing the legal to carry it over [to defeat] the evangelical.

This influence still lingers with me. But surely there is a perversity in that, from which I long to be emancipated, that I may run with alacrity in the new obedience of the gospel and have the comfort of knowing that my labour in the Lord is not in vain. Oh that I were delivered from all which is calculated to freeze up the activities of my nature, and to restrain the free and fearless and (let me add) hopeful consecration of all my services and all my powers to him who poured out his soul unto the death to purify a people unto himself, zealous of good works! Oh that my light may shine before men, and that men might recognise in the followers of Jesus who call on the name of the Lord, that with them indeed there is true wisdom, and in the worth and excellence of their character the only elements of true greatness. I pray for my country, that the righteousness which exalteth a nation may be theirs.

# September

JOHN KENNEDY (1819–1884) was born in Killearnan, Ross and Cromarty, where his father (also named John Kennedy) was minister of that parish. The young John Kennedy was unconverted when he began divinity studies in Aberdeen, but his father's sudden death in 1841 was the means God used to bring him to a serious concern for the salvation of his soul. By the time he returned to Aberdeen to resume studies after his father's funeral, he was a new creature in Christ Jesus.

In 1844, John Kennedy was ordained to the charge of the Free Church of Scotland in Dingwall, where he remained as minister until his death. Dr Kennedy was an important exponent of the deeply practical piety that was widespread in the Highlands during those years. He occupied a very influential position both as a pastor and a leader of the Church in the Highlands. His sermons are examples of a profound discovery of divine truths which he ably communicated to his hearers. It is said that he had no equal in his day as a preacher in the Gaelic language.

Dr Kennedy was prominent in the stand against unscriptural influences that are detrimental to spiritual life. As a leader of the 'Constitutionalist' party in the Free Church he was one of the most forceful campaigners against modernising influences in the Church, and he resolutely opposed the declensions in doctrine and practice within the denomination.

## Source of daily readings

*Sermons by Rev. Dr Kennedy, Dingwall* (Inverness, 1883).

## Biography

Alexander Auld, *Life of John Kennedy, D.D.* (London, 1887).

# 1 September

For by grace are ye saved through faith; and that not of yourselves: it is the gift of God.
*Ephesians 2:8*

'Ye are saved.' This does not mean that they were fully saved. It assures them, however, that they were heirs of a full and everlasting salvation, and that they shall speedily and surely enjoy their inheritance. 'He that believeth shall be saved.' It is not said to them, 'Ye *have* been saved.' But they are assured that the process of their salvation had begun—that they were born again of God, that they were vitally united to the Lord Jesus Christ, that they were the 'righteousness of God' because 'in him' as members of his mystical body, that the Holy Spirit dwelt in them and was carrying on as the sanctifier the work begun in their regeneration, and that his work would be perfected in the day of Jesus Christ. It says to them, 'Salvation has come to you. Ye have a right to it in all its perfectness. Ye are being saved by a work of grace within you. Ye are being saved, and shall yet be fully and for ever saved.'

What a prospect of ineffable brightness lies before these! Salvation from all the consequences of their guilt, from all the corruption of their hearts, from all the troubles of their lot, from all tribulation in the world, from all the devices and assaults of Satan, from all hidings of their Father's face, from all strokes of his rod, from all sickness arising from delay, from all the pain of thirst, from all the chilling sense of alienation, from being before the glass in which they can only darkly see instead of being face to face with the glories of the Father's house. From all this they are soon and certainly to be delivered.

# 2 September

For by grace are ye saved through faith; and that not of yourselves: it is the gift of God.
*Ephesians 2:8*

'It is the gift of God.' He has bestowed true faith on all who have it. It would come from no other source. It rests with him to determine who shall have it. He gives it whomsoever he will. Thus spake the Son to the Father, 'I thank thee, O Father, Lord of heaven and earth, that thou hast hid these things from the wise and prudent, and hast revealed them unto babes.' And for this distinguishing grace the only reason assigned is in the words, 'Even so, Father, for so it seemeth good in thy sight.'

When Simon Peter professed his faith in Jesus as the Christ and the Son of God, he was at once told, 'Flesh and blood hath not revealed this unto thee, but my Father which is in heaven.' Thence, even from heaven, came the faith of Peter, and from the Father there. And from the same source came the faith of all who have 'believed to the saving of the soul'. The Spirit produced it by his regenerating power. He, by a work in secret, bearing directly on their passive souls, 'quickened them, when they were dead in sins'. And by means of the word of the truth of the gospel, applied with power, elicited in the exercise of faith the life to vital union to him. They were thus 'quickened together with Christ' and called effectually to him. Therefore, and on this account alone, they believed in Christ and obtained a place among the saved.

# 3 September

Not of works, lest any man should boast. For we are his workmanship, created in Christ Jesus unto good works, which God hath before ordained that we should walk in them.
*Ephesians 2:9–10*

Are there any of you, feeling your need of faith, persuaded that it cannot be 'of yourselves', and rebellious and hopeless in the measure in which you feel shut up to God? Do not imagine, if you are ever saved, that you can evade a crisis in which you must feel yourself in absolute subjection to the sovereign will of the Father, and in absolute dependence on the efficient grace of the Spirit. Do not desire to deal with Christ so as to evade a consciousness of this. He never will take a place that interferes with the sovereignty of him who sent him, nor with the promise and work of the Holy Ghost. He was ever careful in his teaching to ascribe all salvation to the good pleasure of the Father, and to conserve the province of the Holy Spirit. But he was careful, too, to tell that all things were delivered unto him by his Father, and that he had power to send the Spirit to do his work of grace, while in acting according to that arrangement and in the use of that power, he referred to the appointment of him whose anointed he was, and to the grace and power of the Spirit by whose fulness he was sealed.

Do not shrink from realising that all things are of God, and that salvation can never be yours except as you are the subject of the Spirit's work of grace. But fix your thoughts on Christ, with his commission to save, as given him by the Father. Think of him as having all the fulness of provided grace abiding in him. Think of his power to baptise with the Holy Ghost.

# 4 September

*And she shall bring forth a son, and thou shalt call his name* JESUS: *for he shall save his people from their sins.*
*Matthew 1:21*

I am now to ask each one of you, 'What is Jesus to you? Is he your Saviour? Can you claim him as your own? If not, is he the object of your desire? Are you content with him as the only one who can save you from your sins? Do you feel pained at heart because of the power that works to keep you away from him? Are you crying to God for an eye to see his beauty, for an ear to hear his voice, for a heart to accept himself and his great salvation?' What is your answer to such questions as these?

There are some of you, I fear, to whom Jesus is not even a name, representing him who bears it—not even a word, to the meaning of which you give any attention: it is but a sound which, unmoved, you allow to pass you by. Oh, friends, if you knew how indispensable he is to you, you could not be so indifferent about him. If you knew aught of his glory and of his grace, you could not thus despise him. If you thought of how his Father delights in him, when he speaks to you regarding him, you could not dare to insult his Son in presence of his glory. When I ask you today, 'Are you to seek Jesus and his salvation?' your answer is, '*Never.*' That is your present resolution. Or, at any rate, you have no other. You make no approach to resolve to seek him. And under the power which sways you, that is just to let yourself float on the current that bears you away from Jesus, on to everlasting death.

# 5 September

*For the needy shall not alway be forgotten: the expectation of the poor shall not perish for ever.*
*Psalm 9:18*

It is a mistake to imagine that an assurance of an interest in Christ banishes all sorrow from the heart, and that if there be sorrow it must be the result of unbelief. It is quite true that without the hope of glory no Christian can be glad—at any rate, he can have no spiritual joy, though he may have the ease that is found in sleep. But it is quite as true that the man who rejoices 'in hope of the glory of God' has enough in himself to make him sorrowful even when rejoicing. It is then his pain is deepest, because of the corruption he still finds within him, because of how little he has ever rendered to the Lord for all his benefits, and because of the condition of the Church and of the world around him, in contrast to what is before the eye of his hope in the company at home before him.

So bent are some on the banishment of all sorrow from their religion, and at the same time so haunted by the thought that perfect sinlessness must precede perfect joy, that they have conceived the idea of attaining to such a victory over sin, even in this life, as shall allow them to rejoice without trembling. It is quite easy for these dreamers to attain to an unconsciousness of sin. They have merely to form a standard of experience and service for themselves, apart from the Word of God, and thus attaining to an imagined perfection they may have a dreamer's Elysium.[3]

## 6 September

> Remember me, O LORD, with the favour that thou bearest unto thy people: O visit me with thy salvation; that I may see the good of thy chosen, that I may rejoice in the gladness of thy nation, that I may glory with thine inheritance.
> Psalm 106:4–5

---

[3] A mythological place of perfect happiness.

This psalm opens with a call to praise the Lord. And beyond what is presented in his great name as Jehovah, there is no reason given why he should be praised. Praise is due to him because of what he is in his underived, unbegun, unending, unchanging, and unlimited being, and because that infinite being is invested with the beauty of holiness.

Because he is Jehovah he is to be praised, and woe unto all whose hearts remain ever songless before his majesty and glory! An old blind, hard heart will never sing his praise. True praise is 'a new song', and it can only come from 'a new heart', which alone can know and love Jehovah's name.

But the call to praise the Lord is followed by a call to give him thanks. Two reasons are given for the latter, and they are urged only on his chosen people. The one is 'for he is good'; the other is 'for his mercy endureth for ever'. Thanks must be rendered by his people to Jehovah for what he has given, and for what he has promised to them. But in rendering thanks for the past they must rise up from the gift to the divine fountain of goodness whence it came. Give thanks for he is good; not, be glad because you have received good from his hand. And thanks are as surely due to him for what he has promised as for what he has given—for what they hope to attain as for what has already reached them. His people are called to give thanks, for his mercy endureth for ever.

## 7 September

Ho, every one that thirsteth, come ye to the waters, and he that hath no money; come ye, buy, and eat; yea, come, buy wine and milk without money and without price. Wherefore do ye spend money for that which is not bread? and your labour for that which satisfieth not? Hearken diligently unto me, and eat ye that which is good, and let your soul delight itself in fatness. Incline your ear, and come unto me: hear,

and your soul shall live; and I will make an everlasting covenant with you, even the sure mercies of David.
*Isaiah 55:1–3*

In the words of the text there is a view given of the provision of the covenant as presented in the gospel—a description of the people who are called to receive and enjoy it, and the terms of the call which is addressed to them. The words employed to exhibit the grace of salvation are 'the waters', 'wine and milk', 'that which is good', and 'fatness'.

'The waters.' This emblem tells us how indispensable this grace is. Were there no water, there could be no life on earth—no plant, no animal could live. In order to the sustenance of life, this earth is rather a globe of water studded with projecting solid matter than a solid sphere interspersed with water. Only thus could man or beast or plant find it a fitting place to live in. There would be only death on earth without its waters.

But quite as indispensable to you, sinner, it is that you, in order to have life, spiritual and eternal, should be a partaker of the grace of God in Christ. What, apart from this, can deliver you from death and give you life? Would that this were realised by you! And, oh, would that you felt that the alternative is to be a partaker of God's saving grace or miserably to perish for ever! You are shut up to 'the waters' by the exigencies of your case—would that you were so by your consciousness of what you are as a sinner!

# 8 September

Ho, every one that thirsteth, come ye to the waters, and he that hath no money; come ye, buy, and eat; yea, come, buy wine and milk without money and without price.
*Isaiah 55:1*

The waters tell us how free the grace of the gospel is. Men have found a way of taxing water, but as God gives it, it is sufficiently free. When, parched with thirst, you come to a spring or stream, you just stoop down and drink. You never think of putting your hand to your purse for money before applying your mouth to the water. There is none to demand or to receive a price from you, and if your purse is found to be empty, you never think of making that a reason for not taking a drink.

Quite as little need you think of giving aught before receiving what is offered to you in the gospel. It is grace that is before you there, and how can that be aught else than free? It could not be grace if you had to give, so that you might take it. And it is divine grace, with its infinite bounty. And God proclaims it so to be. Oh, surely then it must be altogether free! You need it should be so, and the honour of God's name demands this as well. Oh, is it not well when what is requisite in the interest of God's glory is what exactly meets your case!

And this tells of the abundance of divine grace. I know not, unless it be to teach us the all-sufficiency of the provision of the covenant, why 'the waters' is the form of expression used in giving us the emblem. Let every ocean and sea and lake and river and spring and pool and stream and rivulet on the face of all the earth be combined in one great reservoir, the accumulation of the waters there would suffice but only feebly to represent the infinite fulness of grace in Christ.

## 9 September

Ho, every one that thirsteth, come ye to the waters, and he that hath no money; come ye, buy, and eat; yea, come, buy wine and milk without money and without price.
*Isaiah 55:1*

'Wine and milk.' It is not wine alone, nor is it milk alone, nor is it 'milk and wine'. They are both together, and in the order 'wine and milk': wine that cheers, and milk that nourishes. This wine must be that of which it is said that it 'maketh glad the heart of man', and which is prescribed to 'those who are of heavy hearts'.

This is one emblem of what is proffered in the gospel. It points to the precious blood of Christ. That is wine that made glad the heart of God, and without which no mans heart can know true peace and joy. To this you must first have recourse when you come to Christ. Apart from this you can find no ground of acceptance with God. But there is what suits and suffices there. If you get an eye to discern its preciousness, as it looks at it in the light of Emmanuel's glory, if you get a heart to accept of it as God's righteousness to you, if your conscience is satisfied with it as, in the light that shineth through your understanding, it comes to it with an assurance of its being well-pleasing to God. And with a promise of forgiveness, and if you get the hand of faith to appropriate it to yourself, then you will know that this wine, because it first was pleasing to God, can make your heart exceeding glad.

Then may you partake of the milk that can nourish you—the saving grace of the covenant, sealed by 'the precious blood of Christ'. This is 'the sincere milk of the word', to be found in the doctrines and promises of the gospel.

# 10 September

Wherefore do ye spend money for that which is not bread? and your labour for that which satisfieth not? Hearken diligently unto me, and eat ye that which is good, and let your soul delight itself in fatness.
*Isaiah 55:2*

'That which is good.' It comes as good from God, and it is the only thing that is really good for you. It is excellent good as it comes from God, a meet expression of his infinite love. And it is an excellent good as it meets all your wants, as you are sinful, and can satisfy all your aspirations, as one who is to exist for ever. Oh, what apart from this can be a satisfying good to you or to me? But here is wisdom for the foolish, righteousness for the guilty, sanctification for the unholy, and redemption for the helpless.

Here is a fulness of God's providing, in order to the perfect salvation of the lost. The 'all' of God's providing must suffice to meet the 'all' of your need. Nothing can be awanting [lacking] to you that is not to be found in 'that which is good'. And if once you have it, it can never be taken away. Eternal life shall be yours—perfect ability according to the measure of your being, and an opportunity endless as its duration, for glorifying and enjoying God. What can compare with this? In the good that comes from God is God himself. He in all his glory shall be thine, as thine inheritance, and he in all his grace shall be thine, that he may perfect thy salvation, in order to a full enjoyment of thy portion, if thou acceptest the 'good' which is proffered to thee in the text.

# 11 September

Ho, every one that thirsteth, come ye to the waters, and he that hath no money; come ye, buy, and eat; yea, come, buy wine and milk without money and without price. Wherefore do ye spend money for that which is not bread? and your labour for that which satisfieth not? Hearken diligently unto me, and eat ye that which is good, and let your soul delight itself in fatness. Incline your ear, and come unto me: hear, and your soul shall live; and I will make an everlasting covenant with you, even the sure mercies of David.
*Isaiah 55:1–3*

The call addressed by God begins with the first syllable: 'Ho.' The next word is 'come', followed by a call to 'buy', an invitation to 'eat', then by the words 'hearken diligently unto me', and it closes with the wondrous words, 'let thy soul delight itself in fatness.'

'Ho' is a divine shout, uttered by the voice of God, as with a trumpet blast from heaven. It is intended to arrest sinners as they are hurrying past the provision of grace in the gospel towards everlasting destruction.

And yet, how many pass on unheeding, without any impression of the earnestness and authority of God. As the careless crowd, on their way to market in Jerusalem, passed the cross on which Jesus was suspended and was about to die, 'wagging their heads' and reviling, so do many still pass on to death, treating with contempt the Christ and the call of God in the gospel. You, sinner, can act the same part with those revilers of old, for Christ is as surely near to you in the gospel as he was to them in the flesh. He is lifted up before you in the gospel quite beside you, as surely as he was lifted on the cross quite beside them. You can pass him by as surely as they did. And passing him by you are, careless sinner, while the Lord is calling to arrest you. He speaks to you from heaven, to bring you to a stand that you may cease rushing heedless hellwards. Oh, will you not give ear! Are you to fight still against the authority of God shutting you up to Christ crucified as the only object of hope to which you can repair?

## 12 September

Ho, every one that thirsteth, come ye to the waters, and he that hath no money; come ye, buy, and eat; yea, come, buy wine and milk without money and without price.
*Isaiah 55:1*

'Buy' is the next word, and it seems a strange word in such a call. It tells you that there must be a personal transaction between you and the Christ of God, and between you and God in and through him.

But how can there be any such transaction as is implied in buying and selling between a sinner and Christ? In buying you get what was never yours before, and in selling to you one gives you what was his own before. May there not be a transaction such as this between you and Christ, and between Christ and you? And when you buy you obtain a right to what you received, which will be sustained in any court of law where decisions are according to righteousness, if your right to your purchase should be challenged. Is it not a right to salvation, such as will be sustained in the court of heaven, that Christ gives to all who transact with him in faith? And is it not expressly said that to buy from Christ is to 'buy without money and without price'? Is not this the kind of buying that suits your state as a sinner? It verily suits your condition, whether it suits your disposition or not. 'He that hath no money' is the one to buy from Christ. The market of free grace—the gospel fair—is the only one at which such a one can buy. But there none besides can be a purchaser. It is by becoming a debtor that you become a buyer in dealing with Christ.

# 13 September

> Ho, every one that thirsteth, come ye to the waters, and he that hath no money; come ye, buy, and eat; yea, come, buy wine and milk without money and without price.
> *Isaiah 55:1*

'To eat' is to have spiritual enjoyment in the doctrines of the gospel, and to be appropriating in faith its promises of grace. There may be the former without the latter. Faith may operate, on the teaching of gospel truth, so as to secure some spiritual enjoyment in the exhibition given of the glory and grace of God in redemption, without any conscious approbation of promised grace. And yet this may be true eating. It tells in the way of intensifying one's desire after further attainment in knowledge, faith and love, and actually tells in the transformation of the soul. But there flows from this a desire to make use of the exceeding great promises to which all who are in Christ are entitled on the ground of his precious blood. Enabled to appropriate the grace of the promise in time of need, they are encouraged, and in this encouragement their soul has its strength renewed. They verily eat in this exercise of faith. There is no reality in any feeding if it be not here.

All who come and buy are called to eat. Why should they not? Till they came and bought they could only steal in laying an appropriating hand on the blessings of the covenant as brought near in the promises of the gospel. And yet, how common is such theft! There are not a few who proclaim that they have peace, and who have clamant joy and zeal, who owe all they have to theft. They have appropriated the love of God to themselves on the ground of its being universal, and, on the same ground, the redemption from death, which they associate with Christ, and thus delude themselves into the persuasion that all is well with them, and venture to claim all the promises as theirs. Of course, this makes them very joyful, but it is stolen wine that cheers them. Friends, remember that a right to eat is the result of transacting in faith with a personal Saviour, without or apart from whom ye can do nothing.

## 14 September

And the Spirit and the bride say, Come. And let him that heareth say, Come. And let him that is athirst come. And whosoever will, let him take the water of life freely.
*Revelation 22:17*

The call of the gospel as is given in Old Testament scripture does exactly correspond with the form of the call we find in the last chapter of the New Testament: 'The Spirit and the bride say, Come. And let him that is athirst come. And whosoever will, let him take the water of life freely.'

Here, as in Isaiah, the emblem of water is used to show the indispensableness, freeness, and abundance of the grace of God as revealed and brought near by the gospel. It is the water of life—life-giving and life-promoting—issuing as a river out of the throne of God and of the Lamb. Its fountain is in the sovereign, eternal, infinite and unchanging love of God. It can proceed out of the divine throne because the Lamb, who is in the midst of it, was slain, and it flows out in the dispensation of the Holy Ghost. All that is involved in this wondrous outflow is to be found in Christ as revealed and offered in the gospel. A call to Christ is, therefore, a call to 'the water of life'.

'And the Spirit and the bride say, Come.' Not, 'The Spirit says and the bride says,' but both speak together. In the Bible the Spirit speaks, but it is through inspired men who were espoused to Christ. He speaks, too, in the preaching of the gospel, but it is by men who are betrothed to the Lamb. The Spirit speaks not apart from the bride, and the bride cannot say, 'Come,' apart from him.

'And let him that heareth say, Come.' It is not said, 'Let him that heareth come,' for he that heareth has to pass the call in from his ear to his heart. He has to say 'Come' to his soul, and to the Lord.

# 15 September

Ye that fear the LORD, praise him; all ye the seed of Jacob, glorify him; and fear him, all ye the seed of Israel. For he hath not despised nor abhorred the affliction of the afflicted; neither hath he hid his face from him; but when he cried unto him, he heard.
*Psalm 22:23–24*

There are some among you who are saddened by the felt want [lack] of love to Christ, and who would fain be brought to know and trust and love and serve him. But you are sometimes afraid that you will be left among his despisers. And you know that unless the Father draw you, you will never reach his anointed one, as a true believer, to lean on him and, as a willing subject, to take your place at his feet. But your fear of not attaining to this is evidence of your desire to be a willing debtor and a willing servant to Messiah. If that be your desire, it shall be granted unto you—yea, this which you seek is already yours.

But if you cannot take this comfort to yourself, you may, at any rate, hopefully express your desire to God. It cannot but be pleasing to him that you should desire to love him whom it was his delight to deliver out of all his affliction. The feeblest groan, expressing a desire for love to his Son, is music in the Father's ears. And remember that, what you would fain receive, it is in the power of him whose name is Jesus to impart. He can fulfil the promise, 'Thy people shall be willing in the day of thy power.' For the exercise of this power, if not as one of his people, at least as one of those who are rebellious, you may lift up your cry. And remember that it is part of the work of the Holy Spirit to glorify Christ, and to take what is Christ's and the Father's and to show them to all who fain would know and trust and love both the Son and him who gave him.

## 16 September

> Blessed are they which do hunger and thirst after righteousness: for they shall be filled.
> *Matthew 5:6*

The description of those who are blessed given in the text is that they hunger and thirst after righteousness, and the promise given to them as such is that they shall be filled.

The word 'righteousness' indicates the object of their desire, and 'hunger and thirst' describe the feeling with which they regard it. There is no specification of what the righteousness is. It is not *the* righteousness, as if it were something specified and outstanding; it is not *a* righteousness, as if it were one and not manifold. It is set before us in a general form, because it is intended to represent what the object is at which they aim in all departments of their exercise— in their attempts to know and to be rightly affected by their past sins; in their desire to discover, and to reach and rest on, the one ground of acceptance with God; in all their exercise in connection with a sense of indwelling corruption; in the worship of God; in the discharge of their duties towards their fellow men; and in their experience of tribulation in the world. All these are departments in which their souls are exercised. And in connection with each one of them, righteousness is the object after which they hunger and thirst.

Hunger and thirst describe the feeling with which that object is regarded. Not reasonless is the use of both these words. They hunger, and in the measure in which their desire is not gratified they feel weak, and not unfrequently the weakness passes into faintness. Such is the effect of unsatisfied hunger both on soul and body. But they thirst too—they have a keen burning desire, which stimulates them to eager longings for the wished-for righteousness, and makes them diligent in the use of means.

## 17 September

Blessed are they which do hunger and thirst after righteousness: for they shall be filled.
*Matthew 5:6*

Those who hunger and thirst after righteousness differ from people who are content with themselves in three respects.

Firstly, they desire to aim at the glory of God. To render him the honour due to his name is their desire, and they count themselves unrighteous in the measure in which they find that this is not the motive of their service.

Secondly, they desire to be conformed in their worship to the rule of service prescribed in his Word by the Lord. All is will-worship that is not rendered with a careful regard to the Word of God as the rule, and they who offer such service are challenged by the Lord with the question, 'Who hath required this at your hand?'

Thirdly, knowing their shortcoming in service—and knowing this just because they desire to glorify God by doing his will—these seek grace whereby they may serve God acceptably with reverence and godly fear. Hungering and thirsting after righteousness, they are given to prayer for grace to help them to attain it.

True worshippers are lowly worshippers. Oh, what a course of blundering their past service appears as they inquire to what extent they were aiming at the glory of God as their end, and were walking according to the rule of his Word! And sometimes they are tempted to think that they but expose themselves to righteous mockery in venturing to hope that they shall yet be worshipping in spirit and in truth.

# 18 September

> They shall hunger no more, neither thirst any more; neither shall the sun light on them, nor any heat.
> *Revelation 7:16*

The Lord will so preserve and sustain the believers' hope of being righteous that it cannot perish within them. He will sometimes so strengthen their desire after righteousness that they cannot but be conscious of its movements, and thus according to the measure of their pain will be the measure of their hopefulness. But the more they attain the desire to accord to the Lord his place and his rights, the further they find themselves from the perfection to which they aspire, and not infrequent is their experience of temptation to despair of ever reaching an attainment so high.

But they shall at last be fully satisfied. All their fears and faintings, all their hunger and thirst, shall completely and for ever pass away. There never shall be a reason up there [in heaven] why there should be any hiding of their Father's face, any estrangement from their Elder Brother, any coldness towards them on the part of any one inhabitant. And utterly and for ever excluded from their home shall all be who were wont to trouble them. Oh, what a change shall this be felt to be by those who passed sin-laden, afflicted, hungry and athirst through the vale of tears to their eternal home!

'Filled.' Oh, yes, filled to overflowing shall they for ever be, when the light of God's face shall be an eternal brightness over them, the beauty of perfect holiness upon and around them, and an eternity of perfect blessedness before them. Nought to cast a shadow on their joy shall be found in the place into which nothing that defileth shall enter, and nothing to produce a sigh can there be, where no inhabitant shall ever say, 'I am sick,' and where they shall hunger and thirst no more.

# 19 September

> He shall glorify me: for he shall receive of mine, and shall shew it unto you.
> *John 16:14*

As a friend, Christ is 'the chiefest among ten thousand'. Sweet and fruitful was the disciples' experience of his being so, since first they knew him as their friend, when he effectually called them to his fellowship. Most patiently he bore with their ignorance, their perverseness, their unbelief, and their hardness of heart. Most carefully did he watch over them—as carefully as if he had nought besides their welfare to think of. Most painstaking and wisely tender was his way of teaching them, correcting their errors, adapting his doctrine both to their capacity and to their circumstances, and seasonably warning them of coming trials.

And now, in the near prospect of his own awful sufferings, he remembers his disciples. Even in Gethsemane, in the intervals between his wrestlings, he comes to them with words of instruction. Oh, this wondrous mingling of prayer to his Father and instruction to his disciples—this meekness of submission to the will of him who gave him the bitter cup to drink, and this loving care of the 'little flock'! How like him was this, and how incomparable is he in this above all besides! And the wondrous sermon of this and the two preceding chapters, and the wondrous prayer of the chapter which follows! Oh, what excuse can there be for suspecting the friendship of him who, just as he was entering into the darkness and horror of the sufferings, which were to close only in his dying the death of the cross, could thus teach and pray for his poor disciples? Never was love so tried as his, and never was love so commended.

## 20 September

> He shall glorify me: for he shall receive of mine, and shall shew it unto you.
> *John 16:14*

Christ has been fully glorified by the Father. There has been nothing left undone on the part of him 'who raised him from the dead, and gave him glory', in response to the intercession, 'Glorify me with thine own self with the glory which I had with thee before the world was.' But the scene of that glorifying is heaven. Love would desiderate more than even this for Christ. It cannot he satisfied without there being a glorifying of him on the very earth on which he was abased and died. The text meets this crave of love. And the glorifying is to be the work of a divine person. And he is to be glorified when preached as 'Christ crucified' in the gospel. And those in whose eyes he is to be glorious as the crucified one are they who had for him once such contempt and hatred as were in the hearts of those by whose wicked hands he was nailed to the tree.

Friend, does this satisfy thee? Not yet! What wouldest thou have besides? I fain would that he should be glorified in his saints when he presents them all, as members of his mystical body, holy and without blemish in the light that shall shine from the great white throne, before an assembled universe.

'Glorified in his saints'—once guilty, loathsome sinners, now perfectly holy! What a consummation! And nothing will satisfy thee but thy being one of them.

Oh, friend, thou seekest much, but seek no less. Oh, what ravishing bliss shall it be to all lovers of Christ when they are assured that, in their perfected salvation, Christ manifests his glory, and that they are to his praise, just in the measure in which they once were poor and needy, guilty, lost and loathsome!

# 21 September

> He shall glorify me: for he shall receive of mine, and shall shew it unto you.
> *John 16:14*

This text is fraught with encouragement to all who would fain appreciate and trust and love the Lord Jesus. Well did Jesus know what would suit the felt wants and the spiritual desires of his disciples. He knew that they would all feel—painfully feel—their lack of esteem for him, and that love to him in their hearts panted for his being glorified in and by them. And this felt want and this living desire he meets by the promise of the text. This is drink that suits the thirst of all true lovers of Christ.

Friend, you must owe him all. You must be a debtor to him for knowing his name and for trusting in him, as surely as for all that he bestows in answer to the cry of faith. At your worst, trust him for all, and he will never fail to do above all that you can ask or think. There is hope, even for you who esteem yourselves to be the most ignorant, unbelieving and unloving of all to whom Christ is preached in the gospel. Does he not claim a right to send the Comforter? Is not the promised Comforter possessed of almighty power and infinite love? What can he not do in order that sinners may be brought to esteem Christ as the standard-bearer among ten thousand, and altogether lovely? Lift your cry to him who has promised the Comforter, as did the blind man who appealed for mercy to Jesus in the days of his flesh, and a saving and satisfying view of his glory shall be yours from him who was anointed to open the eyes of the blind.

## 22 September

> Awake, O sword, against my shepherd, and against the man that is my fellow, saith the LORD of hosts: smite the shepherd, and the sheep shall be scattered: and I will turn mine hand upon the little ones.
> *Zechariah 13:7*

O what a feast is in this text for the sheep of the flock of which Messiah is the Shepherd! Here he is in the marvellous glory of his person, as the man who is Jehovah's 'fellow'. Here he is in the infinite merit of the death he died. Here he is in matchless love. Here he is in the efficiency of his finished work, the Lord of hosts being pledged to put forth his power in order to give him in the salvation of 'the little ones' a satisfying reward of all his travail!

Oh, friend, is there not enough here, specially when around all this and through it shines forth, in its highest and fullest manifestation, the glory of the Lord of hosts? Oh, seek grace to be more eager in desiring and more diligent in partaking of this wonderous feast. Oh, how little thou hast known and trusted and loved and praised and obeyed and suffered for 'the man' who is the fellow of the Lord of hosts, and who for thy sins was smitten, that his chastisement might be the chastisement of thy peace, and that thou through his stripes might have healing.

Oh, cleave to him, for he is thy only refuge, thy only guide, thy only Healer, the 'friend that sticketh closer than a brother'. Seek to know his voice and to follow him. Be content to pass in his company even 'through the fire'. And seek to be so purged as to be made ready for being with him, as he is in the midst of the throne on high, so showing himself from out of the glory in which he dwells, that he shall be recognised by thee as the Lamb slain or as the Shepherd smitten, while his glory and his love shall so affect thee that to sing his praise as thy Redeemer shall be thy blissful exercise for ever.

## 23 September

> For the grace of God that bringeth salvation hath appeared to all men, teaching us that, denying ungodliness and worldly lusts, we should live soberly, righteously, and godly, in this present world.
> *Titus 2:11–12*

'The grace of God that bringeth salvation.' Salvation is the gift of grace. Thus only can it be fitly expressed towards sinners. It first of all gave the Saviour. He, as given, came to seek and to save that which was lost. He could not be given without salvation being brought in him to all to whom he came near. And the salvation must be one that meets the sinner's whole case. It is the salvation of God, and it must be perfect. It is the grace of God that brings it, and therefore there can be nothing awanting to it which a poor sinner needs. Divine blood, divine grace, divine power combine to make it perfect.

There are three ways in which the grace of God may be said to be bringing salvation. Firstly, in the mission of Christ to redeem from all iniquity and to seal the everlasting covenant. Secondly, in the revelation and offer of the gospel, in which Christ is preached. And thirdly, by the ministration of the Spirit, when he comes into a soul to work there as the Spirit of life and of faith in the day of effectual calling.

Firstly, in the mission of Christ. He could not be sent without salvation being brought to those to whom he came. He was a divine, and a divinely appointed, Saviour, who appeared as the Son of man on the earth. There was in him almighty power pledged to the work of salvation, and he was moved by a love to his people that was infinite and eternal, and by a zeal for the glory of him who sent him, which no experience of trial could abate.

## 24 September

> For the grace of God that bringeth salvation hath appeared to all men, teaching us that, denying ungodliness and worldly lusts, we should live soberly, righteously, and godly, in this present world.
> Titus 2:11–12

Grace brings salvation in the offer of the gospel to all to whom the word of this salvation is sent. Christ is preached in the gospel in his wondrous person as Emmanuel, with all that makes him all-sufficient and suitable as a Saviour. He is preached as Christ, the anointed One whom the Father sealed, and who has therefore a right to save. He is preached as Christ crucified, who by his death on the cross removed all that could interpose between the grace of

God and the work of salvation. And he is preached as an exalted Prince and Saviour, by the power of whose life sinners shall be drawn unto him, and by which he shall save to the uttermost all who come unto God through him.

He of whom all this is true is brought nigh to all who hear the gospel of the grace of God. So near is he thus brought that he is at the very door of the sinner's heart. While he is there, all salvation is there, and there is no power in hell, and there is only one power on earth, that can keep you from having that salvation as your own— even the strength of your own unwillingness.

## 25 September

> For the grace of God that bringeth salvation hath appeared to all men, teaching us that, denying ungodliness and worldly lusts, we should live soberly, righteously, and godly, in this present world.
> *Titus 2:11–12*

The grace of God brings salvation by the ministration of the Spirit of life and of faith, when he comes into a soul in the day of effectual calling, there to work and dwell. Though mountains of guilt interpose between a sinner and God, the Spirit may, in the right of Christ, exercise his saving love in coming over them all. Though hosts of enemies encompass him and have the sway within him, the Spirit can reach him and cast out the spirits of darkness from their place of power. And though enmity to God have possession of his heart and the power of death holds him helpless under bondage, the Spirit can subdue his enmity by quickening him and bringing him under the constraining influence of the love of Christ.

This is a work of which all the objects of divine love shall be made the subjects. To them all shall salvation thus be brought by the grace of God. And till it is thus brought unto you, never can the salvation which is in Christ be yours through your being brought to receive him by faith according to the terms on which he is offered in the gospel.

The grace of God is the teacher. The grace of the Father, or the Father in his grace, is teaching. 'They shall be all taught of God,' says Christ, and adds, 'Every man therefore that hath heard and hath learned of the Father cometh unto me.'

The Son was the teacher of those whom he gathered around him while he was in the flesh on earth, for they were called his disciples, and on one occasion we read that he opened the understandings of some of his disciples. The grace of God in the Son, or the Son in his grace, is teaching. And all saving teaching is by the Holy Ghost. What eye hath not seen, nor ear heard, nor heart received, God reveals by his Spirit, 'for the Spirit searcheth all things, yea, the deep things of God'. Thus most emphatically true is it that the teaching is *of God*. And it cannot be of him without being of *grace*. Oh, if so, then, there is hope for you, poor simpleton!

## 26 September

> Wherefore the rather, brethren, give diligence to make your calling and election sure: for if ye do these things, ye shall never fall.
> *2 Peter 1:10*

Friend, if your soul is in a backsliding condition, what you first need is to be brought back—with a heart broken for and from your sin—to God, in the exercise of living faith. Then is the time to be careful to add to your faith all those graces which flow from the faith which is the gift of God. And in order to your return and to your fruitfulness, how urgently you need the gracious aid of the Holy Ghost! Not till he has secured both these to you is there an opportunity of giving you the comfort of knowing that you have been called. His work must be certified by the production of its fruits, ere he can assure you that that work has been done.

More is needed than that your calling and election should be certified by their appropriate fruits, in order that you may be assured that you are of the 'chosen generation'. The Spirit must shine on his own revived work within you as evidenced by its fruits, in order to your discovering what can be a good reason to hope that you have known the grace of God in truth. He must, in the light of truth, show to you the correspondence of your exercise with that of the saints and of their Head, and by the divine authority of applied truth seal that before the bar of your conscience as evidence of your calling and election. He must help you against all that would distort your judgment and would shut you out from the comfort of being assured as to your salvation. And he can accompany this with such an application of the word of promise as shall give you, from the throne of God, an overwhelmingly sweet assurance of your having been loved from the beginning, and therefore of your being loved to the end.

# 27 September

*And he said unto them, Out of the eater came forth meat, and out of the strong came forth sweetness. And they could not in three days expound the riddle.*
*Judges 14:14*

This riddle presents to us the mystery of the cross. 'God raised unto Israel a Saviour, Jesus.' He was manifested to destroy the works of the devil, and to procure redemption for a people who were both prisoners and slaves. These two designs could only be accompanied together, and only by death. As no meat could come out of the eater unless the eater had been slain, so there could be no redemption to Israel unless Christ, by his death, had destroyed him that had the power of death. But the meat was not produced by 'the eater', though it came out of him. The lion was dead, and could no more be an eater, and only in his dead carcase could the honey be stored by the swarm of bees whose work it was to gather it.

All that is meat and sweetness as the result of 'the death of death in the death of Christ' is due to the grace of God, which found in him who died and rose again a place in which the blessings of the everlasting covenant might be stored, and a way by which the Holy Spirit might come forth to dispense them. Let it be no difficulty to your mind to think of a living Samson while looking on the dead lion. Samson only risked his life, while Christ actually laid his down. Yet do not think that you have in this what utterly unfits the one for being an emblem of the other. The actual death of Christ only secured redemption by destroying him that had the power of death.

## 28 September

> But as for me, I will come into thy house in the multitude of thy mercy: and in thy fear will I worship toward thy holy temple.
> *Psalm 5:7*

The house of God is the place where he is to be worshipped by his people. There his great presence is to be approached. There, as on his throne, he presents himself in order the homage of his people. There, as on his mercy seat, he is accessible, for the way into the holiest is now open to his Israel and he has promised to bring them near. All are called to come, that they may obtain a right of access to him in every time of need, but they who are effectually called alone have obtained that right. Even they can avail themselves of their privilege only as the Spirit guides them. But he hath been promised, and shall be given to them, and they themselves and their worship shall be accepted of the Lord.

He makes Bethesda a Bethel by his presence with his people there. He has promised to be present with them. He distinctly tells that his design in building the house was 'that the Lord God might dwell among them'. And how is he to be present? Not merely because, being omnipresent, he cannot be away from his house—the Church. Not as if in some mystic way his presence was connected with the place in which his people meet to worship him. Not as if in a place set apart for his worship there was a special local abiding presence of the Most High. His people's hearts are the temples of his gracious presence. With them the high and lofty one who inhabiteth eternity has promised to dwell. This presence he has specially promised to them in connection with the service of his house. He has promised to be in the midst of those who meet together in his name.

## 29 September

> Wherefore he is able also to save them to the uttermost that come unto God by him, seeing he ever liveth to make intercession for them.
> *Hebrews 7:25*

He hath power, by his Spirit, to awaken the most sleepy sluggard on the earth. He can abase the proudest. He can enlighten the most benighted of all the children of darkness. He can subdue the most rebellious. He can quicken the soul that has been longest dead. He can draw the most distant alien to himself. He can make him one Spirit with himself, thus securing that he shall be 'made the righteousness of God in him'. And then he can effectually use his power with God so as to secure the free, full and final pardon of all his sins, with a God-given title to everlasting life.

And, sinner, he is able to do all this for thee. Oh, dost thou not need all this exercise of Christ's power within thee, and in thy behalf, in order to have peace with God? If so, friend, Christ is able to meet your whole case—your whole case—at its worst. Are you the most openly ungodly, the most defiantly wicked sinner? Are you, because of your peculiar privileges, the sinner whose guilt is more aggravated than that of all besides? Is there a special sin in your past conduct which you cannot think was ever committed except by yourself? Is there, after all you have ever done, utter blindness in your mind and utter callousness in your heart as to what is sin against God? Even could all these things be together true of you, here is one who can meet your whole case, who can do within you and for you all that is required, in order that you may be saved to the uttermost from all your guilt. And has he not been exalted a Prince and a Saviour, to give repentance to Israel, and forgiveness of sins? That is the work which he has been exalted to perform, and which you may ask him whose name is Jesus to do for you. He is able to do it.

## 30 September

> Wherefore he is able also to save them to the uttermost that come unto God by him, seeing he ever liveth to make intercession for them.
> *Hebrews 7:25*

He is able to save when 'the uttermost' is reached at death. What a crisis death seems to be to those who carefully forecast it! What a scaring thing it appears to some, and what a solemn thing to those who have ceased to regard it with terror! Then I shall be rent in twain—soul and body separated while still they cleave to each other. Then my last opportunity of receiving grace on earth shall have utterly passed away. Then shall I, as a naked spirit, actually pass into eternity. How solemn this entrance into the hitherto unseen world, where I must find my eternal place and state!

And in front of that solemn change, that terribly novel experience, how much is hidden which I would have palpable! How much there is within me which, if not utterly removed, must shut me out of heaven! And up to the very last moment I must have all sin present in my soul. Oh, how much it may affect my consciousness on the very eve of dying! How active may conscience then be in condemning, if the blood of Jesus be not then afresh sprinkled on it. And how active, even then, may the powers of darkness be in assailing my hope, while all the time my body may be racked with pain, and reason may be tottering, while hope is fainting. True, friend, all that may be your experience when your time to die has come. You cannot say it shall be so with you then, and you have no right to attempt to forecast the details of the coming experience of dying, nor to make any choice as to these. Leave all that is future in the hands of him who cannot err.

# October

CHARLES CALDER MACKINTOSH (1806–1868) was born in Tain in the Highlands where his father, Dr Angus Mackintosh, was the renowned evangelical minister of the parish.

Charles Mackintosh was an academically gifted child, who was sent to study at the University of Aberdeen at the unusually early age of eleven. He entered the Divinity classes at Glasgow when he was sixteen. Two years later a marked change was noted in his life and deportment and this was followed by evidence that he had drunk abundantly of the wells of salvation.

He was licensed to preach the gospel at Tain in 1828 at the age of twenty-one and became assistant to his father. Due to ill-health Charles Mackintosh left Tain almost immediately but returned in 1830 and the following year became his father's successor. Along with nearly all his large congregation he joined the Free Church of

Scotland at the Disruption. He was translated to Dunoon Free Church in 1854. His health broke down irrecoverably in 1868 and he died in France.

Charles Calder Mackintosh was a godly servant of Christ, esteemed both by discerning Highland Christians and his fellow ministers. His sermons were distinguished by a rich spiritual tone.

## Source of daily readings

William Taylor (ed.), *Memorials of the Life and Ministry of Charles Calder Mackintosh, D.D., of Tain and Dunoon* (Edinburgh, 1871).

## Biography

William Taylor, *Biographical Sketch* in *Memorials of the Life and Ministry of Charles Calder Mackintosh, D.D. (op cit.)*

# 1 October

Is there no balm in Gilead; is there no physician there? Why then is not the health of the daughter of my people recovered?
*Jeremiah 8:22*

Is there one here who may be ready to say, 'Woe is me, what shall I do? Once I thought I was in the fair way to heaven, but now I find that I have been ever in the broad way. Once I thought that I could do much in the matter of my soul's salvation; that I could master the Bible whenever I seriously applied my mind to it; that I could cleanse my heart; that I could watch and pray and keep my heart too. But now I find that I am guilty, and lost, and vile. My sins are as a heavy burden, too heavy for me to bear—most of all, the sin of rejecting a Saviour. And yet so hard is my heart, that it refuses to melt. So bound am I with the chain of sin, that were heaven to be won by one pure prayer, I should be for ever without. I try to pray, but I cannot pray. I try to read and to hear, but there is no light for me in the blessed book of life: it falls upon me as the rain upon the rock! And time is hastening on, and eternity is near. Oh! What shall I do?'

What shall you do, poor soul? Is there no balm in Gilead? Is there no physician there? Is there no hope in Israel for such a case as yours? Yes, what shall you do but cast yourself, as lost, at the feet of Jesus, saying, 'If I perish, I perish.'

# 2 October

For I through the law am dead to the law, that I might live unto God.
*Galatians 2:19*

Being dead to the law implies a ceasing to expect life from it or to look to it for life. Once it was far otherwise. It is one of the strange ways in which the mystery of iniquity in the heart shows itself, one of the strange aspects that the deceitful heart assumes, that while the sinner lies under the curse of the law and is morally unable to yield any true obedience to it, still his desire is to it, he looks to it for protection and life. That is, he trusts in something of his own in the shape of obedience, rather than in Christ.

But the believer in Jesus has abandoned every such ground of trust, and made the righteousness of the Redeemer his only refuge. I do not say that he will not feel the workings of self-righteousness and of pride—nay, that this is not a main part of the 'body of sin and death' under which he groans, and with which he must conflict to his dying day. But I say that, to all the suggestions of this accursed principle, and of Satan speaking through it, his renewed nature will reply, 'God forbid that I should glory, save in the cross of our Lord Jesus Christ, by whom the world is crucified unto me, and I unto the world. In the matter of my acceptance with God, I cast everything from me, that I may be found in Christ.'

## 3 October

> But grow in grace, and in the knowledge of our Lord and Saviour Jesus Christ. To him be glory both now and for ever. Amen.
> *2 Peter 3:18*

Oh, believer, are you humbled because of your little growth in grace? Are you ashamed of the unsteadfastness of your walk with God? Would you live to God? Then aim increasingly at living by the faith of his Son. Then employ increasingly the blessed Spirit of all grace to show you the things that are Christ's—the glory of his person, the preciousness of his blood, and the riches of his love.

If you would grow in humility, it must be in this way. It must be a believing contemplation of the Saviour that will produce it. If you would grow in repentance and self-denial and deadness to the world, it is this that will produce it. If you would be changed into the image of the Lord, it is this alone that will produce it.

Oh then, seek to dwell in view of Calvary. Let the tempter find you there. Let trial find you there. Let death find you there. It is but little of its glories that is perceived by the holiest saint on earth—the full unclouded view of them is reserved for the upper sanctuary. But as the saints there are all one in saying, 'Worthy is the Lamb that was slain, to receive power, and riches, and wisdom, and strength, and honour, and glory, and blessing,' so on earth they are all one in seeking this from the Lord—that they may grow in the knowledge of Christ crucified, and in the experience of the sanctifying efficacy of that knowledge.

# 4 October

> For my thoughts are not your thoughts, neither are your ways my ways, saith the LORD.
> Isaiah 55:8

If that which gave comfort to one of the holiest saints on earth in the near approach of death—'Christ Jesus came into the world to save sinners, of whom I am chief'—touches no sympathetic chord in your breast; if these blessed words are words of indifference to you—if you feel no personal interest in them—we know why it is so, and we are called to declare it unto you. It is because you are still dead in trespasses and sins, so that the very sense of your condition has yet to be discovered to you. We know too what is the necessary tendency, what the fearful issue of such security. It is death eternal.

Oh then, awake to a sense of your condition! 'Awake, thou that sleepest, and arise from the dead, and Christ shall give thee light.' Awake, ye that live without God and Christ in the world! Awake, ye that live as if this world were your home! Awake, ye that go about to establish your own righteousness! God's avenging law is in pursuit of you, and if it find you without the covert of the Redeemer's blood, your future misery is sure. Let the world say what it will, unless this blessed book be a fiction, the world 'lieth in the wicked one' and is devoted to destruction. Let the world say what it will of the mercy of God and of the uselessness of fear and anxiety in regard to an eternal state, sooner or later the pride of our hearts must be subdued, and we prostrated at God's feet. Better, surely, to be so when he is on the throne of grace and the royal hand of mercy will raise us up, than to be shivered by the rod of iron.

The song of the redeemed in heaven is, 'To him that loved us, and washed us from our sins in his own blood.' And if you would ever join that blessed throng, you must learn something of the wonders of redemption now.

# 5 October

> For ye know the grace of our Lord Jesus Christ, that, though he was rich, yet for your sakes he became poor, that ye through his poverty might be rich.
> *2 Corinthians 8:9*

He became poor in assuming our nature. He became truly bone of our bone and flesh of our flesh. And who can estimate this grace or fathom this condescension? Great, indeed, is the mystery of godliness, God manifest in the flesh. He took it upon him, and assumed it into intimate and indissoluble union with his divine person. And though he took it sinless, as pure from all stain as it was in Adam when he was created, yet he took it after it had become fallen and sinful.

He appeared 'in the likeness of sinful flesh'. Here indeed was poverty and humiliation. This is more a subject for thought and contemplation than for language, but surely the little that many nominal Christians find to wonder at in the incarnation of the Son of God is a proof that they have never fixedly contemplated or rightly understood it. 'Flesh and blood hath not revealed it unto thee, but my Father which is in heaven.'

Believer, adore that grace that led the Lord Jesus to take on him not the nature of angels, but the seed of Abraham, and that led him to become your brother, like unto you in all things, yet without sin. Believers, draw near and adore, while you hear the joyful sound that to you has been born a Saviour, Christ the Lord. And see here too how the ineffable condescension and humiliation of the Son of God has dignified and ennobled poverty, and stamped all the vain pomp and glory of this world with beggary. Are you poor? Remember that Christ was poor.

## 6 October

> For he hath made him to be sin for us, who knew no sin; that we might be made the righteousness of God in him.
> *2 Corinthians 5:21*

It is done 'once for all'. Sin is put away, and the believing sinner is as completely in a state of acceptance with God as he will be in heaven. This is a sure truth, and therefore, seeing what a foundation is laid in it for the exercise of hope and joy, we need not wonder that such joy should be in exercise. We should rather expect it, when it is given to one to realize the glory of the righteousness of God, and God's way of accepting sinners in his dear Son.

Yet, while there is a foundation laid for the continued and growing exercise of hope and joy to the end, it may be through an inward and unintermitting struggle that one is enabled to exercise the hope of his personal interest in Christ and of his completeness in him. It may be, as it is, in connection with watchfulness and prayer and the laborious use of the means of grace—striving in and through them to see Jesus. There can be no assurance of hope except in so far as faith is exercised on the Saviour in the gospel. The faith of yesterday will not avail for today, and neither assurance nor faith is a thing which the believer can lay hands on when he pleases. There is enough of such easy assurance and easy faith, deceitful assurance and false faith. The believer feels his need of the putting forth of the power of the Holy Spirit to enable him to see Jesus in the gospel, and to exercise faith in him for righteousness.

# 7 October

> This is a faithful saying, and worthy of all acceptation, that Christ Jesus came into the world to save sinners; of whom I am chief.
> *1 Timothy 1:15*

There was an eminent saint, an eminent minister of Christ now in glory, who in his dying sickness was sorely exercised in regard to the state of his soul. The enemy thrust sore, and he was brought very low. His sins possessed him, God's face was hid from him, and hope had well-nigh expired. While in this anguish of spirit, one night he dreamed a dream. He was not one of those who put any trust in impressions or in dreams apart from the law and the testimony. But God can still make use of this means for instruction and for admonition.

He dreamed that he saw heaven opened, and a company approach and go in, and the door was shut. In this company he beheld Abraham and Isaac and Jacob, and many of the Old Testament saints, and some whom he himself had known, but he could not get in along with them. There was a pause, and again the door was opened, and again a company approached, and in this company he knew many, but he could not get in along with them, and he began to tremble exceedingly. A third time the door was opened, and another company approached, and they went in one after another, and terror began to seize upon him, and his knees smote one against another, when all at once, looking round, he saw Manasseh—Manasseh who had made Jerusalem stream with blood. 'And', said the dying saint, 'I crept in at Manasseh's back.' He died, having nothing to trust to but this—but it was enough. This is a faithful saying, and worthy of all acceptation, that Christ Jesus came into the world to save sinners, even the chief.

# 8 October

> Against thee, thee only, have I sinned, and done this evil in thy sight: that thou mightest be justified when thou speakest, and be clear when thou judgest.
> *Psalm 51:4*

Who is the repenting sinner? He is one who, but yesterday, had his heart filled with worldliness, selfishness, pride, unbelief, and enmity against God, and who stood out in rebellion against him—and all this, perhaps, under the garb of discipleship. But now his sins possess him; he has no cloak for them. His whole past life has been sin. His lust, and atheism, and profanity, and unthankfulness, and want of love to Christ, and countless other sins, have taken hold of him, so that he cannot lift up his head. He has broken a law which is holy, and just, and good. It is against God he has sinned—the Creator, the Preserver, the Lawgiver, the long-suffering God, the Redeemer.

And withal [additionally], his heart is evil, it is desperately wicked. See how the Word, the formerly despised Bible, makes his knees smite together! You may see this, but no human eye can see how its light penetrates to the darkest recesses of the heart, how its fire consumes his self-righteousness, how its sword kills false hope. He condemns himself. He abhors himself. He ascribes righteousness to God, though he should cast him from his sight for ever. For this belongs to true repentance—not merely remorse, or a sense of the evil of sin as bringing misery in its train (such was Judas's repentance); not merely sorrow for sin because we hope that God has pardoned, or will pardon, our sins (such sorrow may consist with love to sin and opposition to the sovereignty of God), but a recognition of the glory of the attribute of justice in God, as manifested in the requirements and the sanctions of his law.

# 9 October

> Simon Peter, a servant and an apostle of Jesus Christ, to them that have obtained like precious faith with us through the righteousness of God and our Saviour Jesus Christ.
> *2 Peter 1:1*

With respect to the preciousness of faith, I would notice, first, its author. It is God's command to us to believe on the name of his Son Jesus Christ. It is our solemn duty to comply with his command, and faith is our act, the exercise of our minds and hearts. But the ability thus to exercise them is of God. The spiritual illumination and the holy disposition implied in faith are the effects of the Holy Spirit's gracious operations on the mind and heart.

Consider especially these words, 'Unto you it is given'—literally, 'freely given'—'in the behalf of Christ, not only to believe on him,' etc., in connection with the words that precede and follow our text: 'them that have obtained like precious faith with us, through the righteousness of God and our Saviour Jesus Christ'. That is, faith is God's gift, and it is for Christ's sake it is bestowed. To deny this truth, avowedly or virtually, is to deny the work of the Holy Spirit, and to subvert the gospel of Christ. Those who teach men that they believe of themselves, or believe at any time they please, are leading them in the way to destruction. We cannot be too jealous of [apprehensive about] the preaching that overlooks the necessity for the Holy Spirit's agency to work faith in the heart, or that overlooks the truth that *every* spiritual blessing—faith, as surely as forgiveness—is the purchase of the blood or righteousness of God our Saviour, and bestowed by the Father in his sovereign grace.

## 10 October

Unto you therefore which believe he is precious.
1 Peter 2:7

Its foundation shows its preciousness. Just in proportion to the magnitude of the interests involved in belief of the gospel is the importance of a sure ground of confidence that it is no 'cunningly devised fable'.

Now, the foundation of faith is that the gospel is God's testimony. It does not rest on the testimony of man—of any individual holy man, or of any association of good though fallible men. I do not believe because the Church believes. That would be a poor, shifting foundation on which to rest one's hopes for eternity.

Nor does my faith rest on the conviction to which I have reached after the examination of the evidences of Christianity, that it is of God—though that conviction is, in its own place, of great importance, and though it will invariably follow a candid and serious examination of such evidences.

Nor does faith rest on internal feelings and exercises. I do not see or feel, and therefore believe. I do not find a good heart within, and on this ground expect mercy. I do not find myself prepared for Christ, and on this ground, in connection with what Christ has done, look for salvation.

I find no good heart within to encourage me to approach God. I have no previous experience of his mercy to embolden me to trust in him, but, under the pressure of guilt and misery, I approach God on the bare warrant of his own Word.

# 11 October

*All scripture is given by inspiration of God, and is profitable for doctrine, for reproof, for correction, for instruction in righteousness.*
*2 Timothy 3:16*

Faith rests on the testimony of God: 'Thus saith the Lord.' Faith is exercised when God is recognised as speaking in his own Word. Hence the transcendent importance of the truth concerning the inspiration of the Holy Scriptures.

Men calling themselves Christian teachers are labouring in our day, more or less openly, in the work in which avowed infidels in former generations spent their strength, namely, that of undermining the Church's faith in the trustworthiness of the Holy Scriptures as God's written revelation of his will for our salvation. If the Bible be not God's own book, written by holy men as they were moved by the Holy Spirit, then there is no infallible foundation of faith. If it be not truly God's pure and sure Word for our salvation, so that we can and ought to surrender ourselves implicitly to its guidance to be illuminated, comforted, and moulded by it, then the foundations of hope are taken away. Because there are disputed passages, and various readings of some passages, and because there are other things left to try us, men who hate the humbling doctrines of the cross begin again the old work of fighting against God's Word. But he who so wondrously watched over it and preserved it for his Church in past generations will watch over it still. And, unaffected by such cavils and calumnies, souls thirsting for salvation will still come to its living waters and drink. God will make his powerful and melting voice to be heard in his own Word.

## 12 October

And the Holy Ghost descended in a bodily shape like a dove upon him, and a voice came from heaven, which said, Thou art my beloved Son; in thee I am well pleased.
*Luke 3:22*

The object of faith shows its preciousness. Faith having for its foundation the word or testimony of God, terminates indeed on the whole of God's revealed will, more immediately on the truth concerning man's lost condition and the way of salvation by Jesus Christ, but peculiarly on Christ himself. It is not the mercy of God separated from Christ, nor even the righteousness of Christ apart from Christ, but Christ himself. The object of saving faith, then, is not bare truth, however glorious that truth may be, but, in its primary and peculiar acting, it is the essential Word, the living Truth, Christ himself.

It is the nature of faith, or rather the way of God in dealing savingly with a sinner, to lead him forth from himself to Christ in the gospel. Within, he finds nothing but guilt, darkness, misery. But, guided by God's testimony, he goes forth to Christ. God says, 'This is my beloved Son, in whom I am well pleased. Behold the Lamb of God, which taketh away the sin of the world.' 'Open thy mouth wide, and I will fill it.' 'My Father giveth you the true bread from heaven.'

What the self-emptied sinner seeks is what will meet all the wants of his sin-laden, immortal spirit in the prospect of eternity—what will meet his guilt, his distance from God, his spiritual nakedness and pollution and poverty. On this side of Christ, he will seek for this in vain. But, guided by the Word and Spirit of God, he sees Jesus—the Sun of righteousness breaks forth on his night of gloom and darkness. He sees one uniting the glories of divinity and the beauties of humanity in his wondrous person.

# 13 October

> Simon Peter, a servant and an apostle of Jesus Christ, to them that have obtained like precious faith with us through the righteousness of God and our Saviour Jesus Christ.
> *2 Peter 1:1*

Let Christians seek to grow in the knowledge of the necessity and excellence of precious faith, and be encouraged to exercise it, and to glorify Christ by casting every burden upon him—the burden of sin, of affliction, of a very narrow path of duty. The foundation abideth, though you may be tossed. Faith must needs be tried. But Christ prays that it may not fail.

Does sin oppress you—the remembrance of sin, or a sense of present sin? He is the Lord your righteousness, and your peace. Are you troubled with a dark mind? He is the light of dark souls. Or with an obdurate heart? With him is the Spirit of grace and of supplications. Are you weak? In him is everlasting strength. Are you poor? With him are unsearchable riches. Are you unstable, and have you a treacherous heart? Yet he abideth faithful, and he has promised restoring grace.

Glorify Christ, by giving him all your works to work in you. He is the same now as when he took David out of the fearful pit, as when he kept Peter from sinking, as when he brought Paul to say, 'I can do all things through Christ which strengtheneth me.'

But do you possess this faith? If not, become partakers of it. The word of faith is preached to you; the object of faith is presented to you. He speaks to you the same gracious words which he addressed to sinners in past times, and invites you to the same hopes. He asks you to receive him as your all, that he may do all for you.

# 14 October

Forasmuch as ye know that ye were not redeemed with corruptible things, as silver and gold, from your vain conversation received by tradition from your fathers; but with the precious blood of Christ, as of a lamb without blemish and without spot.
1 Peter 1:18–19

That gospel makes known the propitiation effected by the blood of the incarnate Son of God, the sacrifice of a suitable and all-sufficient surety accepted by the Judge and exhibited in his Word to be relied upon and trusted in by sinners.

Here is something suited to give relief and peace. Here is what the law-pursued and conscience-struck sinner is seeking after. Here is one ready to be his Mediator, one whom the offended God has appointed to this work and in whom he delights, one who has mediated by his own blood, who has stood between sinners and the storm—bearing it in his own body on the tree—one ready to make over to him, however guilty and vile, all the merit of the sacrifice which is of a sweet-smelling savour to God, so that all his guilt shall be taken away and that he shall be enabled, while smiting on his breast, to look up to God and to say, 'Christ—yea Christ whom I have pierced—hath died, and thine own testimony is that his blood cleanseth from all sin.'

And therefore, when the reality and the infinite value of the atonement are apprehended, when the Judge is seen as satisfied and as on a throne of grace waiting to be gracious, that which he has provided for sheltering the sinner and for purging the conscience is enough to meet all the requirements of conscience and to give him hope in his presence. And so, while he looks to the precious blood of Christ and essays to trust in it for the purging away of all his sin, there begins to flow in a blessed rest and quiet on the conscience.

# 15 October

*And, having made peace through the blood of his cross, by him to reconcile all things unto himself; by him, I say, whether they be things in earth, or things in heaven.*
*Colossians 1:20*

His peace flows directly and altogether from the blood of Christ, to the exclusion of any ground of hope in the sinner. As, without any evidence and apart from any evidence of a work of grace on his heart, he has a warrant as an ungodly sinner to enjoy peace in looking to the blood of Christ, so it is substantially in the same way, on the warrant of the same gospel, in the exercise of the same faith similarly exercised, that this peace is renewed in the believer's experience from day to day.

He must examine himself whether he be 'in the faith', and he ought to be encouraged by all his past experience to look afresh to Jesus with hope and expectation. But his soul-prosperity and the vigorous exercise of faith for all the exigencies of the Christian life must depend on his continued application, in the exercise of simple faith, to the Lord Jesus in his sacrifice for cleansing and peace-making. He applies, not as one under condemnation—it is his infirmity or his sin if he does this. But, although a justified man and a child of God, he applies as a sinner needing the blood of Christ to cleanse his soul from the guilt he is continually contracting and to preserve peace as much as when he first looked to it for a full pardon and for peace. He needs to look to it not as a sanctified man but as a sinner. The more close his walk with God, the more will this be his exercise. The stronger his faith, the simpler it will be.

# 16 October

Cast away from you all your transgressions, whereby ye have transgressed; and make you a new heart and a new spirit: for why will ye die, O house of Israel?
*Ezekiel 18:31*

'Make you a new heart.' These words have a startling sound. The truths they teach are little thought of, and hard to be believed. Many may acknowledge in general that it is their duty to repent, and they may experience no difficulty in acknowledging this, just because they have false and unscriptural views of what repentance is, because they think of repentance as a something that they can originate in their own minds and hearts when they please. But when the same great change is brought before them as consisting in this—a new heart—and when the words of God, 'Make you a new heart,' are really contemplated and considered by the sinner, then either he will be altogether perplexed as to the meaning of such language, or he will find his heart rising up against God for addressing him in such words as these. And I would just notice some of the objections which may suggest themselves to such an individual.

It may be thought—it has been thought, and said, 'Am I not unable to do anything spiritually good? Am I not told this in the Word of God? Is it not the very first truth which I am called to learn, that I am as unable to do anything spiritually good as a dead man is to perform the functions of natural life? Then how am I under obligation to possess this heart?'

Now, it is a solemn question: On what does our obligation rest to love, to believe, to obey God? It rests not on our present disposition of heart, but on our relation to God as his creatures, who are possessed of a reason, of a conscience, and of a will.

# 17 October

> Cast away from you all your transgressions, whereby ye have transgressed; and make you a new heart and a new spirit: for why will ye die, O house of Israel?
> *Ezekiel 18:31*

But it may again be thought and said, 'Why does God *command* me to make me a new heart, when he knows that I am unable to do this—as unable as to create a world?' *Why?* Because he is gracious; because it is possible to obtain a new heart; because the way of salvation and of life has been opened up through his dear Son; because there is hope in him for the chief of sinners; because God makes use of the threatenings and the expostulations of his Word in saving souls, in drawing them to himself; and because he will have you to know, as a truth—that will meet you on the great day of account—that he has no pleasure in your death.

'As I live, saith the Lord God, I have no pleasure in the death of the wicked; but that the wicked turn from his way and live: turn ye, turn ye from your evil ways; for why will ye die?' As surely as we are bound to believe that God is unchangeably just and good, and that he is infinitely gracious, we are bound to believe that he is sincere when he says to the sinner, 'Why will ye die?' It were blasphemy to deny this; it is a great sin to question it. It is the expression of the compassion and the pity of the heart of God, when he says, 'Why will ye die?'

# 18 October

> Cast away from you all your transgressions, whereby ye have transgressed; and make you a new heart and a new spirit: for why will ye die, O house of Israel?
> *Ezekiel 18:31*

Surely we must learn that if it be a duty to possess a new heart, then it must be a duty to use the means towards it. The Lord the Spirit stirs the soul up to activity, and from first to last, from the beginning of his gracious work to the close, it is in felt weakness that his strength is perfected, in utter helplessness that the strength of Jehovah the Spirit is perfected. Yes, men may pervert this blessed doctrine and may make it the minister of sloth. But when the Holy Spirit begins to work savingly on the heart of any sinner, then that soul ceases thus to pervert it. The more he feels that he cannot pray, the more he prays. The more he feels that all his doings and his earnestness will go for nothing unless divine mercy interpose, arrest and deliver him, the more earnest he is, the more laborious, in striving to enter in at the strait gate. And the more emptied he is of self-sufficiency, the more is he brought to look with hope to the promise of the Holy Spirit, and the more is he prepared for understanding and realizing its preciousness.

Therefore, fellow sinner, fellow traveller to eternity, here is a work—greater and more glorious, we admit, than the creation of a world—to be wrought in you, without which you must perish. It is no dream. It is the truth of God that a state of never-ending existence awaits you, and everything hastens that period when the final separation shall be made between the righteous and the wicked.

## 19 October

> For my yoke is easy, and my burden is light.
> Matthew 11:30

It will be found very instructive to notice the connection in which these words are introduced by the Redeemer. He had denounced woe against Chorazin and Bethsaida. Most of his mighty works had been done in those cities. Yet, where we should have expected that most fruit would be brought forth, there was almost none. And so the Redeemer pronounced their doom, saying that in the great day they would be found guiltier than Tyre and Sidon, and even than Sodom, and that they should receive the greater condemnation. He had at the same time thanked his Father that it seemed good in his sight savingly to make known the mysteries of his kingdom unto babes, while they were hidden from the wise and prudent. Then, stretching out his arms of mercy, he invited all that labour and are heavy laden to come to him for rest.

These three things, then, are alike true: that men's destruction is of themselves, that their salvation is of God, and that Christ is a free Saviour to whom all are equally invited to come. We may find it hard—I should rather say impossible—in this world to understand the perfect harmony of the glorious sovereignty of him who has mercy on whom he will have mercy with the absolute freeness of the gospel, and with our free agency and full accountability for our reception of it. Yet each of these is a Bible truth, and it will be your wisdom to accept them as from the lips of God.

## 20 October

> For my yoke is easy, and my burden is light.
> *Matthew 11:30*

How can that yoke be easy, an essential part of which is to deny ourselves, to take up the cross and follow Christ in the narrow way?

It is easy, in the first place, because it is *his* yoke. It is the yoke of him who is our rightful Lord, who is infinitely worthy of the love of the whole heart and the services of the whole being, who has the claims of Redeemer as well as Creator, who is holy, who is gracious, who is God all-sufficient, whom all the angels of God worship. It is his yoke, of whom his forerunner, who knew his glory, said that he was not worthy to unloose his shoe-latchet; of whom another of his servants said that he esteemed his reproach, however much he might suffer in confessing his name, greater riches than the treasures in Egypt. If it be an honour to serve the best and highest of earthly kings, what an honour is it to serve him who is King of kings, Lord of lords, and at the same time the friend and brother of his people!

Secondly, it is the yoke of liberty. They who bear it are his redeemed ones, who have been delivered with a great deliverance. They have been blessed with freedom from the condemning sentence of the holy law which bound them over to eternal death. They have been blessed with freedom from the servitude of sin, which once they served, till in the light of the cross they saw its evil and its vileness; with freedom from the tyranny of Satan, who once led them captive at his will.

# 21 October

*For my yoke is easy, and my burden is light.*
*Matthew 11:30*

But some one may say, 'How can this truth—that Christ's yoke is easy—consist with the Christian life being one of suffering and self-denial, with the gate to life being strait and the way narrow?'

It might be enough to answer, in the language of Paul, that 'the sufferings of this present time are not worthy to be compared with the glory which shall be revealed in us', and that the exercise of that hope by which believers are saved is more than sufficient to counterbalance any present suffering in the way. But more than this: there is no part of the suffering which is appointed for Christians in serving Christ in this world, which is not needful with a view to their present spiritual good and usefulness and to their eternal happiness. They are assured of this by their Lord, and they have some experience of it.

Is the conflict with sin which occasions (as we know from Paul's experience) acute suffering? The Christian is thus prepared more and more for estimating what a great thing salvation—a holy salvation—is. Or is it the conflict with his spiritual enemies? He thus makes increasing acquaintance with the sympathy of the great High Priest, who was 'tempted in all points like as we are, yet without sin'. Or is it the conflict with trial of other kinds? 'If we suffer, we shall also reign with him,' says Paul. If the believer lived up to his privileges, he would see special love in the most rugged steps of the journey.

## 22 October

> For my yoke is easy, and my burden is light.
> *Matthew 11:30*

Dear friends, what is our experience? Is our religion a task, a burden which in some, or many, of its observances we would shake off if we could? Or is it the source of true peace and happiness to us? Is our service the service of slaves, or of freemen and children? No doubt there may be some enjoyment found in a religion of self-righteousness, in a religion, the great end of which is to pacify conscience and to feed and pamper self. But this is not Christ's yoke, and this enjoyment is not the true rest.

But supposing that we profess to have taken Christ's yoke upon us, knowing the implicit dependence upon him and the entire devotedness to him that are implied in it, then what is our experience? Do we find Christ a hard master, or have we experienced some true rest in his service? Do we love the Word of Christ better than any other book, and the day of Christ better than any other day? Do we love Christ's house? Do we love his person, though not as we would? And the more we are enabled to rely upon him exclusively and to devote ourselves to him, to seek as our chief aim that he may be magnified, the more intensely we are engaged in his work, and the more we are energetically employed in seeking to have sin mortified, do we the more experience that his yoke is easy and his burden is light? This is an evidence that we have proved his word, and know it experimentally to be true.

## 23 October

> Fear not, little flock; for it is your Father's good pleasure to give you the kingdom.
> *Luke 12:32*

True discipleship is consistent with only broken rest in Christ, with the experience of only a scanty measure of rest in Christ, particularly on the part of the young or the tried disciple. One may say, 'I *do* see things in a new light—how vain the world is, how great the soul and salvation are, how solemn eternity is! I *do* see that the great end of life is to find Christ and to follow him. I *do* see a loveliness and excellency in the Saviour that make him infinitely worthy of the trust and love of sinners. And I *do* desire to have him as my Priest and Teacher and King. But I cannot say that I have attained to settled peace. Instead of this, I am troubled in a new way. I often fear that my sins are not forgiven.'

You are not to expect a peace that would leave you independent of coming afresh every day to the blood of Christ for cleansing. That would be false peace. It were well for you if you were never so satisfied with your coming and your faith as that you should give it Christ's place.

Another may say, 'I am very ignorant of the mysteries of the kingdom of heaven, and slow of heart to understand. I never felt my ignorance as I do now.' If this is because you have begun to come in contact with the great things of God, it is well. Christ can give you light. Christ can carry you on in the knowledge of himself.

# 24 October

Fear not, little flock; for it is your Father's good pleasure to give you the kingdom.
*Luke 12:32*

What obligations are Christians laid under to commend the yoke of Christ to others by a consistent, humble, fruitful walk, by a suitable deportment under trial, by speaking well of his name—especially to the young, and by trying to win others to his service! Oh, commend the precious Saviour, dear friends!

Though some of us may be—and have reason to be—ashamed when we place ourselves side by side with some of the Bible worthies, or with some of the characters in the *Pilgrim's Progress,* yet surely every Christian would desire to add his amen to the testimony which one of Bunyan's pilgrims gives for Christ when he is in the river of death: 'This river has been a terror to many, yea the thoughts of it also have often frightened me. The waters, indeed, are to the palate bitter, and to the stomach cold; yet the thoughts of what I am going to, and of the conduct that waits for me on the other side, do lie as a glowing coal at my heart. I am now at the end of my journey; my toilsome days are ended. I am going now to see that head that was crowned with thorns, and that face that was spit upon for me. I have loved to hear my Lord spoken of; and wherever I have seen the print of his shoe in the earth, there I have coveted to set my foot too. His name has been to me sweeter than all perfumes.'

# 25 October

So when they had dined, Jesus saith to Simon Peter, Simon, son of Jonas, lovest thou me more than these? He saith unto him, Yea, Lord; thou knowest that I love thee. He saith unto him, Feed my lambs.
*John 21:15*

As it was for the church that Christ lived and died, so it was for her that he rose again. He left his Father's throne of glory and came into a far country, that he might earn and purchase her redemption and deliverance. His love for her was such that the waters of many temptations and the floods of affliction and of his Father's wrath could not quench it. For the joy that was set before him in her complete deliverance he endured the cross. For her he became obedient even unto death.

And in all his humiliation the prospect in the distance of this beauteous and ransomed bride rejoiced his spirit, and carried him exultingly through. As he died for her offences, so he rose again for her justification. If he is now at the right hand of the Father, it is that he may make intercession for her. If he has all power in heaven and on earth, it is that he may give eternal life to her for whom he laid down his life. And as the severest pang of his sufferings could not prevail to make him think the purchase too dear, so he rejoiced in their completion mainly because his church's deliverance was effected.

If we would see into the heart of Christ, let us contemplate him on the day of his resurrection. He had burst the prison gates and come forth a conqueror. He stood the head of a redeemed world. He had spoiled principalities and powers. A name above every name awaited him.

# 26 October

So when they had dined, Jesus saith to Simon Peter, Simon, son of Jonas, lovest thou me more than these? He saith unto him, Yea, Lord; thou knowest that I love thee. He saith unto him, Feed my lambs.
*John 21:15*

It is no longer self-confident boasting Peter, but humbled, broken-hearted Peter who speaks. He had learned a lesson of humility. He had learned the deceitfulness of his heart. The exceeding sinfulness of his sin was present to his mind, so that he blushed in remembering his woeful pride and presumption. And instead of thinking he stood foremost in faith and love, he now deemed himself unworthy to be called a disciple, feeling that if again permitted to call Christ 'Lord and Master', it would be a miracle of mercy.

Yet still he felt that he loved him, that Christ was dearer to him than all besides, that without him this world would be to him a blank and void. He knew that he harboured no known rebel to his Lord in his heart, and if such an Achan lurked unsuspected there, it was his desire that Christ should drag it forth and slay it before him. He knew also that he had sorrowed for his sin as he had never sorrowed for any earthly losses or trials, and in the view of this he was able to look Christ in the face and to say, 'Lord, *thou knowest* that I love thee.' He appealed to the Searcher of hearts, and left it with him to say if it were not so.

In this reply we may see also the workings of the Spirit of adoption. He felt how grievously he had sinned. It led him to throw himself into the arms of the Lord Jesus, in the self-same spirit with that which led David to say, 'Let me fall into the hand of the Lord, for his mercies are great.' 'Yea, Lord, thou knowest that I love thee.'

# 27 October

Abide in me, and I in you. As the branch cannot bear fruit of itself, except it abide in the vine; no more can ye, except ye abide in me.
*John 15:4*

These words were first addressed by Christ to the eleven, who were 'in him', not by profession only but in reality, and to whom he had a little before spoken such words as these, 'Let not your heart be troubled: ye believe in God, believe also in me.' 'I will not leave you comfortless; I will come to you. Yet a little while, and the world seeth me no more; but ye see me: because I live, ye shall live also.' 'Peace I leave with you, my peace I give unto you: not as the world giveth, give I unto you. Let not your heart be troubled, neither let it be afraid,' and of whom he had just said (Judas having previously left them), 'Now are ye clean, through the word that I have spoken unto you.'

He makes use of the simile of the vine-stock and the branches to illustrate the union that subsists between him and his people. The vine-stock and the branches make up one tree: Christ and his people are one. No doubt Christ speaks of certain branches in him being taken away, cast forth and withered. But these are branches that by bearing no fruit unto perfection show that they are not truly united to the vine, and do not partake of its life and fatness. The mysterious union on which salvation turns has never been made up between them and the Saviour, through his Spirit quickening them and their coming to him for life. We must be living souls, living branches in the living vine, in order that the union may be indissoluble.

## 28 October

> Abide in me, and I in you. As the branch cannot bear fruit of itself, except it abide in the vine; no more can ye, except ye abide in me.
> *John 15:4*

It is not enough to be in Christ. We must abide in Christ. As it is not enough for a *sinner* to know that Jesus is the common Saviour, or to know that all whom the Father hath given him shall come to him; as his knowledge of these things will but increase his condemnation unless he comes to Christ for salvation, so neither is it enough for the *believer* to know that nothing shall separate him from the love of Christ. For, if it be a blessed truth that the love of Christ is unchangeable, it is just as sure that those who are interested in it 'work out their own salvation' and do not 'draw back to perdition'.

All care and anxiety about the soul do not leave a man once through grace he is in Christ. The fear of the wrath to come should indeed be removed by faith in the blood of atonement, but there must be the same care to continue in Christ that there was to find Christ. And no comfort can be drawn from the unchangeableness of his love unless we are thus striving to 'abide in him'. Our first care must be to attain to a state of salvation through union to Christ. Our continued care must be to have our salvation advancing and the spiritual life in us increased through daily experience of the power of Christ as the life.

## 29 October

> Abide in me, and I in you. As the branch cannot bear fruit of itself, except it abide in the vine; no more can ye, except ye abide in me.
> *John 15:4*

What is implied then in abiding in Christ? There must be a deep continued sense of need of Christ, and an abiding perception of his all-sufficiency and fulness as a Saviour. The poverty of spirit to which the blessing is attached by our Lord in the Sermon on the Mount is characteristic of the Christian, not at the outset of his course only, but while he is in this world. It will leave him at death, when sin will leave him. Then he will be perfected in humility and perfectly blessed in the enjoyment of Christ, but he will be no longer poor in spirit. Till then, he will be growing in this grace. The richer in grace, the poorer will he be in spirit, because he will be increasingly humble, because there will be increasing sensibility to sin, and a more and more enlarged apprehension of how much he has to attain. And thus, as he grows in grace, he will more and more need the same Saviour who received him at first, when he came in his guilt and his rags and his misery, and who showed him mercy.

But along with a sense of need of Christ, there must be a continued and growing perception of the suitableness and fulness of Christ, through a spiritual understanding of the record concerning him. Without this the Christian, with his deep exercise, would be of all men the most miserable. The blessedness of the poor in spirit lies in this, that theirs is the kingdom of heaven to enrich and ennoble them.

## 30 October

> Where there is neither Greek nor Jew, circumcision nor un-circumcision, Barbarian, Scythian, bond nor free: but Christ is all, and in all.
> *Colossians 3:11*

'Christ is all' in the estimation and choice of every believing sinner. He has been seeking rest for his troubled spirit in many ways of vanity—oh, what has he not tried?—till, having spent all and ready to give over, he obtains, through the teaching of the loving

Comforter, a glimpse of the sufficiency and the grace of Christ manifested on Calvary, and he proves him, and finds that he is 'able to save to the uttermost'.

For his guilt, he finds atoning blood; for his unrighteousness, everlasting righteousness; for his strengthlessness to resist sin, almighty grace; for his blindness, eyesalve which restores sight to the soul; for his vileness, bowels of mercy and compassion; for his defencelessness, the care of the Good Shepherd; for his sorrows, the sympathy of the great High Priest; for his waywardness and inconstancy, the love of the unchanging friend; for his heart, a portion that will fill it for ever; for his destitution of all good and his utter unworthiness, a Saviour to be his without money and without price. And now what things were gain to him, he counts loss for Christ. He has found the pearl of great price, and sells all that it may be his. To know Christ, to be united to him—so united to him, by a union not of man's forming, but of the Holy Spirit's forming, as that Christ's merits shall be counted to him, and that Christ shall be in him as the spring and perfecter of the spiritual life—this is the one thing he desires of the Lord.

# 31 October

> Where there is neither Greek nor Jew, circumcision nor uncircumcision, Barbarian, Scythian, bond nor free: but Christ is all, and in all.
> *Colossians 3:11*

May the children of Zion be joyful in their King! Well may they cease from hewing out broken cisterns that can hold no water, or from trusting in anything for salvation and happiness but Christ alone. Well may they rejoice for what they have in him—for 'all things are theirs'—much more for what he is in himself! And they *do* trust in him, they *do* love him, they *do* glory in him—though not as they would, for in this world their views of Christ are often greatly bedimmed by sin; at the best they see through a glass darkly. They are compassed with infirmity, warring with corruption.

But, oh! Which of them would exchange the hope which he has from Christ and in Christ, faint though it may be, for a thousand worlds? Which of them will hesitate to give his testimony to the sufficiency, the grace, and the transcendent excellency of Christ? Which of them has not some wondrous deliverance to speak of, which only matchless Christ could have effected for his soul in the time of his distress? The full meaning of the words 'Christ is all, and in all' is not known, then, to the saints in this world. They will begin to know it when they have crossed the dark valley and entered on the joy of their Lord. At the resurrection day, when the redemption of the church will be completed, they will begin to understand the meaning of these words: 'The Lamb which is in the midst of the throne shall feed them, and shall lead them unto living fountains of waters: and God shall wipe away all tears from their eyes.'

# November

JONATHAN RANKEN ANDERSON (1803–1859) was born in Paisley. After a period of deep conviction of sin, God brought him to faith in the crucified Saviour at the age of sixteen.

He began studies at the University of Glasgow, distinguishing himself both in the Arts course and the Divinity classes. In 1834 he became minister of Kirkfield Chapel in Glasgow. A notable revival of religion occurred under his ministry in 1840. He was translated to the new John Knox congregation in the Kingston area of the city in 1842.

Jonathan Ranken Anderson joined the Free Church at the Disruption in 1843 and became a tutor in Hebrew at the Glasgow Free Church College. In 1852 he left the Free Church, concerned at the laxity he observed in doctrine and practice in the denomination. Many of his congregation followed him, and he also ministered to large groups of like-minded people in various parts of Scotland, particularly in Caithness and the Northern Highlands. His sermons were greatly appreciated for their depth and discriminating spiritual content.

## Source of daily readings

Herbert B. Pitt (ed.), *Life and Sermons of the Late Rev. J.R. Anderson, Minister of the Gospel, Glasgow*, Vol. II (Glasgow and Trowbridge, 1937).

## Biography

Herbert B. Pitt, *Sketch of the Life of the Late Rev. Jonathan Ranken Anderson, Minister of the Gospel in Glasgow* in *Life and Sermons (op. cit.)*, Vol. II.

# 1 November

> I am the door: by me if any man enter in, he shall be saved, and shall go in and out, and find pasture.
> *John 10:9*

To a man who is in any measure duly alive to the state of guilt and misery in which he comes into the world, and in which if he leaves it he shall eternally wish that he had never been born, it must appear a question of the greatest magnitude, how he may be delivered from it and brought into a state of peace and happiness.

When this question is raised by an individual thus affected, it is not every answer that will meet and settle it. An enquiry into the matter, that is proposed merely to gain information to avoid the reproach of being ignorant of that which everybody ought to know, or to serve some present or merely worldly purpose, is very easily put to rest.

But when a man is under the pressure of conscious guilt, when he is grieved with the deprivation of fellowship with God, when he is bowed down and afflicted with the views that rise up before him and the corruptions that rankle within him, and in these circumstances puts the question, how he may escape the wrath which is to come, it needs an Interpreter, one of a thousand, to solve his enquiries and to allay his fears. He feels it is with God he has to do. It is against him he has sinned, from him he is banished, and by him he is condemned. And therefore he judges that no plan of escape can be trusted to, which does not bear upon it the seal of his approbation, and that no way of safety ought to be entered upon, which has not been opened by the power of his grace.

# 2 November

*I am the door: by me if any man enter in, he shall be saved, and shall go in and out, and find pasture.*
*John 10:9*

In the text, there are some things evidently presupposed, to which it is needful that we turn our attention.

And first, it is presupposed that men are in a state of danger. Were you to pass the Asylum for the Blind and read on the gateway the inscription which bears the name of that institution, you would at once conclude that in our city there were individuals destitute of the sense of sight. In like manner, when we read (as in the text) of a door of salvation, what can be plainer than that there must be some who are in danger? And is not this fact recorded and illustrated on every page of the Word of God? In our world there are men in danger, and most imminent danger, not only of temporal calamities and bodily sufferings, but of eternal destruction and spiritual plagues. But where are they? They are here, in our city, in our assembly. We—*we*—are the men, 'for all have sinned, and come short of the glory of God', and 'cursed is every one that continueth not in all things which are written in the book of the law to do them'.

But, secondly, it is presupposed in the text that an asylum has been provided for those who are in danger. A door is the entrance to some enclosure, be it a temple, a house or a sheep-fold. And this is fully taught in the holy Scriptures. Indeed, this is the burden of these invaluable writings, and from Genesis to Revelation the theme for substance is, 'Glory to God in the highest, and on earth peace, goodwill toward men.'

# 3 November

*I am the door: by me if any man enter in, he shall be saved, and shall go in and out, and find pasture.*
*John 10:9*

We are thus brought to consider in the second place, the entrance to this asylum: 'I am the door.' The speaker here is the Lord Jesus Christ, the Son of the Blessed, who is of one essence with him, and equal to him in the glory and majesty of the divine nature. He did, however, in amazing condescension, become incarnate, and by a mystery of wisdom and power and love, which we cannot fathom, did assume the nature of man into personal union with himself. In this wondrous constitution of person did he stand and, with a majesty and grace peculiar to himself, declare, 'I am the door.' The honour he thus wears is very high; the office he fills is arduous. But when we reflect on the dignity of his person and the variety of his endowments, we cannot doubt that he is perfectly equal to the work assigned to him. He is the 'Wonderful, Counsellor, the Mighty God, the Everlasting Father, the Prince of Peace'.

But why is this glorious one called the door? In seeking the answer to this question, let it be observed that the state of salvation into which sinners are to be brought is a state of covenant love with God, of federal union to the Lord Christ, of fellowship with God the Holy Ghost, of communion with all saints, and of true and eternal purity and blessedness. Now, Christ is called the door because it is through him, and for his sake, that any of the children of men are introduced to this privileged condition.

# 4 November

*Having therefore, brethren, boldness to enter into the holiest by the blood of Jesus.*
*Hebrews 10:19*

Christ is the door because by his Surety work he hath taken away sin, and thus obtained a good and valid title to eternal life. He did come under the law in its precept, and never was he discouraged, deep as was the conflict and severe as were the labours, till he said, 'It is finished.'

In consequence of this glorious work, which will be the wonder and study of saints and angels through eternal ages, he was himself exalted into ineffable glory: 'Thou wilt show me the path of life: in thy presence is fulness of joy, at thy right hand are pleasures for evermore.' The everlasting doors of the heavenly glory were opened to him because he appeared with his own blood, the shedding of which was the consummation of his work. Just as the high priest passed through the veil of the temple, once a year, with the blood of sacrifices, so is Christ's blood and righteousness which it completed, made that on the ground of which sinful men are admitted to a state of grace here and of glory hereafter: 'When we were enemies, we were reconciled to God by the death of his Son.' 'Having therefore, brethren, boldness to enter into the holiest by the blood of Jesus, by a new and living way, which he hath he hath consecrated for us through the veil, that is to say, his flesh.' 'By his knowledge shall my righteous servant justify many: for he shall bear their iniquities.'

## 5 November

*And their sins and iniquities will I remember no more.*
*Hebrews 10:17*

How happy the change that is wrought, when the sinner enters the door and finds himself safe! He sees that he is in a large room, even the covenant of eternal love, its immeasurable compass and its immense fulness. He discovers that by his reconciliation to God he has made a covenant, so to speak, with the very beasts of the field; yea, that his very enemies are at peace with him. He learns that all danger is passed away. The heavens that thundered with Jehovah's wrath now drop down salvation. The earth that brought forth only thorns and briers now yields the lovely fruits of righteousness. The pit that yawned to devour him is now closed. The law which threatened him with vengeance is now completely satisfied, and conscience, which vexed him, is now pacified. His sins are mortified, the world subdued, the devil chained up, and all things are under the control of the wisdom and power of his covenant God, and made to work together for his good. And therefore he feels that he may go in and out with safety and with comfort.

He lives, it is true, in an enemy's country and in a sinful world, but it is a city the walls of which are salvation, and the gates praise. He walks forth amidst foes, visible and invisible, but it is attended by a host of angels, yea, surrounded by the Lord of angels, for 'as the mountains are round about Jerusalem, so the Lord is round about his people from henceforth, even for ever'.

## 6 November

> He maketh me to lie down in green pastures: he leadeth me beside the still waters.
> *Psalm 23:2*

The last benefit here mentioned is, 'He shall find pasture.' The pasture is mediatorially the Lord Christ, in his glorious person and finished work. To us there is no saving nor soul-satisfying discovery of God, but in Christ Jesus. And as he has been pleased to communicate himself through Christ, we must seek the enjoyment of him through the same channel.

Now, the Scripture is full of Christ, and in everything that is said of him, may the believer see that of the blessed God which is fitted to nourish and refresh his soul. 'I have manifested thy name unto the men whom thou gavest me out of the world.' And what he thus manifested to them, the apostle John wrote, he declared to their converts, 'that ye also might have fellowship with us; with his Son Jesus Christ'. 'And these things', he adds, 'write we unto you, that your joy may be full.'

The pasture is, efficiently, the fellowship of the Holy Ghost. There is no discovery of God to us but in Christ. And we now remark that there is no application of Christ for the support and comfort of the soul but by the Spirit. The treasures of Christ are indeed immense and rich and suitable, and the soul of a believer is poor and needy and desolate. But, it needs the Spirit to take of these treasures and show them to the soul, and to bring the soul up to a participation and enjoyment of them. The apostle, accordingly, who implored for those to whom he wrote, 'the love of the Father, and the grace of the Lord Jesus Christ', implored also, as essential to the possession of the other two, 'the communion of the Holy Ghost'.

## 7 November

> But he is a Jew, which is one inwardly; and circumcision is that of the heart, in the spirit, and not in the letter; whose praise is not of men, but of God.
> Romans 2:29

Let the self-righteous take warning from this subject. You know some little of your danger, and some little, too, of salvation. You feel that if something be not done, you must perish. But, ignorant of God's righteousness, and going about to establish your own righteousness, you do not submit to the righteousness of God. Not that you leave Christ out of your creed altogether: this were too gross an error to be committed by the professed members of the Church. But then he is not the door, but your prayers, your church-goings, and perhaps a few other things of the like kind. Now, we may let you heap these up as high as you please. The more you have of them, if you trust in them, the wider will be the gate through which you will have to pass to hell. No class of people are farther away from the door to grace and heaven than you. There is more hope of a fool, of an infidel, of a heathen, than of you. Oh, that you would ponder the words, 'Except your righteousness shall exceed the righteousness of the scribes and Pharisees, ye shall in no case enter into the kingdom of heaven.'

We are once more favoured to hear of glorious Christ, and in him, of eternal life. Ah, how blind must you be not to see him; how stupid not to regard him; how obstinate not to submit to him; how infatuated not to receive him! Christ, the door formed by divine wisdom, furnished by divine grace, and opened by divine love.

# 8 November

> But this man, after he had offered one sacrifice for sins for ever, sat down on the right hand of God.
> *Hebrews 10:12*

We have to enquire who this man is, of whom the text speaks. He is the Son of God. That points to his true and proper nature. It is expressive of the original and essential dignity of his person, and points to the ineffable relation which he holds to the Father. In this aspect he is held forth in this very epistle as the brightness of the Father's glory, and the express image of his person, insomuch that he who sees the Son sees the Father also.

But again, and taking up another line of illustration of this man of whom the text speaks, let us look at the state in which he appears. He is in himself in the form of God, and we can no more apprehend the state that pertains to him and becomes him, than we can apprehend his infinite nature. He challenges the children of men to tell, if they can, where it becomes him to dwell. 'Where is the house that ye will build for me, and where is the place of my rest?' It belongs to him, equally with the Father and the Holy Ghost, to dwell in himself. There is no temple costly enough from without the Godhead wherein he could dwell, and hence, in the highest discovery that is made of him, there is seen no temple. 'The Lord God is the temple.' It is therefore very wonderful to find that one so exalted should appear in the form of man, in the likeness of sinful flesh, and for a season sojourn amongst men.

## 9 November

But this man, after he had offered one sacrifice for sins for ever, sat down on the right hand of God.
*Hebrews 10:12*

What Christ has done? 'After he had offered one sacrifice for sins.' In the view of his person there is presented the link that connects what he is with what he is here said to have done. It pertains only to priests to offer sacrifices, and it were not an unimportant definition of what a priest is, to say, he is one who offers sacrifices. Thus you see the propriety of adverting to the office he fills ere we come to the consideration of what, in the discharge of the functions of the office, he has done.

In turning, then, to this part of our subject, our attention seems due firstly to that for which the sacrifice is offered. It is 'for sins'. Now, we would never have heard of sins, but for the revelation of the divine will in the holy Scripture. You will find no mention made of sins, properly so-called, anywhere else. All creation is dumb on this point. The ingenuity of man is at fault here: though on occasions men appear to be using expressions that point to this thing, it will be found on close enquiry that it is something else they mean. It is very plain, then, that unless you are brought to this source of light, you must be entire strangers to what sins are. The source of light may be outwardly exhibited to you, but if there be nothing else, you will still remain as much strangers to sins as you were before. You must be brought subjectively near to the source of light.

# 10 November

> For then must he often have suffered since the foundation of the world: but now once in the end of the world hath he appeared to put away sin by the sacrifice of himself.
> *Hebrews 9:26*

You must consider him as sitting upon the throne of judgment, as having sins before his eye, and weighing what they are and what they deserve at his hand, because he is more concerned in sins than any of us, or than all creatures put together. He has a heavier stake in being right and upright in this matter than all creatures in heaven or earth. If he judges unjustly or unfairly in this matter, he would be, if it were possible, the greatest sufferer. He would suffer more than all creatures put together. This serves to show that, if his curse is said to be due to every one sin, and all sins committed, then it is quite according to the demerit of sins. I have said those who have their souls opened in the way I have noticed, have a struggle to maintain on this matter. If it were possible for the eye of Jehovah to lose sight of himself for an instant, he would for that instant lose sight of the infinite demerit of sin, and think of it as you do.

What is the inference? If your souls and mine are away from the apprehension of his essential infinite beauty, we are sure to stumble with regard to the demerit of sin. The Lord Jesus was brought very near to this awful fire in the day when his Father dealt with him as a sacrifice for sin. He looked into it in a way that it is impossible for us to express or apprehend. He beheld the wrath that was kindling like a tempest against him, in a way that made his soul exceedingly sorrowful even unto death, so that his sweat was as it were great drops of blood falling to the earth.

# 11 November

For then must he often have suffered since the foundation of the world: but now once in the end of the world hath he appeared to put away sin by the sacrifice of himself.
*Hebrews 9:26*

He gave himself a sacrifice. And in what pertains properly to the priest's office, we have this farther precious truth exhibited, that the Lord Jesus Christ consented to take upon himself what the Father caused to meet upon his head. Thus the Father, as judge, places sin to the account of the priest, and the priest, in discharging the functions of his office, lays these sins upon himself as the sacrifice. Thus being made sin, though he knew no sin, according to the law, he must die.

The death in prospect was so terrible to him that he seemed, once and again, as if he would shrink from it. The language he is represented as employing is most instructive. We know no way in which it could be more emphatically made known, what a terrible thing it is to sin against God. You think it is a light matter, because you are far, far away from the consuming fire. But the moment you come near to it, either in a work of grace, in clear saving convictions, or at last in an undone state, to perish for ever, it will no longer appear a light matter to you. 'And he went a little further, and fell on his face, and prayed, saying, O my Father, if it be possible, let this cup pass from me: nevertheless not as I will, but as thou wilt.' What thou willest, that I am resolved and prepared to do.

## 12 November

> For then must he often have suffered since the foundation of the world: but now once in the end of the world hath he appeared to put away sin by the sacrifice of himself.
> *Hebrews 9:26*

See for what purpose the death of Christ was endured: he put away sin by the sacrifice of himself. But you will not understand what is meant by putting away sin, if sin be not present to you.

Have you ever seen sin before God, as a thick cloud, intercepting the light of his countenance from your souls, and shutting out your prayer from his ear? Have you ever seen sins beneath the eye of your own conscience, your conscience looking at them and troubling you because of what it discovers? Have you ever seen your sins in the light of the Word, that Word opening them up, as if it would tell all that is within you and all that is done by you? Have you ever seen your sins prospectively on a deathbed, at the judgment seat, in eternity? If not, how can you understand what is meant, by putting away sin? A weighty matter, an arduous work! Jesus Christ did it. He did no more: it took him, it took all he was, and all he had. The curse did not leave one leaf of that plant of renown. It burned him all up: it did not leave one particle of sap—it completely exhausted it, just like the fire that came upon Elijah's sacrifice.

He put away sin by the sacrifice of himself, and when the sacrifice of himself is appropriated to your souls by faith, being applied by the gracious effectual work of the Holy Ghost, then your sins are put away.

# 13 November

And this is life eternal, that they might know thee the only true God, and Jesus Christ, whom thou hast sent.
*John 17:3*

The soul that possesses the knowledge of the Father, and of his Son Jesus Christ that is eternal life, hath communion with the Father in the sweetness of his love.

To the carnal heart, nothing is more distasteful than the love of God. You will be astonished to hear this, but so it is. Let men form their own ideas of God and his love, and they will delight in them. But all this is mere idolatry, the worship of the fancies of their own imaginations. But let the God of glory be declared to them, and let his love as it is revealed be set before them, and they are mad with rage. They sink into sullen indifference, or are lifted up in insolent contempt. The peculiar glory of divine love is its sovereignty and its holiness.

And I put it to you, whether there be not persons here who cannot brook these views of it. We may declaim as long as we please on the love of God, and not offend them. But the moment we speak of him as, in his love, taking this man and leaving that, giving this blessing and withholding that, they are almost ready to stone us.

We may illustrate our point in another way. The great enemy never disturbs those who preach and those who believe that God loves those who are sober and upright and industrious, and hates those who are drunkards, revellers, and given to all manner of wickedness. But let men preach that God loves sinners, even the chief, not because of their sins, but because of his own good pleasure, and Satan rages like a lion.

# 14 November

For it pleased the Father that in him should all fulness dwell.
*Colossians 1:19*

They that have the knowledge of the Father, the only true God, and Jesus Christ, have communion with the Lord Jesus Christ. And they have communion with him in his grace. 'For it hath pleased the Father'—and that in his love, of which we have been speaking—'that in Christ should all fulness dwell.' As he himself is the fountain of love, in which love he designs all the good that sinners receive, so Christ is the fountain of grace, as the medium through which his favour flows to lost men. And accordingly, to fit the soul for communion with the Lord Jesus Christ in this character, there is communicated a knowledge of him in his person as God-man, in his character as the Messiah, in his mission and work as the Saviour of sinners.

Now, where this knowledge is, there is communion with Christ in his grace. And a believer has communion with Christ in the riches of his grace. I might speak of the communion which the soul has with Christ in his personal grace, or that peculiar beauty that adorns his character. But this was spoken to under the head of the objects of knowledge, when it was shown that he is the fairest of the sons of men, yea altogether lovely. I therefore speak at present of what we may call his official grace. By grace, remember, is understood unmerited favour: the name is applied sometimes to the favour, and sometimes to the effects it produces. Now in both views the grace of Christ is infinitely rich. He bears infinite favour to his people, and he bestows infinite favours upon them.

## 15 November

*For God sent not his Son into the world to condemn the world; but that the world through him might be saved.*
*John 3:17*

To show the absolute freeness of this grace, men have actually need of grace to receive it. The grace of Christ is given without money and without price, but what is it that receives this? It is the grace of faith. If you were to give a beggar a little money, and to give him at the same time the inclination and power to receive it, you would have some illustration of our subject. And yet it would we a very faint one, for the grace of Christ is bestowed not only upon those who have no inclination to receive it, but upon those who have a strong aversion to it.

Now what becomes of your objections and your difficulties? You will tell me of your sinfulness, and corruption, etc., but what of that? It is indeed no reason why Christ should bestow his grace upon you, but neither is it a reason why he should withhold it from you. In yourselves by nature, you will never see anything that is a ground of hope. But what you do not see in yourselves, you may see in Christ, for there is in him both the grace and the foundation on which he bestows it. 'This is a faithful saying and worthy of all acceptation, that Christ Jesus came into the world to save sinners; of whom I am chief.'

## 16 November

*As thou hast given him power over all flesh, that he should give eternal life to as many as thou hast given him.*
*John 17:2*

We have many amongst us that profess to have some knowledge of God and his Son Jesus Christ: they surely are not to be reckoned as altogether ignorant of this subject.

Now, my friends I have to ask you, does your knowledge ever lead to communion with the Father and his Son Jesus Christ? Does it ever lead you to feel your want of this, and urge you to desire and seek after it? I am pretty sure that the consciences of many, at this moment, whisper that they do not know what I mean by communion with God. Some people say they have this knowledge, who have no prayer. Is it not so, you that never bend the knee in the closet nor in the family? Some say their prayers, and there the matter ends, but whether they have communion with God or not, they cannot tell.

Now, brethren, it is needless to mince the matter. We tell you plainly, that such of you as are in this condition have not a particle of true knowledge. And the only difference between you and the most ignorant heathen is that you have a mass of carnal knowledge to condemn you, which he has not. All knowledge in religion that does not come from God and lead to God will be swept away with the besom of destruction.

I know there are amongst us those who admit the truth of all I say, and who will be ready to take occasion from it to mourn over their sad state, for they have been taught to make no account of any knowledge which does not lead to communion with the Father and his Son Jesus Christ.

## 17 November

And I will pour upon the house of David, and upon the inhabitants of Jerusalem, the spirit of grace and of supplications: and they shall look upon me whom they have pierced, and they shall mourn for him, as one mourneth for his only

son, and shall be in bitterness for him, as one that is in bitterness for his firstborn.
*Zechariah 12:10*

The Spirit of grace is very glorious in himself, and most glorious is the work which he accomplishes in the economy of redemption. The fulness of Christ is open to him, and thence does he receive those unsearchable treasures which it hath pleased the Father should dwell in him.

In his infinite condescension, he comes with them to the children of men, as they lie in the kingdom of darkness, polluted with sin, and condemned to destruction; who, so far from having any desire after such a visit or any regard for the end for which it is paid, are full of the most bitter hostility to the whole subject.

We need not wonder that the entrance of such a person into this region of corruption and death should create a strange sensation and produce a deep commotion. It is like carrying the light of a torch into a den of thieves, the very sight of which occasions the greatest consternation and alarm. For, when the Spirit of grace comes to a soul, the great adversary awakes, and struggles to retain his prey. The lusts of the flesh, like so many owls, are disquieted and stirred up, and the whole powers of darkness are thrown into a state of agitation. Nor is it until the Lord of glory appears that there is anything like order or peace restored.

## 18 November

Then said I, Woe is me! For I am undone; because I am a man of unclean lips, and I dwell in the midst of a people of unclean lips: for mine eyes have seen the King, the LORD of hosts.
*Isaiah 6:5*

The Holy Spirit enlightens in the knowledge of the glory of Christ, namely, the glory of his person, his offices, his state. Secondly, he enlightens in the knowledge of the grace of Christ—its nature, sufficiency, freeness, efficacy, immutability.

The first effect commonly produced by this illumination is a sense of great darkness as to the glory of Christ. Hence Saul, after the vision on the way to Damascus, was blind three days and three nights. We therefore hope well of those amongst us that complain of their blindness to the glory of Christ, and mourn their incapacity to believe on his name. It will be a great astonishment, as well as a heavy grief to us, if such persons are not saved. 'The Lord openeth the eyes of the blind.'

A further effect of this divine illumination is a feeling of extreme vileness and worthlessness. We have an instance of this in the prophet Isaiah who, on seeing the glory of Christ, cried out, 'Woe is me! for I am undone; because I am a man of unclean lips, and I dwell in the midst of a people of unclean lips.'

We may apply this for the encouragement of those who are groaning under a sense of their desperate wickedness, and who perhaps never feel it more sensibly than when the glory of Christ is set before them. 'Behold, I am vile; what shall I answer thee? I will lay mine hand upon my mouth' (Job 40:4).

Another effect of divine illumination is to produce great self-loathing and hatred of sin. We have this exemplified in the case of Job. 'I have heard of thee by the hearing of the ear: but now mine eye seeth thee. Wherefore I abhor myself, and repent in dust and ashes.'

# 19 November

Then said I, Woe is me! for I am undone; because I am a man of unclean lips, and I dwell in the midst of a people of

unclean lips: for mine eyes have seen the King, the LORD of hosts.
*Isaiah 6:5*

The man who has been convinced of his sin by the Spirit of grace sees that he has, by his first apostasy in Adam, by his life of ungodliness, and more than all by his rejection of Christ, offered an infinite offence to the divine Majesty.

His case becomes more desperate, when, to quiet his troubled conscience and to pacify him whom he has offended, he sets himself to keep the law, and finds that the more he strives to be better, he only grows the worse; and that the higher he seeks to rise in holiness, the deeper he sinks in corruption. He now sees that, though all his past sins were forgiven and forgotten, he would scarcely have received the boon when he would plunge himself anew into debt, and become as miserable as before.

And by and by he discovers that God cannot accept for his justification anything that has the least stain of sin in it, nor can he accept of obedience to part of his law, without obedience to the whole. Nor can he accept of righteousness at all unless it be for the past, the present and the future. By these views, the man is brought to his wits' end. He wonders if ever there was a creature in such a dilemma: awakened to the demands of the law, anxious to settle them, but at every step dishonouring God, breaking the law, despising Christ, and ruining his own soul. Oh, the depth and bitterness of the cry he raises, 'What must I do to be saved?'

## 20 November

All we like sheep have gone astray; we have turned every one to his own way; and the LORD hath laid on him the iniquity of us all.
*Isaiah 53:6*

In this condition of conviction of sin the Son of God incarnate, in glory ineffable, with riches unsearchable, from love unspeakable, steps forward, and says to the Father—the God whom sinners have offended, and at whose hand they deserve nothing but wrath to the uttermost, 'I will go into their room. Let all their sins be laid upon me; I will bear them. Let all their obedience be upon me; I will render it. Let all their concerns be upon me; I will manage them.'

The Father loves the Son. He knows his worth, his sufficiency, his grace, and he accepts him as the substitute of poor, bankrupt, perishing sinners. 'Sacrifice and offering thou didst not desire. ... Then said I, Lo, I come: in the volume of the book it is written of me, I delight to do thy will, O my God: yea, thy law is within my heart.'

Let us look at the origin of Christ's substitution. And here we find a very deep and solid foundation on which to rest in it with confidence, for it originated in the infinite wisdom of God himself. 'I have found David my servant.' 'I have laid help upon one that is mighty.' 'The Lord hath laid upon him the iniquity of us all.' We have thus the strongest assurance that his substitution is acceptable, for it is of the creditor's own choice. To question the sufficiency of Christ to be the substitute of any sinner who lays hold of him, is to despise the wisdom of the Father and the worth of Christ. We accordingly find the Father testifying, 'This is my beloved Son, in whom I am well pleased.'

## 21 November

> They are all gone out of the way, they are together become unprofitable; there is none that doeth good, no, not one.
> *Romans 3:12*

The Spirit of grace shows the soul that God is glorified by his wonderful work. By which I do not mean that any glory is given to his nature which did not before belong to him, for 'Who hath first given to him, and it shall be recompensed unto him again?' I mean that the glory of his name is manifested, or made to appear in the eyes of an admiring universe.

The thing that presses heavily upon truly awakened sinners is that, by their sin, they have dishonoured the name of God. And the only way in which they think his name can be vindicated is in their eternal perdition, for they see and feel that it is a righteous and seemly thing in God to cast for ever away from him those who have wickedly cast him away from them.

In the work of Christ, however, a higher vindication of the name of God is accomplished than can be by the perdition of your souls, or that of all the creatures that ever existed. For what does that perdition say, but that sin is so very hateful to God, that he will destroy his own creatures in whom it is found? And to every person capable of appreciating it, it must be an awful sight to see men that were originally made in the image of God, and fitted for his service, eternally banished from his presence. And they must return from the contemplation of the sad spectacle with the conviction that it is indeed an evil and a bitter thing to sin against God.

## 22 November

> Now we know that what things soever the law saith, it saith to them who are under the law: that every mouth may be stopped, and all the world may become guilty before God.
> *Romans 3:19*

The Spirit of grace shows the soul that the law is magnified by the work of Christ. The effect of a real work of conviction is to make a man jealous for the honour of the divine name. Salvation he cannot receive, far less enjoy, but through a channel which maintains it.

But it has the farther effect of making him most tender about the claims of the divine law. And the very man who before condemned its authority, set its curse at defiance, and trampled upon its requirements, cannot have peace, will not take salvation, unless in every point it be fully maintained and honoured.

Thus it is that he shows to all who are able to interpret aright his experience, that he is partaker of a new nature, for before he would have rejoiced if the law were abolished altogether and he were allowed to take his full swing of iniquity, without any fear of the judgment to come. But now he is grieved that his heart rebels against it, that his life is opposed to it, and that instead of obeying it, he does nothing but transgress it. To such a man, the Spirit's view of the righteousness of Christ is peculiarly precious, for he sees in it wonderful satisfaction to the penalty of the law. In the death of Christ there is exhibited the rare sight of one bearing the wrath of God due to sin, with a heart full of supreme love to him whose hand is lifted up to inflict the stroke.

## 23 November

> All we like sheep have gone astray; we have turned every one to his own way; and the LORD hath laid on him the iniquity of us all.
> *Isaiah 53:6*

The Spirit of grace shows the soul that the work of Christ is exactly suited to the condition of sinners. The reason why men fall into such grievous mistakes in regard to the work of Christ is that, trusting to their own foolish hearts and despising the light of the Word of God, they sadly err in regard to their natural state. The Socinians imagine that a created Saviour will suit them. The Papists think that good works will profit them. Nominal Protestants dream that an orthodox creed will save them. Pharisees think that morality will be of some use to them. And multitudes who belong to an evangelical church think if they believe, no matter where they get their faith nor what be its nature, that will do. Now, however these may differ from one another, they all agree in taking erroneous views of men's natural condition, and therefore the work of Christ is either wholly set aside or is mutilated and perverted to suit their corrupt fancies.

The light of the Spirit of grace pierces through these abodes of darkness, and lays open to the soul the truth of what the Scripture says of men, that they are apostate, fallen and ruined, that they are in themselves, and as to their power, utterly undone and helpless, and yet that unless divine justice be satisfied by the endurance of the wrath due to sin, and the performance of the obedience required by the law, no flesh shall be saved. To a man thus enlightened, the work of Christ appears with peculiar beauty and preciousness, as being exactly the thing which he feels he needs.

## 24 November

> But before faith came, we were kept under the law, shut up unto the faith which should afterwards be revealed.
> *Galatians 3:23*

The Spirit of grace shows a man that in Christ there is salvation from condemnation. The apostasy of man began in the blinding and deceiving of the heart: his recovery begins in the opening of his eyes, and putting truth into his inward parts. The apostasy hence led him into sin, and by sin into condemnation. In Christ there is the pardon of sin, and the consequent freedom from condemnation: 'In whom we have redemption through his blood, the forgiveness of sins, according to the riches of his grace.' By the apostasy, men lost their righteousness: in Christ they are furnished with a righteousness, and therein are accepted in the sight of God, 'accepted in the beloved'.

I beg you not only to ponder the truth I now declare, but to consider the place in which I have put it. The first thought that arises in many people's minds on the discovery of their sins is, 'We must seek, with the help of God, to do better for the time to come.' Now, friends, this is one of the high roads to hell, and if you are not driven from it, you will go as certainly and as speedily to hell as in your former practices. I deny not but the really awakened may attempt to get peace in this way, but they will soon find that they are becoming worse and worse, for the Lord, in mercy, will burn them out of every such expedient and shut them up to the true way of salvation.

# 25 November

> It was meet that we should make merry, and be glad: for this thy brother was dead, and is alive again; and was lost, and is found.
> *Luke 15:32*

A penitent sinner can never rest till he is in the bosom of the blessed God, folded in the arms of Jesus Christ. He there hears the Father say, 'This my son was lost, but is found.' My beloved people, know ye what this is? This is heaven upon earth.

Closely connected with this, and inseparable from it, is the soul's communion with his Son Jesus Christ. How can the Father open his arms to receive such a culprit? How can he embrace him in his love—his warm, satisfying, refreshing love? The reason is: his eye is upon the Lamb that hath been slain. How can the poor sinner venture so near the divine majesty? How can such a vile reptile, who feels that his proper place is the lowest hell, and that he has done all he could to provoke God to destroy him: how can he venture to look the Father in the face? By faith, he sees the Lamb of God. There the eye of the Father and the eye of the soul meet in one and the same place. The Father rests in the Lamb of God, that taketh away the sins of the world. The penitent soul coming back to the Father, rests in the Lamb of God, that taketh away the sins of the world. There is reconciliation. 'Bring forth the best robe' (Luke 15:22–24). Oh ye angels in the presence of God, well may you long for a sinner to be brought to repentance! It is a new feast to you. They have there some fresh discoveries made of the glory of the blessed God. 'There is joy amongst the angels in heaven over one sinner brought to repentance.'

## 26 November

> As the living Father hath sent me, and I live by the Father: so he that eateth me, even he shall live by me.
> John 6:57

We have to enquire respecting this meat: where this meat is to be found.

Firstly, it is set forth primarily in the counsels of Jehovah. It was meet that within the Godhead the first sight should be got of this marvellous meat. 'I am Alpha.' I am first in my place, I am first in the sight of everything worth seeing, and here is the great sight, 'God manifest in the flesh'. He was set forth in Jehovah's counsels. Through the weakness and infirmity of our nature we are permitted to speak of his counsels as distinct from his nature, from himself, although we must never conceive of them as possibly separable. Under this aspect we judge that it is quite according to the analogy of faith, agreeable to the Scripture truth, and not stepping beyond the commission of the Christian ministry, to exhibit this meat as seen in the counsels of God, and to say to you who are capable of having fellowship with the Father and with his Son Jesus Christ, 'Behold the Man!'

Secondly, this meat is set forth in the proclamation of the gospel. Upon the mountain of the gospel ministry—upon the mountain of the precious truth that is always found where the gospel ministry is—will the Lord make a feast to all people. Isaiah 25:6: 'And in this mountain shall the LORD of hosts make unto all people a feast of fat things, a feast of wines on the lees, of fat things full of marrow, of wines on the lees well refined.' Isaiah 55:1–3: 'Ho, every one that thirsteth, come ye to the waters, and he that hath no money; come ye, buy, and eat; yea, come, buy wine and milk without money and without price.'

## 27 November

> And in this mountain shall the LORD of hosts make unto all people a feast of fat things, a feast of wines on the lees, of fat things full of marrow, of wines on the lees well refined.
> *Isaiah 25:6*

There is the eating of the meat. This eating is of grace. Romans 9:16: 'So then it is not of him that willeth, nor of him that runneth, but of God that sheweth mercy.' The Lord has to make the feast, and he makes it in his grace. The Lord provides the guests, and he provides them in his grace. The Lord has to take charge of the eating on the part of the guests, else they will make nothing of it. This eating is of grace. Ephesians 2:5: 'By grace ye are saved.'

This eating is through faith. Far be it from our minds to take in the carnal notion of physical mastication, as if in this matter men were to act like cannibals. We say this eating is of grace, but grace works in the way of faith. It is by faith that it might be by grace, or that it might appear to be of grace. Faith is peculiarly fitted to magnify grace, to illustrate its nature, demonstrating that what faith gets, it gets by grace. What faith does, it does through grace. What faith enjoys, it enjoys by grace. It is by faith that it might be by grace, to cut off all occasion of glorifying on the part of the creature. Now faith, being a grace of the Spirit of God, and being in the soul a supernatural principle, carrying the man altogether above and immeasurably beyond the power and reach of nature, it penetrates into the mysteries of the kingdom, apprehends the things set forth, and has a special eye to the person of Christ and to his undertaking to save sinners, his obedience unto death, and the glory that followed.

## 28 November

> And in this mountain shall the LORD of hosts make unto all people a feast of fat things, a feast of wines on the lees, of fat things full of marrow, of wines on the lees well refined.
> *Isaiah 25:6*

Under what aspect is this meat set forth in the gospel? It is set forth as meat from heaven, it is the gift of God, that is so much. And it is set forth as meat for sinners, so that the inscription upon the meat may be said to be twofold. One pointing to him who provides the meat: 'Thanks be unto God for his unspeakable gift' (2 Corinthians 9:15); 'For God so loved the world, that he gave his only begotten Son, that whosoever believeth in him should not perish, but have everlasting life' (John 3:16). And another inscription pointing to those for whom it is provided and who are welcome to receive it, who are clearly sinners of this world. God gives the meat in his love, and God gives the meat in his love to sinners.

This is a peculiar kind of love that is manifested in the gift of Christ. 'God so loved the world as to give his only begotten Son.' There thus appears in the Word, at any rate, however blind and insensible we may be to it, to be a making over of this meat in a free, gracious proclamation to sinners of mankind. But one must read the proclamation that is made, one must enter into its import and intention. One must credit what God testifies. One must meet him at the point where he meets sinners. Here is work for the Holy Ghost: none else can accomplish it. 'No man can come to me, except the Father which hath sent me draw him; and I will raise him up at the last day. It is written in the prophets, And they shall be all taught of God. Every man therefore that hath heard, and hath learned of the Father, cometh unto me.' (John 6:44–45).

# 29 November

> When the Son of man shall come in his glory, and all the holy angels with him, then shall he sit upon the throne of his glory: and before him shall be gathered all nations: and he shall separate them one from another, as a shepherd divideth his sheep from the goats: and he shall set the sheep on his right hand, but the goats on the left.
> *Matthew 25:31–33*

To be prepared for the eternal world is the first and last lesson in the school of Christ. It runs through the whole of his holy Word, and it is distinctly impressed upon the parables which hold so prominent a place in the doctrines he taught. It is no doubt true that it inculcates the necessity of constant watchfulness, but it is lest his disciples be taken by surprise by the summons to depart hence. He teaches the necessity of a faithful and diligent cultivation of the talents committed to their care, but it is with a special view to the return of their Master, who will call for a return at their hands, and give to every man according to his works. Now, what he so evidently teaches in the parables he spake, he lays before his disciples in plain and impressive terms in the passage now read.

This whole passage points to the judgment day. The scene it describes will then take place, and the procedure it presents before us will then go forward in all its weight and solemnity. We are first of all introduced to the Judge. A remarkable title he bears: 'the Son of man'. Still he is an infinitely exalted person that bears this title. It is one which in infinite condescension he assumed; it did not originally and properly pertain to him. It was by the mysterious step of the incarnation that he who is, was and shall be the Son of God became the Son of man. He acquired it by deep abasement, unparalleled ignominy, and inconceivable sorrow.

## 30 November

> When the Son of man shall come in his glory, and all the holy angels with him, then shall he sit upon the throne of his glory: and before him shall be gathered all nations: and he shall separate them one from another, as a shepherd divideth his sheep from the goats: and he shall set the sheep on his right hand, but the goats on the left.
> *Matthew 25:31–33*

We have the manner in which the Judge will come: 'in his glory'. There is a glory essential, infinite, and eternal that belongs to him originally. He is equal in power and glory with the Father, and this glory is his, and lies at the foundation of every other he possesses. But for this, he would not have been capable of receiving the glory that belongs to him as Mediator.

In the eternal Sonship of Jesus Christ you see the proper basis of his office, his work, and his glory. All that is his as the Son. Accordingly, they who err with regard to the glory of his person, err grievously with everything else concerning him. The Jews looked upon him as the son of Joseph. They could not therefore understand how he could give them his flesh to eat. And no man can by faith taste of the Lamb roasted with the fire of divine justice for the deliverance of sinners, that hath not by faith of divine operation caught something of the infinite glory of him who is the Lamb of God that taketh away the sins of the world.

He hath received glory of the Father in human nature. It was promised to him, and he fulfilled the condition of the promise in the purchase of redemption for sinners, and this promise will reach its full accomplishment. There have been a few beams of this glory given to the children of men. 'The Word was made flesh, and dwelt among us, (and we beheld his glory, the glory as of the only begotten of the Father), full of grace and truth.'

# December

R OBERT SMITH CANDLISH (1806–1873) studied at the University of Glasgow and became a tutor at Eton College after graduation. He then served as an assistant minister in two Glasgow congregations before becoming the minister of Edinburgh's leading church, St George's. He played an important role in the years leading up to the Disruption in 1843.

In 1847, after the death of Thomas Chalmers, Dr Candlish was appointed his successor as Professor of Divinity in New College, Edinburgh. His now vacant congregation called Alexander Stewart of Cromarty as his successor, but Mr. Stewart died before he could be translated. In these circumstances Dr Candlish resigned his professorial appointment and returned to his former charge. Following the death of Principal William Cunningham, Dr Candlish was appointed Principal of New College in 1862, and he discharged the duties of that office along with his pastoral work till his death.

Next to Thomas Chalmers, Dr Candlish was the main churchman raised up in the providence of God to expound and defend the principles of the newly formed Free Church of Scotland. He played a leading role in organising the new denomination.

Robert Candlish wrote extensively on a variety of subjects. Some of his most influential writings were exegetical commentaries on books of the Bible.

## Source of daily readings

Robert S. Candlish, *The Gospel of Forgiveness: A series of discourses* (Edinburgh, 1878).

## Biography

William Wilson, *Life of Robert Smith Candlish, D.D.* (Edinburgh, 1880).

# 1 December

*If I have told you earthly things, and ye believe not, how shall ye believe, if I tell you of heavenly things?*
*John 3:12*

I sometimes wonder that I am so little affected and impressed by the great love of God in the gift of his Son to be the propitiation for my sin—that I am so slow to take in all the terror and all the glory of that amazing substitution: the eternal Son taking my nature and my place under the law which I have broken, made sin, and made a curse for me.

I may not question the reality of the transaction, but somehow I find myself little alive, less than I used to be, to its awful meaning and dread necessity. I am beginning again to ask why there should be so much ado about my deliverance and my safety, and consequently to see less and feel less of the love passing knowledge that prompts and pervades the whole gracious plan. Is it so with me now? Ah, it is a sad sign of declension, a most alarming symptom of unbelieving unthankfulness, that must surely and swiftly harden my heart!

Let me be startled at once. Let me thoroughly search and try myself, and instantly ask God to search and try me. And let it be very specially on this precise point that I search myself and ask God to search me: the state of my conscience and its conviction of indwelling sin, the corruption of my nature, and my inveterate, because inborn, carnality. May there not be creeping over me a growing insensibility to that sore evil, in some one or other of the forms in which it must continue to meet me, as long as the war of the flesh against the Spirit lasts? Alas! May not that warfare itself be slackening in its energy, if not inclining to a truce? May not that explain the melancholy mystery of my lessening warmth of gratitude to God for his unspeakable gift? For let me be well assured that all through my spiritual life, from its first beginning in the new birth to its final consummation in perfected holiness, the principle involved in the Lord's question must apply: 'If I have told you earthly things and ye believe not, how shall ye believe if I tell you of heavenly things?'

# 2 December

> If I have told you earthly things, and ye believe not, how shall ye believe, if I tell you of heavenly things?
> *John 3:12*

Christ is telling me of these heavenly things, and the Spirit is bringing home to me Christ's telling me of them if, with eye opened by the Holy Ghost, I get but a glimpse of that love in which the whole plan of redemption originates, and of which even it is an inadequate expression. If thus taught of God, I see into the heart of God and obtain some faint idea of the longing of that heart for the world's salvation and for mine; if I am divinely moved to apprehend that it is that very love that the great Father reveals to me and presses on my acceptance in his dear Son, beseeching me to be to him what his Son is, and to let him be to me what he is to him.

Ah, if thus I am made to see the great Father in heaven loving me with a love like that, providing for me an atoning sacrifice that satisfies highest justice and expiates deepest guilt, and so reconciling me to himself, fully, freely, in his Son, may not such a discovery of what God is to me open my eyes to what I am to him? May it not convince me that I do indeed need to be born again, if I am to know and believe such love as that?

Ah, sinner, wilt thou not be moved by that love now? Wilt thou not contrast what is in God's heart towards thee with what is in thy heart towards God? Wilt thou not be filled with shame and grief when thou thinkest how dead and insensible thou hast been when such love as that has been set before thee and pressed upon thee?

Wilt thou not cry out in earnest, 'Create in me a clean heart, O God, and renew within me a right spirit. Fulfil thine own promise: "A new heart will I give thee, and a right spirit will I put within thee. And I will put my spirit within thee."' O Lord God, gracious and loving Father, purge me with hyssop and I shall be clean. Take not thy Holy Spirit from me.

# 3 December

> In the last day, that great day of the feast, Jesus stood and cried, saying, If any man thirst, let him come unto me, and drink.
> *John 7:37*

Christ is saying to you, 'Come unto me and drink.' Here is one exhorting, intreating you to make a very simple experiment, to adopt a very simple cure. Do not tamely submit to a burden so intolerable. Do not rest in a state so unworthy of a reasonable being. Your conscious uneasiness indicates something wrong. Do not hastily conclude that the wrong is irremediable. At least listen to the suggestions of the Saviour, for you have no right to suppose that your case is beyond relief till you have tried all expedients, and this among the rest.

You have been pitching your tents in a dreary desert or in a city of vanity. You have reaped many a harvest and kept many a harvest home. You have decked and garnished the hard realities of sordid, commonplace existence with many rich tokens of your Maker's bounty, and in gathering in the fruits of all your labour that is under the sun, you have done your best to rejoice, and you have called your neighbours to rejoice along with you.

But in this feast of tabernacles, to which at the very best your plan of life may be compared, have you discovered, have you recognised the Lord himself in the midst of all, and have you acknowledged him as the centre and source of all? And is it any wonder that when he, who is himself alike the author and the end of the whole feast, is unobserved and unregarded by you—or noticed only as one giving good counsel to the busy crowd, or as the voice of one crying in the wilderness—you receive not the full measure of joy that the scene and the circumstances might seem fitted to yield? That you are conscious of a void, a vacancy—something wanting, something you fain would grasp, but cannot? Cannot? No, you cannot, until you hear, as even now you may hear his voice, 'Come unto me, and drink.'

# 4 December

> I am the good shepherd, and know my sheep, and am known of mine. As the Father knoweth me, even so know I the Father: and I lay down my life for the sheep.
> *John 10:14–15*

The work of the Good Shepherd is closely connected with his laying down his life for the sheep. He spoils principalities and powers, making a show of them openly in his cross. Through death he destroys him that has the power of death, that is the devil, and delivers them who through fear of death are all their lifetime subject to bondage. But the death through which he effected this release is his giving himself as a ransom for many, not to the adversary, but to the Father—to God, the holy lawgiver and righteous judge. For it is the Father's justice, the wrath of God lying upon us, that makes us helpless under the prince whose service we have chosen, and whose lie we are fain to try to believe. That is the secret of his hold upon us.

But Jesus, our shepherd, by satisfying that justice and himself enduring that wrath, emancipates us from the thraldom under which the hopeless sense of condemnation keeps us. Redeeming us from the sentence of divine law and justice, he delivers us out of the hand of all our enemies. So he meets the wolf by laying down his life for the sheep. The transaction itself is with the Father, though one of its results is that the wolf is foiled. The immediate and direct bearing of the transaction is on the relation of the sheep to God. The Saviour-shepherd offers himself a sacrifice to God for you, the sheep. The sacrifice is of infinite worth and value. He gives his life for yours—a ransom infinitely sufficient in itself and in his manner of giving it.

## 5 December

> Remember the word that I said unto you, The servant is not greater than his lord. If they have persecuted me, they will also persecute you; if they have kept my saying, they will keep yours also.
> John 15:20

You are not of the world, as he was not of the world. Therefore you may expect that the world will hate you as it hated him. True, it is no part of your duty to give needless offence, or wantonly provoke and challenge opposition, nor may you always interpret the world's ridicule or resentment as an infallible sign of your being persecuted for righteousness' sake.

You are sent by Christ into the world as he was sent by the Father into the world. You are to make thus your disciples out of the world, as he makes you his disciples out of the world. Therefore you must ever keep ahead and in advance of your disciples. You must see to it that you can be to them as your disciples what Christ is to you as his disciples: competent masters, fit to teach and train them up to Christ's own saved standard of perfection. What an argument against concession and conformity! What a motive to the highest aspiration after a pure, holy, spiritual, heavenly walk! Ah, what unfaithfulness to him who so loves the world as to give his only begotten Son, that whosoever believeth in him should not perish, but have everlasting life! What ingratitude to the Son, who has redeemed you out of the world! What cruelty to the world itself—to your brother, neighbour, friend, does your feeble, faltering, timid, doubtful witness-bearing involve! How does it concern you, if you love the Master, and those whom the Master loves, to 'let your light so shine before men that they at they may see your good works, and glorify your Father which is in heaven'!

# 6 December

> Jesus saith unto him, If I will that he tarry till I come, what is that to thee? follow thou me.
> *John 21:22*

He says, 'Follow me.' Follow me in the following up and following out of that work with reference to which I said that thou couldst not follow me then. Follow me now, as loving me, and prepared to feed my sheep and to die with me now; nor consider thy lot hard if thou shouldst have to glorify God by a bloody death, and thy beloved friend should tarry, if I will, till I come. 'What is that to thee? Follow thou me.'

It may be allowed to thee so far to feel an interest in the future of thy friend. Thou wouldst have his course in following me marked out as clearly as thine own, and, if possible, associated with thine own. Thou wouldst know what he is to do, and by what death he is to glorify God, not for thine own satisfaction merely, but it may be for his. But what if I will that he is to glorify God by not dying at all? Leave all that to me; what is it to thee?

Let thine eye be singly intent on thine own walk. Thou art not to follow John, nor is John to follow thee. Nor are you two, John and thou, to follow me in any way that you may concert [contrive] and arrange between you. Thou must needs glorify God by a cruel, horrid death. He may peacefully pass away, or tarry till I come. What is that to thee? Follow thou me. He is in my hands as thou art, and thou needest give thyself no concern about any difference of lot, or any temporary separation that such difference may cause; thou glorifying me by a cruel death, he, if I will, tarrying till I come. No, for then you both shall meet, and meet to part no more. Then, when I come, when the dead shall be raised, thou being among them, and the living shall be changed. John, if I will, being among them, and all shall forever be with me, the Lord.

## 7 December

> The law of the LORD is perfect, converting the soul: the testimony of the LORD is sure, making wise the simple.
> Psalm 19:7

The law of Jehovah is perfect, converting the soul. Its very perfection fits it for being the instrument of the Spirit in effecting that result. Its being perfect makes it converting. For what is the view which the sinner naturally takes of the law, considered as the embodiment and enactment of what Jehovah requires? Is it not really this, that it may admit of abatement and relaxation in his favour? He is always reckoning on some modification of its demands, some accommodation of its terms, to suit his convenience and meet his case. And it must be so. The carnal mind, being enmity against God, is not subject to the law of God, neither indeed can be. Jehovah and the sinner, Jehovah's law and the sinner's carnal mind, are at widest variance. To bring about anything like a good understanding, there must be a bending, a turning, a submission, on one side or the other, either on the side of Jehovah's law, or on the side of the sinner's carnal mind. On which side shall it be? Need I say which side of the alternative we all naturally prefer? It is Jehovah's law that must yield, and not my carnal mind. It is the law that must give in to me, not I to the law.

Conversion, change of some sort, there must be. I feel this. My conscience makes me feel it. I can have no rest until some sort of agreement is brought about between Jehovah's law and my mind. And not being willing to yield to the law, I make the law yield to me. Thus I get some peace, such as it is. The perfection of the law is love. But I live on at ease, unloving and unloved, because I fancy that something less, or something else, than love may do.

# 8 December

Who can understand his errors? cleanse thou me from secret faults.
*Psalm 19:12*

Ah, friends, be sure that there is no security against sin regaining its ascendency over you in your merely aiming at keeping it out of your heart and mouth—as if the heart could be kept pure by being kept empty, and the mouth could be kept clean by being kept shut and silent. Fill the heart with holy thoughts. Fill the mouth with holy songs and sayings. Let there not be merely the absence of corrupt musings from your heart and vile utterances from your mouth. Let it not be counted enough that the Lord, when he searches your heart, should find no cherished thoughts of evil to be condemned, and when he listens to the voice of your lips, should hear no blasphemies or ribaldries or outbreaks of passion to offend his ear. Let him find, when he comes, an acceptable meditation in your heart, acceptable words in your mouth.

Is he not well entitled to this? Is he not your strength and your Redeemer? Your strength, giving you ability for this very thing, your Redeemer who has bought and purchased you expressly with a view of redeeming you from the guilt and power of sin by the shedding of the precious blood of his Son, strengthening you with might by his Spirit in the inner man? He fits your mouth for speaking acceptably, your heart for meditating acceptably, and, as your strength and your Redeemer, he furnishes the very theme of meditation and speech which is most acceptable in his sight.

Let mouth and heart therefore be ever busy. That is what you pray for. You ask the Lord, your strength and your Redeemer, to keep your heart and mouth ever busy. Let mouth and heart be occupied, pre-occupied—so pre-occupied and pre-engaged that 'secret faults' may never at any time be able to win a word from you or to win a thought from you.

# 9 December

> Blessed is he whose transgression is forgiven, whose sin is covered. Blessed is the man unto whom the LORD imputeth not iniquity, and in whose spirit there is no guile.
> Psalm 32:1–2

There are here a privilege, a character, and a blessing. The privilege is that of 'the man unto whom God imputeth righteousness without works' (Romans 5:6). The character is that which Jesus recognised and owned in Nathanael (John 1:47). The blessing attached to both is substantially the full peace and free access described in Romans 5:1. Thus, all the three Old Testament thoughts of privilege, character and blessing receive a New Testament interpretation and application. But the Old Testament experience, as regards these thoughts, must be our guide and mould, for the psalm is an experimental one.

The psalmist's own experience is therefore all in all. And the psalmist being, without doubt, David himself, gives us all the benefit of it. He tells us plainly of the trial through which he has come. He had been keeping silence, suppressing conviction, evading honest confession. It may have been some special sin about which he was thus practising reserve, or the reticence may have had reference to his spiritual state generally. The point is that he has not been speaking to God about himself, or about something in himself fitted to cause uneasiness. There has been a shrinking from fair dealing with God, either about his state generally, or about a specific sin, and that implies guile—self-deception at least, if not wilful hypocrisy. He has been excusing or justifying himself. But he has not found rest. In very mercy God has not suffered him to find rest. His own conscience resents the attempt to impose on its veracity and stifle its voice. And the Spirit, quickening his conscience, reproves and convicts him. He is so self-condemned that he cannot get rid of the sense of a more terrible condemnation. 'For if our heart condemn us, God is greater than our heart and knoweth all things' (1 John 3:20). He is constrained, graciously constrained, to try a more excellent way, the way of full, unreserved, and unqualified confession. Then comes the blessedness of a glad relief from his own conscious or half-unconscious guile, and a calm, quiet sense of the Lord's pardoning and justifying grace.

## 10 December

> But to him that worketh not, but believeth on him that justifieth the ungodly, his faith is counted for righteousness.
> *Romans 4:5*

Let the Holy Ghost show you what sin is—what, under the government of a righteous God it must be held to be, as an act of rebellion against his righteous sovereignty and a breach of his holy law. And thou, my brother, sin-smitten, heart-broken, art thou in darkness, in difficulty, for this very cause? Consulting now for thy God as well as for thyself, for his truth and right even more than for thine own safety, dost thou refuse the comfort of forgiveness because thou canst not imagine it possible that such sin as thine can be suffered to pass unpunished?

Look, see! 'Behold the Lamb of God that taketh away the sin of the world!' The sin is thine no more. It is not imputed to thee. It is taken from off thee and laid on the great Sin-bearer. It is not ignored. It is not overlooked. It is not treated as if it had no reality and no guilt. It is as a great fact, a terrible reality, laid upon the head of the Holy One of God. It is thine no more, because it is his. It is not spared. He in bearing it is not spared. In his person it is visited to the very uttermost.

Wilt thou not be satisfied, O doubter, now? Wilt thou not look on him whom thou hast pierced? Wilt thou not believe that God is just, when he is the justifier of them that believe in Jesus?

For now we reach the crowning and comprehensive summary of the apostle: 'to whom the Lord imputeth righteousness without works.' Righteousness—his own righteousness; the righteousness brought in by his own dear Son; the righteousness of his holy personality as God-man; his perfect fulfilment of the law's requirements, as the Father's servant, on our account; his endurance of its sentence of penal death as made sin, made a curse for us.

# 11 December

> I acknowledged my sin unto thee, and mine iniquity have I not hid. I said, I will confess my transgressions unto the LORD; and thou forgavest the iniquity of my sin. Selah.
> *Psalm 32:5*

Mark the Lord's manner of dealing with you when you are enabled, through grace, to break the spell of this miserable reserve and concealment and disguise, and come out naked and open into the open presence of the Holy One. You have not been suffered to find peace in the way of keeping silence. Alas, too many find peace in that way—excusing themselves, soothing their consciences, explaining away, at least as applicable to themselves, the warnings of coming wrath. But it has not been so with you. You have been awakened. Your sin has found you out. Judgment has come upon you. And all your endeavours to obtain rest while keeping away from God, making the best of yourselves, have ended only in a deeper inward feeling of helpless guilt and sinfulness, and a more awful apprehension of inexorable and inevitable retribution.

But now you try a more excellent way (verse 5). It is the way of the poor prodigal. And you find in it all that he found. The Father meets you as he met him. He sees you afar off, and runs to meet you. He is beforehand with you. He anticipates your confession. He does not wait for your acknowledgment of sin and your humiliation in his presence. 'I said, I will confess my transgressions unto the Lord; and thou forgavest the iniquity of my sin.'

# 12 December

> I will instruct thee and teach thee in the way which thou shalt go: I will guide thee with mine eye.
> *Psalm 32:8*

'I will guide thee with mine eye.' It is a most benignant, kindly, gracious mode of guidance. It is opposed to the guidance of mere force, or what tends toward the use of force, compulsion or constraint, violence or the threat of violence.

It is such guidance as a favourite and faithful servant—or still better, a loved and loving child—can understand and appreciate. It is fatherly guidance apprehended by a filial heart. For if I have a son who loves and trusts me because I love and trust him, I expect him to watch my countenance, not merely to wait for my express command, far less to brave the rude compulsion of my power, but to observe my very look, to take a hint from the glance of my eye. Does he see me, ever so faintly, hinting, by the slightest frown, my dislike, or suspicion, or doubt, of any path on which he is tempted to enter, any work or play in which he might otherwise have desired to engage? He waits not for positive prohibition. He demands no proof of express unlawfulness. Enough that his filial heart discerns, as if instinctively, a father's anxious scruple. He asks no questions; he urges no arguments. He submits to the guidance of my eye. And he accepts that guidance in regard to what I would have him to do, as well as what I would have him to avoid. For he understands me. He is of my counsel, my intelligent and sympathising confidant. He perceives what my heart is bent on, and, without being forced or bidden, he is on the alert even to anticipate my wish.

Surely such a manner of guidance on the part of God is blessedness indeed for those who can apprehend and realise it. And who are they? Not those who are ever asking, 'Must I? May I? Must I forego this pleasure? Submit to this sacrifice? Undertake this toil and trouble? May I for once venture on this liberty? Enter this gay hall of pleasure? Allow myself in this doubtful thing?' Ah, that is being really as the horse or mule which have no understanding, who own only the guidance of bit and bridle! It is the spirit of bondage. But ye have not received the spirit of bondage again to fear, but the spirit of adoption by which you cry, Abba, Father. 'All things are lawful for me, but all things are not expedient.' 'Lord, what wouldest thou have me to do?'

## 13 December

Blessed is the man whom thou choosest, and causest to approach unto thee, that he may dwell in thy courts: we shall be satisfied with the goodness of thy house, even of thy holy temple.
*Psalm 65:4*

The blessing of a good harvest is regarded in this Psalm as subordinate to spiritual privileges, and chiefly valuable because it is a sign of their continuance. 'Blessed is the man whom thou choosest, and causest to approach unto thee, that he may dwell in thy courts: we shall be satisfied with thy goodness of thy house, even of thy holy temple.' This exclamation will appear very natural if we consider that the people are here supposed to be celebrating the feast of harvest or of tabernacles.

It is a joyful occasion to the devout Jew, especially to him who comes from a distance. One principal reason why he delights in the return of harvest is because it brings round propitiously the season of his stated visit to the holy temple. More particularly since an abundant harvest is expressly mentioned in the law as a special mark of the Lord's favour to his chosen people, the experience of such a blessing seems to give them more assurance of their warrant to approach God and more confidence to dwell in his courts. Above all, when there has been reason to fear that there might be no harvest at all, or one scanty for drought or ravaged by war, it must be cause of peculiar joy that not only has God crowned the year with his goodness, but that he satisfies them also with the goodness of his house, even of his holy place.

You cannot suppose that, in his dealings of tenderness with you, God has in view merely your temporal or bodily comfort, or that the goodness with which he crowneth the year is designed merely to fill your mouths with food and gladness. No, but by this seasonable kindness he would so melt your hearts and draw them to himself. He would so excite and enlarge your desires after him, that you should be satisfied with nothing short of the goodness of his house, even of his holy place.

## 14 December

> By terrible things in righteousness wilt thou answer us, O God of our salvation; who art the confidence of all the ends of the earth, and of them that are afar off upon the sea.
> *Psalm 65:5*

Then also, in that harvest home the church obtains an explanation of all that has been dark and distressing in the Lord's dealing with her—how by terrible things in righteousness he has been answering her as the very God of her salvation. Amid whatever noise and tumult may have caused the dwellers in the uttermost parts of the earth to be afraid at his tokens, the Lord then gives his church such evidence of his power, and such an insight into his purposes, as enables her to hold fast her own confidence in him and to commend him as the confidence of all the ends of the earth, greatly to be feared, but yet causing universal joy.

That harvest home is the time of an abundant outpouring of the Spirit, the windows of heaven being widely opened, and gracious showers copiously descending over all the world. That is the crowning blessing: the fulness of the joy of the joyous feast of tabernacles.

And it is a joy and blessing that may be yours individually now, as it is to be that of the universal church at last, if only, entering into the spirit of this Psalm, you are willing to vow and pray and confess, to dwell in God and wait for God, and seek the gift of the Spirit, in the full assurance of that other Psalm: 'They that sow in tears shall reap in joy. He that goeth forth and weepeth, bearing precious seed, shall doubtless come again with rejoicing, bringing his sheaves with him.'

## 15 December

> O satisfy us early with thy mercy; that we may rejoice and be glad all our days.
> Psalm 90:14

Thou hast taught us to know thee—to know thee not only in the terror of thy wrath, but in the riches of thy grace, as the sure dwelling place of thy people in all generations. Greatly art thou to be feared, in thine unchangeableness! From everlasting to everlasting thou art God. But how lovely art thou, and how loving! Thou hast so opened to us thy heart, and so opened our hearts to thee, that we cannot now consent to let thee go.

Return, O Lord, once more visit us with the light of thy countenance There may be no change—we ask for no change—in thy dealings with us. Let us still have the wilderness for our earthly portion instead of Canaan. But so far let it repent thee concerning thy servants, that we may realise a change in thy disposition toward us, and may feel that thou art not now angry with us, but pacified towards us; that we are no longer under thy just sentence of wrath, but find grace and favour in thine eyes. 'O satisfy us early with thy mercy.'

Yes! It is thy mercy we seek. That will satisfy us. Let it be ours, O Lord. Let it be ours speedily, soon, early, now. Whatever fruit of it is to come in the shape of ulterior good may be postponed. But thy mercy itself! Let it be early—now. Now in the early morning of that new pilgrimage on which we are entering. Now, in the early commencement of our subjection to vanity by reason of sin. Only let thy mercy be thus early ours. It is enough. We shall be satisfied.

## 16 December

Let thy work appear unto thy servants, and thy glory unto their children.
*Psalm 90:16*

This is a prayer for the Holy Spirit, and for the Holy Spirit as discharging his double office. On the one hand, opening up to us more and more from without—or as it were, objectively, through the instrumentality of the Word—the work of the Lord, giving us larger and loftier views of its character and nature. 'Let thy work appear unto us.' And on the other hand, opening up in us, within, and as it were, subjectively, by an immediate touching of our inner man, the eye of the mind, the soul, the heart, so as to make it more capable of not only understanding the work of the Lord more clearly in all its bearings, but perceiving, recognising, and appreciating, with livelier sympathy, his glory in it.

'Let thy work appear unto thy servants, and thy glory unto their children.' For it is not enough that his work appears, unless his glory in it appears also. Hence there must be a double action, so to speak, of the Holy Spirit. He acts by means of outward revelation, withdrawing more and more—through his blessing on your study of the Scriptures—the veil that hides the wondrous working of the Lord. And he acts by means of inward renewal, intensifying your new-born and new-created faculty of discerning spiritual things, so that you see more and more, in all the wondrous working of the Lord, his wondrous glory.

The petition, therefore, of this verse betokens a gracious state of things, as between God and the people who with Moses make it their own, and a gracious frame of mind on their part towards God. Thy work, they say, O Lord, and not ours, is what alone is worthy of our regard. And by the help of thy Spirit, we would see in it thy glory—thy glorious character, thy glorious self. 'Let thy work appear unto thy servants, and thy glory unto their children.'

## 17 December

> Jesus answered and said unto them, This is the work of God,
> that ye believe on him whom he hath sent.
> John 6:29

Jesus tells you what he is doing on the earth, that you may join yourself with him in the doing of it. He takes you into his counsels and unfolds to you his manner of working, that you may frame and fashion your manner of working in accordance with his.

You are to work the works of God. How? The Jews once asked, and they got for answer, 'This is the work of God, that ye believe on him whom God hath sent.' That is your first work, your first participation in God's work, that ye believe in him whom he has sent—your believing corresponding to his sending. Christ being to you what he is to the Father, believe in the Lord Jesus Christ and be saved. Would you have the Lord to establish that work? See that you make sure of it yourselves. Let there be no unsteadfastness, no doubt or hesitation, about your working thoroughly this work of God: believing on him whom he has sent.

And then let all your subsequent working, of whatever sort, be in harmony with his working. Let it become part and parcel of it. In all you think and say and do, let it be God working in and by and through you. Then no thought or word or work of yours will perish or be lost. The Lord will establish it. Vain thoughts, idle words, worldly deeds, he cannot establish. They are as grass. But thoughts that grasp his thoughts, words that echo his words, deeds that aspire to fellowship in his own great deeds of love: Lord, thou canst, thou wilt establish these. Oh then, let my thoughts, words, deeds be ever thus godly, thus godlike!

## 18 December

> He that dwelleth in the secret place of the most High shall abide under the shadow of the Almighty.
> *Psalm 91:1*

Where is the secret place of the most High? Where but within the veil, where the covenant of peace is ratified, and things hid from the wise and prudent are revealed unto babes. Into that secret place you may freely enter, and in it you may permanently dwell. Christ leads you in, rending the veil, that is to say, his flesh. Sprinkling you with his own precious blood, he takes you along with him as he passes from the cross, from the grave, to the bosom of his Father in heaven.

And as he now abides there evermore, so you also abide with him there continually. There he reveals to you the Father; he gives you an insight into the heart of the most High. And bidding you know and believe that the Father loveth you even as he loveth him, he asks you to make this God most high your habitation, as he is his: your home as he is his, the home of your full confidence the home of your warm affection, the home of your habitual resort, the home of your familiar fellowship. Dwelling there, you acquaint yourself with God and are at peace. You know his name and put your trust in him. You are no more servants merely, not knowing what your master doeth. You are friends of the Son, and all things which he hears of his Father he makes known to you. The secret of the Lord, the secret of his gracious covenant, the secret of his moral government, the secret of his whole providential administration, is with you as with the righteous, as with them that fear him. 'Your life is hid with Christ in God.'

## 19 December

> I will say of the LORD, He is my refuge and my fortress: my God; in him will I trust.
> *Psalm 91:2*

'I will say of the LORD, He is my refuge and my fortress.' To say this is much. To be brought to say it from the heart is the fruit of a gracious work of the Holy Ghost.

By nature, I seek a shelter from the Lord, a defence against the Lord. A hiding-place from God is what I desire. I look for it, and think that I may have it among the trees of the garden—the world's flatteries, or the forms of godliness. There I would fain lurk, putting them between my guilty conscience and my offended God. Or let me have some means of meeting my God when he comes to reckon with me: let me entrench and fortify myself in excuses for my sin and pleas of self-justification. Such is the propensity of the natural mind.

If it be otherwise with me now, it is through the Holy Ghost working in me. It is the effect of a great change of heart—it is to me a new nature. Once I sought a hiding place from God—now God is my hiding place, God is my refuge. From the assaults of my enemies coming to accuse me, to slay me—from my own heart condemning me—I welcome as my refuge the Lord himself, the very God against whom I have offended.

Formerly, I was bold enough to defy the God of judgment. I strengthened myself against him in my imaginary innocence, or my comparative integrity and goodness of heart. Now I give myself into his hands, that he himself may be my defence. I look to him to make me a partaker of his own righteousness—that perfect righteousness of his which none can challenge or assail—the righteousness which he brings near to me in the person of his Son, my strength and my Redeemer. This now is my fortress: Jehovah my righteousness, Jehovah my strength.

## 20 December

> With long life will I satisfy him, and shew him my salvation.
> *Psalm 91:16*

This world is not all a battlefield, a dreary and dangerous pilgrimage, to the Lord's faithful servant. Even to him—rather, one should say, chiefly to him, to him alone reasonably— length of days may be an object of desire. Why should that man grasp many years to live here, who, let him go the whole round of earth's pleasures, must be always conscious of an aching void, an unsatisfied thirst, a feeling moving him to adopt the cry, 'Who will show us any good?'—to echo sadly the complaint, 'Vanity of vanities; all is vanity'?

But you, O man of God, are not fated thus to have the cup of contentment ever brought to your very lips, to be ever turned aside or dashed down before you drink it. You know what that saying means: 'Godliness with contentment is great gain.' You see the Lord's goodness in the land of the living. You have much to make you glad in the prospect of a long life of usefulness and comfort, if that should be the mind of God concerning you. Nay, should length of days bring with it to you only length of toil and care and grief, you will still say that even with such a long life the Lord is satisfying you—for all the more, in such a life, through your calling on him and his being with you in trouble, he will be showing you his salvation. And if, on the other hand, it shall please him whose soldier and pilgrim you are, to cut short your career on the very threshold of your entrance on it—if he shall commission the plague to smite you or the sword to cut you down, your labour scarcely begun, your mouth scarcely opened—you will remember that the promise is not an absolute promise of long life. It is: 'With long life will I satisfy him.'

## 21 December

> My righteousness is near; my salvation is gone forth, and mine arms shall judge the people; the isles shall wait upon me, and on mine arm shall they trust.
> *Isaiah 51:5*

This righteousness of God, as preliminary to his salvation, is brought near to fallen man and his tempter in paradise. Here let me remind you of the terms in which the original promise of mercy was couched. In point of fact, it was not strictly speaking a promise at all, but a threatening. It spoke only of judgment. To the serpent God said, 'The seed of the woman shall bruise thy head.' Thus God brings near his righteousness. And the only ground upon which his doing so (in the form of this intimation of the tempter's sentence and doom) can be held to carry in it any grace at all, is just the law or principle of our text—that when he bringeth near his righteousness, his salvation will not tarry. The execution of his work of righteousness upon the seducer implies, as a consequence, according to this law or principle, the deliverance of his victims.

This righteousness of God is brought near to the redeeming man, the Lord from heaven, the man Christ Jesus, accomplishing his ministry of propitiation. For the deliverer is to be himself a partaker in the calamity of those whom he delivers. He is to make common cause with them. He is to deliver them by representing them, by taking their place, and allowing that righteousness of God which would have had its proper effect or work in their death, to be consummated in him as dying in their stead. Righteousness must come first: his fulfilling all righteousness as a preliminary to his being able to save unto the uttermost all that come unto God by him.

The righteousness of God is brought near to me, a poor sinner, in the Spirit's gracious work of conviction and faith. Righteousness is brought near to me—God's perfect righteousness—not to condemn, but to save!

## 22 December

> But now the righteousness of God without the law is manifested, being witnessed by the law and the prophets
> *Romans 3:21*

In Christ and his finished work of obedience and atonement, the righteousness of God is brought near, as fully and finally satisfied and glorified, and therefore having in it a righteous salvation for me—for me, a sinner—of sinners the chief. In him and in his work, the whole of that judicial procedure—even up to the highest demands of the law's perfection and down to the utmost depths of the law's penalty—which must open the way for the coming of God's salvation, is strictly and thoroughly accomplished. He is therefore himself 'the righteousness of God', and as such, God brings him near. He is near. 'My righteousness,' says Jehovah. Let him be mine! 'Oh, let him only be mine!' do I, poor sinner as I am, amid the doubt and darkness of conscious guilt, cry out. And then may the full light of God's own salvation flow in abundantly on my long benighted soul.

It now only remains to identify this righteousness of God which our texts describe as the precursor of his salvation, with that which the New Testament represents as the ground of our justification before God. I quote one single passage: 'But now the righteousness of God without the law is manifested, being witnessed by the law and the prophets.'

The apostle has conclusively proved the righteousness of man to be in every view insufficient, all righteousness of man—of man's providing or working out—being out of the question as having any worth or efficacy to meet the demands of God's violated law and justice, or give the sinner any ground of hope. And now, that being so, the righteousness of God is manifested in the person and work of his Son Jesus Christ, fulfilling the whole law on our behalf, and expiating the guilt of our breach of it by his own endurance of the penalty in our stead.

## 23 December

Let the wicked forsake his way, and the unrighteous man his thoughts: and let him return unto the LORD, and he will have mercy upon him; and to our God, for he will abundantly pardon. For my thoughts are not your thoughts, neither are your ways my ways, saith the LORD.
*Isaiah 55:7–8*

This statement may be viewed first as giving the reason that makes the sinner's repentance necessary. 'Let the wicked forsake his way, and the unrighteous man his thoughts. For my thoughts are not as your thoughts, neither are your ways my ways, saith the Lord.'

Secondly, as confirming the assurance of full and free forgiveness. 'Let him return unto the Lord, and he will have mercy upon him, and to our God, for he will abundantly pardon.' He may be sure of this, 'for my thoughts are not your thoughts, neither are your ways my ways, saith the Lord'.

Thirdly, as an assertion of the stability of the divine purpose and the certainty of its fulfilment (verses 10–12). It is the purpose of one whose thoughts are not your thoughts, and whose word in the moral economy will infallibly be as effectual as is his reign in the material earth, and who, out of the songs of a renovated world, is determined, whether you believe or no, to make for himself a name.

Considered in the first of these lights, the text places the necessity of repentance not on the footing of a mere arbitrary or discretionary appointment on the part of God, but on the footing of his essential nature. It is not merely because God says it that the wicked must forsake his way and the unrighteous man his thoughts, but because God is what he is. Not as if it were a required and stipulated condition of God's favour, but because even God, being such as he is, cannot arrange it otherwise: the wicked must forsake his way and the unrighteous man his thoughts.

## 24 December

For as the rain cometh down, and the snow from heaven, and returneth not thither, but watereth the earth, and maketh it bring forth and bud, that it may give seed to the sower, and bread to the eater: so shall my word be that goeth forth out of my mouth: it shall not return unto me void, but it shall

accomplish that which I please, and it shall prosper in the thing whereto I sent it.
*Isaiah 55:10–11*

Not only do God's thoughts and ways towards you transcend your actual ways and thoughts towards him, they transcend also all that could have ever entered into your heart. You never could have imagined beforehand such a mode of dealing with returning sinners as God is pleased to adopt. And even now that he has revealed it, and is giving you a spiritual discernment of it, you cannot fully realise it. For there is nothing in your nature that is an adequate counterpart to it; nothing so nearly the same as to afford you an adequate measure of it. It is true, you can form a notion of kindness, generosity, self-sacrificing affection, and bountifulness and liberality, but the full meaning of the comparison between the heavens as higher than the earth, and his ways and thoughts as higher than yours, you can know only if you can know first what is lowest in the earth, and what is highest in the heavens, and what is the vast space between.

What is lowest in the earth? What but the sinner! What but myself—myself, of sinners the chief, sunk in the lowest depths of corruption and guilt and woe! What is highest in the heavens? Is it thou, O blessed Jesus, thou Son of the living God, thou who dwellest in the bosom of the Father? Higher than thou art, or than is the Father's love to thee, nothing in all heaven ever was or ever can be.

And what are God's thoughts now? What are his ways? What is his plan and purpose of love? Is it not to span and bridge across this immeasurable distance between what is lowest in earth and what is highest in the heavens? The Son, in my stead, takes my lowest place in the earth, that I may share his highest place in the heavens.

# 25 December

> God is faithful, by whom ye were called unto the fellowship of his Son Jesus Christ our Lord.
> *1 Corinthians 1:9*

The faithfulness of God is to be viewed in connection with his calling you, as giving you the fullest possible assurance that he will perform and make good on your behalf whatever purpose or promise your being called by him may be fairly held to comprehend. He will do all that, in calling you, he has become expressly or virtually pledged to do.

The question then is, 'To what are you called? What is the end of your calling?' For, whatever is needed for the accomplishment of that end, the faithfulness of God makes it certain that he will do it. Now it is unto the fellowship of his Son Jesus Christ that you have been and are called. He is faithful in discovering to you your case. He tells you that you need his Son—that without him you perish. Your sin he brings before you, your guilt, your ruin. He does so in very faithfulness. His Word is no prophet of smooth things. His Spirit is no giver of false peace. His faithfulness you may at first dislike. It may seem to you like harshness and severity. You question the truth and fairness of the representations he gives, and the convictions he would force upon you, as to your state and character before him. You cannot feel your condition to be absolutely hopeless, your hearts to be altogether wrong towards God. You think it hard to be told that you can do nothing to right or reform yourselves. You cannot rid yourself of a growing apprehension of failure and defeat, of bondage and wrath.

The hurt is not to be healed as you hoped. The plague is deep. The past cannot be undone. You cannot answer for the future. And alas for the evil that is ever present with you! The testimony of God, you find, is true. The discovery which he makes to you of your criminality and corruption, your sin and death, may not be welcome. But in calling you to the knowledge of it, God is faithful.

## 26 December

> But we preach Christ crucified, unto the Jews a stumbling-block, and unto the Greeks foolishness; but unto them which are called, both Jews and Greeks, Christ the power of God, and the wisdom of God.
> 1 Corinthians 1:24

Consider now this Christ as the power of God and the wisdom of God. He is that essentially, being true and very God, the eternal Son of the Father, the Word which in the beginning was with God, and was God. And as the Word made flesh, Immanuel, God manifest in the flesh, he is still, in his person, character, and work, the power of God and the wisdom of God.

But now, to conceive of him aright in this view, it is necessary to inquire what sort of power, what sort of wisdom he is. Or, in other words, to distinguish carefully power as the power of God, wisdom as the wisdom of God, from the broken images of these elements of majesty which pass for power and wisdom among men. With us, power is commonly violent, and wisdom artful, ingenious, inventive. We measure power by the din and noise and tumult it creates; we measure wisdom by its shrewd guesses and apt contrivances and plans. But nothing of all this is to be found about the holy Jesus! He makes no mighty stir when he exerts his power. He surprises by no mere exercise of ingenuity when he manifests his wisdom. Calmness, simplicity, repose, and what might almost be called unconsciousness, are the features that most distinguish his manner.

There is nothing fitful or capricious in Christ as the power of God, nothing like the putting forth of a giant's or a tyrant's might. There is nothing strained, and refined or artful in Christ as the wisdom of

God. His wisdom is not mere knowing or cunning. Power with him is serene and unimpassioned. Wisdom with him is always self-possessed, calm and clear in the unruffled fulness of its infinite forethought and foresight and insight. And hence the grandeur of his character.

# 27 December

> But of him are ye in Christ Jesus, who of God is made unto us wisdom, and righteousness, and sanctification, and redemption.
> 1 Corinthians 1:30

Christ crucified is to be seen and owned as the power of God and the wisdom of God. Is he really so to you? That now is the question, to which the answer is found in verse 30: 'But of him are ye in Christ Jesus, who of God is made unto us wisdom, and righteousness, and sanctification, and redemption.'

There is here a double work of God: making you Christ's, and making Christ yours; causing you to be in Christ Jesus, as he is, the power of God and the wisdom of God, and causing him to be to you that very wisdom and that very power which he is himself. The work is a divine work, in which the Holy Ghost is the agent—the Holy Ghost shutting you up into Christ, and taking of what is Christ's and showing it to you.

Blessed indeed is the correspondence of these two divine operations to one another. To be by a divine work, yourselves in Christ Jesus, and by a divine work also to have Christ Jesus made all things to you! Yes, I say all things! For what is there that is not embraced in this complete and comprehensive enumeration? Let us briefly note the particulars of this experimental Christianity: Christ made of God unto us wisdom, and righteousness, and sanctification, and redemption.

He is made of God unto you wisdom. He is made of God to you, in your experience, that very wisdom of God which he himself is. For all your wisdom is still only Christ. Christ known, Christ believed, Christ applied to you by the Holy Spirit and appropriated on the warrant of the free call and command of the gospel. Christ, in short, grasped as yours—nay rather, grasping you as his. Thus you become wise, wiser than the ancients, wiser than your teachers, when Christ alone is all your wisdom. Ah, what wisdom—holy, heavenly, divine—does a simple acquaintance with Christ and him crucified impart to very babes!

## 28 December

> But of him are ye in Christ Jesus, who of God is made unto us wisdom, and righteousness, and sanctification, and redemption.
> 1 Corinthians 1:30

Oh, what power, what virtue is there in that holy one to turn the foulest thing he touches into purity and pure peace! Be sure, be very sure, O thou whom indwelling sin is vexing—thou for whom inveterate, inborn corruption is too strong—thou who hast got some sense of the beauty of holiness, some taste and relish for the blessedness of holy love—thou who wouldst fain be rid of those carnal, worldly thoughts and lusts that trouble thee—thou who longest in real and right earnest to have the very same affections in thy bosom towards all things that are in the bosom of thy God: be sure that it is Christ himself who is thy holiness as well as thy peace. For he is made of God unto thee, not righteousness only, but sanctification also. Deal with him, directly and personally with himself, for the one grace as well as for the other.

Abide in him, and let him and his Word abide in you. Take his death as your own; his life also, his risen life, as your own. Die daily in and with him. Be daily renewed after the image of his life. For you are dead, and your life is hid with Christ in God. Mortify therefore your members which are on the earth. You are dead: let them be dead too.

And let Christ, living in you, and shedding abroad in your hearts a sweet sense of the love of God, through the Holy Ghost being given to you—let Christ, made over to you as yours in the gospel, appropriated as yours by faith, lived upon, fed upon, tasted and enjoyed, in a growing experience of living fellowship and living trust—let Christ be more and more apprehended as being himself, in his death and in his life, the principle, the spring, the motive, the end and aim of all your thoughts and all your activities.

# 29 December

> Have mercy upon me, O God, according to thy lovingkindness: according unto the multitude of thy tender mercies blot out my transgressions.
> *Psalm 51:1*

The Psalm opens with an abrupt and impulsive appeal. It is the psalmist's ordinary way: to begin with an outburst of feeling, and then go on to explain more leisurely the experience which led up to it. So is it here. His cry is for mercy. 'God be merciful to me a sinner.' And it is a cry altogether self-abandoning and self-despairing. It is a simple casting of himself, sinner as he is, upon God. It is upon God, 'according to his lovingkindness, according to the multitude of his tender mercies' that he casts himself. The rich and large and bountiful grace of God is his only stay.

He appeals to it in terms expressive of the most emphatic fulness of contrite conviction and believing confidence: 'Have mercy upon me, O God, according to thy lovingkindness: according unto the multitude of thy tender mercies blot out my transgressions.' Two unequivocal signs of grace follow: a desire to be thoroughly washed and cleansed, 'Wash me thoroughly from mine iniquity, and cleanse me from my sin,' and a willingness to appear before God, for that end, without concealment and without guile, 'I acknowledge my transgressions; and my sin is ever before me.'

These are the two features in respect of which the 'godly sorrow which worketh repentance to salvation not to be repented of' differs from 'the sorrow of the world which worketh death' (2 Corinthians 7:10): the desire to be thoroughly cleansed, and the owning of all sin. And they are the distinguishing features of this case—the case of one deeply, deplorably, fallen in sin, but yet hopeful.

# 30 December

> Purge me with hyssop, and I shall be clean: wash me, and I shall be whiter than snow.
> *Psalm 51:7*

'Purge thou me; wash thou me.' To God alone does the smitten soul apply—to God, against whom only he has sinned. He alone is the offended party. To him alone I have to answer. He alone can forgive. To him alone, accordingly, I have recourse—to him directly, to him alone.

'Purge thou me; wash thou me.' I do not go to any priest. If I had sinned merely against the priest, or against such ordinances as the priest has to guard, then the priest might, on due submission, absolve and bless me. I do not go to any of my fellows whom my sin may have touched. They may receive or reject an apology or a compensation. How they may regard and treat me is now comparatively a secondary and subordinate consideration—serious, indeed, in one view, for I would fain have their forgiveness, but not the vital consideration.

It is against God, God only, that I have sinned. And how God may deal with me is the real question. Nor can I go to my own heart. There once I might have reckoned upon a verdict of acquittal, or at least of apology. Now, however, nothing short of the sentence of God can relieve or content me.

But now, if God—the very God against whom, against whom only, I have sinned—does, in the exercise of his undoubted and irresistible sovereignty, purge me and wash me and make my broken bones to hear joy and gladness, who may gainsay or call in question the gracious act? The priest may refuse to absolve me. But if God purge me, I am clean. My fellow-sinners may not acquit or pardon me. But if God wash me, I am whiter than the snow.

## 31 December

> Behold, I come quickly: blessed is he that keepeth the sayings of the prophecy of this book.
> *Revelation 22:7*

Believer in Jesus—simple, single-eyed, meek and lowly child of God—do you feel any difficulty in realising that first coming [of Christ] and all that is involved in it, as not past and gone and obsolete, but present, and pressing upon you daily? Any difficulty, I mean, arising out of the long tract of centuries you have to travel over before you find its date in the history of time? Do you trouble yourself here with the innumerable occurrences that crowd the intervening period? And when you are living in all simplicity and godly sincerity by the faith of the Son of God, who loved you and gave himself for you, does the intrusive suggestion, 'Ah, but that is long gone by,' ever come to mar the force and point of this all-prevailing motive to holiness?

'Never,' you will reply. 'Never, except to be resisted.' You strive against it until, by God's help, you have got rid of it, and find yourself enabled to realise that shedding of blood as a thing of today. I know no chronology and no chronological computation of long eras in dealing with that Saviour, who eighteen hundred years ago trod with his blessed feet the soil of Judaea, and expired on the cross of Calvary. I know no chronology and no chronological calculation of the manifold intricacies of dates and cycles, in that which is my daily, hourly, momentary life of faith; my looking unto Jesus crucified, as the Lamb slain, and embracing Jesus risen as my Lord and my God.

www.ingramcontent.com/pod-product-compliance
Lightning Source LLC
Chambersburg PA
CBHW072038160426
43197CB00014B/2542